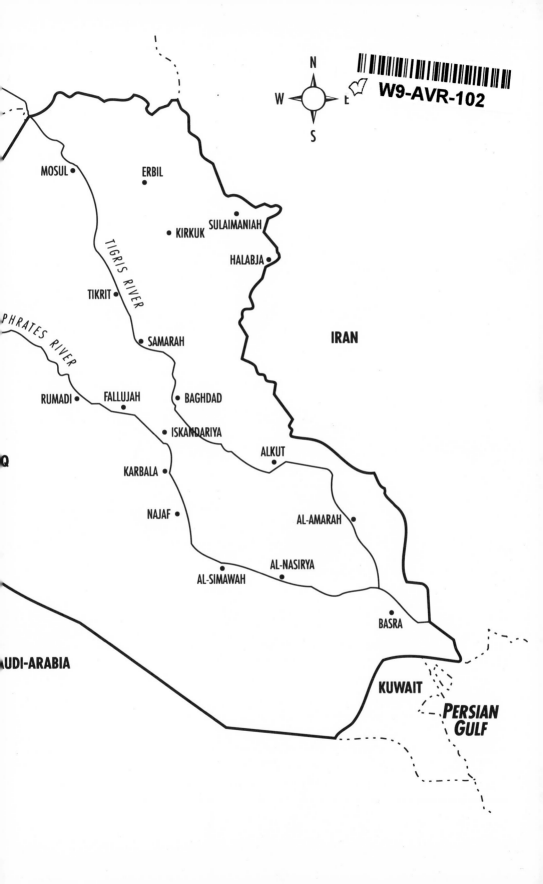

Circle
of Fear

Circle of Fear

MY LIFE
AS AN ISRAELI
AND IRAQI SPY

Hussein Sumaida
WITH CAROLE JEROME

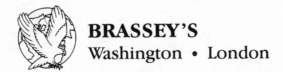

BRASSEY'S
Washington • London

I dedicate this book,
and my life,
to my beloved wife,
Ban

Copyright © 1991 by Hussein Sumaida and Carole Jerome
First Brassey's edition 1994

Brassey's, Inc.

Editorial Offices	*Order Department*
Brassey's, Inc.	Brassey's Book Orders
8000 Westpark Drive	c/o Macmillan Publishing Co.
First Floor	100 Front Street, Box 500
McLean, Virginia 22102	Riverside, New Jersey 08075

Brassey's books are available at special discounts for bulk purchases for sales promotions, premiums, fund-raising, or educational use through Special Sales Director, Macmillan Publishing Company, 866 Third Avenue, New York, New York 10022.

Sumaida, Hussein.
    Circle of Fear: my life as an Israeli and Iraqi spy / Hussein
Sumaida with Carole Jerome.—1st Brassey's ed.
        p.   cm.
    Originally published: Toronto: Stoddart Pub. Co., 1991.
    ISBN 0-02-881099-6
    1. Sumaida, Hussein. 2. Secret service—Iraq—Biography.
I. Jerome, Carole.   II. Title.
HV8242.55.A2S86 1994
327.1'25694'094'092—dc20
    [B]   94-6864
                                                            CIP

Printed in the United States of America

CONTENTS

PREFACE

 THE BOOKS PUBLISHED IN Brassey's Intelligence and National Security Library are chosen because they provide students, scholars, and national security specialists with unique or significant insight into the world of intelligence. *Circle of Fear* is such a book.

Since the mid-1970s, there has been a relative avalanche of books written about intelligence. No longer the province of pulp novels or headline-grabbing exposés, intelligence has moved from the shadows of scholarly attention to a component of security studies and diplomatic history. Indeed, the subject of intelligence as a serious academic pursuit has made remarkable progress over the past two decades.

However, there still exist significant gaps in the field. Understandably, the serious literature on intelligence to date has focused primarily on the Anglo-American and Allied experience during the world wars of both hot and cold variety. In general, we know a great deal about how we and our adversaries operated, what worked, and what didn't.

By contrast, there are few titles one can turn to when it comes to intelligence in the non-Western world, despite the obvious importance of many of those regions to U.S. and Western security. As noted by Middle East specialist John Cooley in his introduction, *Circle of Fear* is one of the few books written in English about an Arab intelligence service. *Circle's* author, Hussein Sumaida, provides his readers with a firsthand account of working against, for, and ultimately against the Mukhabarat, Iraq's most feared intelligence service. Iraq's program to develop weapons of mass destruction was not the only item of Saddam Hussein's rule not fully understood by the West.

As with many books written on intelligence, especially by former operatives, there may be details in Sumaida's account that are not exactly on the mark. Nevertheless, *Circle of Fear* provides unique and valuable material on Iraqi intelligence operations, tradecraft, bureaucracy, and, more generally, the psychology of espionage. In addition, it is useful to compare and contrast Sumaida's description of Iraq and its intelligence services with those of other autocratic states. Despite the obvious differences between the Leninist regimes of the former Soviet empire and Ba'thist Iraq, it is interesting to note how similar the basic institutional mores and pathologies their security services evidenced in their respective efforts to maintain—in John Dziak's phrase—"a counterintelligence state." Indeed, Sumaida's *Circle* is a useful reminder to scholars, intelligence analysts, and operatives alike that the study and understanding of the intelligence apparatus of authoritarian and totalitarian regimes tell us much about the internal dynamics of these regimes as well as their statecraft.

ROY GODSON, Series Editor
Intelligence and National Security Library
Washington, D.C.

INTRODUCTION
TO THE
AMERICAN EDITION

 $\mathbf{D}$ URING NEARLY FORTY
years of work as a correspondent in the Middle East and
North Africa, I have seen a succession of books—good, bad,
and indifferent—about Mossad, the principal Israeli intelligence agency, and its leaders, its agents, and their exploits.
Strangely, this outpouring of material about Israel's secret
warriors has not been balanced by many similar books—
almost none, in fact, in non-Arabic languages—about
Mossad's adversaries, the Arab and Iranian intelligence services and the rulers who give them their orders.

Hussein Sumaida, perhaps the only Iraqi who has gathered information for both his country and Israel and survived to tell the tale, has now taken a giant step toward rec-
tifying this imbalance. *Circle of Fear*, produced with the
help of Canadian journalist and author Carole Jerome, does
far more, however, than merely tell us what it feels like, as a
privileged member of Iraqi dictator Saddam Hussein's elite,
to work in secret for both the Iraqis and the Israelis. He tells
us, with chilling directness, the tale of what it meant to grow
up in a family tyrannized by his father, Ali Mahmoud
Sumaida, a founder of Iraq's ruling Ba'th Party. Physically,
mentally, and morally brutalized by his father, whose fealty
to Saddam's ruthless regime is total, Hussein Sumaida, now
in his late twenties, was the childhood companion of

Saddam's sons, Oday and Kusai, and a witness of the ruthless behavior, in private and public life, of Saddam and of all the terrorized figures of the regime—Saddam's "lackeys" in the author's words.

The author grows to manhood in a Baghdad already under the total sway of Saddam's secret police, the Mukhabarat. He travels in guarded luxury with the family to his father's overseas diplomatic postings in Poland, Zimbabwe, Brussels, New York, and finally Manila, with stops for shopping and sometimes high-risk spying adventures. His father's almost unspeakable cruelty and abuse become to him a kind of personalized microtyranny, a paradigm of Saddam's Ba'th Party police state with its torture, killings—sometimes by Saddam's own hand—of his former friends and subordinates, and its egregious propaganda.

Hussein Sumaida's ultimate rebellion against his father is, at the same time, an act of revolt against Saddam and his Ba'thist system, regarded by the system itself as high treason. In 1984, while studying in Manchester, England, the author seeks and accepts recruitment by agents of the Israeli foreign intelligence service. Mossad sends him to Brussels in 1985 to ask his father's help in getting a job in the Iraqi embassy in London, like other Arab embassies there a principal target of Israeli intelligence.

Sumaida's stark, graphic narrative style makes us feel with him the icy fear of discovery, interrogation, torture, and probable death (he learns that his own father has sent for a Mukhabarat interrogator from Baghdad to question him). His daring, preemptive confession is a gamble with his own life, which is preserved by intervention from an unexpected quarter—Saddam Hussein himself, who insists on locking Sumaida into Mukhabarat operations for life. We learn details of spycraft, and of how Saddam holds on to power and how he deals with real or imagined adversaries. There is data on Iraqi chemical warfare against the Iraqi Kurds and the Iranians during the 1980–88 Iran-Iraq war, and on Iraqi development of biological and chemical weapons as well. The events leading to the invasion of Kuwait in 1990 and the final decisions of the West to halt its outpouring of economic and military aid and to go to war against Saddam in Operation Desert Storm in 1991 become a kind of broad-brush backdrop to the author's decision to flee his country and its hated rulers.

Having decided to flee Iraq, Sumaida also recounts his frustrating experiences with bureaucratic-minded and skeptical American and British immigration and intelligence agents, in contrast to the Canadian officials who were more interested in his information and who provided him and his wife with permanent protection for a new life together. Finally, *Circle of Fear* is also the story of Sumaida's love for Ban, the wife who shares his exile. Moreover, his tender treatment of his long-suffering mother gives us insights into how people survive under a regime totalitarian.

Because of *Circle of Fear*'s insights into history, human personality, and the operations of a brutal totalitarian regime, this book offers the reader great profit. And because of its ruthlessly candid revelations about one man's family and private life, it also provides fascination rarely found outside of quality fiction.

JOHN COOLEY
Mideast Specialist, ABC News

AUTHORS' FOREWORD

I KNOW THAT MUCH OF WHAT I relate in this story does not reflect well on me. So be it. I did not write this book to justify or explain my own faults, crimes and misdemeanors. I wrote it to give others a very rare look inside my country, Iraq, and to share with them what I have learned on my odyssey. It's a personal story that holds a global lesson or two.

Iraq has for decades been a closed book for outsiders. Reporters have been allowed access to political events and figures, but almost never to ordinary people. And people have been afraid to talk openly inside this republic of fear, as one writer phrases it. I call it a small portion of hell. My story takes you into the daily life of my country, to evoke the human element that historians and journalists cannot know, and without which nothing can be fully understood. I add my contribution to theirs.

But because of my unusual background, I can also offer an even rarer look inside the machinery of fear, the Mukhabarat. This all-pervasive apparatus of intelligence and secret police will not be conquered in one hundred hours, like Saddam's pathetic army. My story is a confirmation of the power and the banality of this secret world of espionage and terror. There are no James Bonds in this real world.

I offer as well a view of Israel that is probably unique, coming as it does from an Iraqi Arab who worked inside the Mossad. This heresy brought disillusionment, but also new understanding.

Lastly I offer this book to my own people, as a looking-glass.

Regardless of what happens to me, I feel it is important to have told the whole story. Only as more and more people gain knowledge can the circles of fear be broken.

HUSSEIN SUMAIDA

* * *

When the publishers approached me to write this story about an Iraqi renegade and spy, war between the United States and Saddam Hussein was fast approaching. Clearly, the assignment had immediacy, offering a unique perspective on Iraq. And I needed the money.

But as young Hussein Sumaida unfolded his tale to me, I realized that this was a person of unusual intelligence and sensitivity, with a great deal of historical and political knowledge in addition to his own story. Whether reflecting on the nature of violence or his love for Ban, he often did so in almost lyrical turns of phrase. This book is authentically in his own voice.

This made my task easy, because it coincided with one of my main goals as a journalist: to illuminate political events through the everyday life and the character of the people who live them. And Hussein and his story give a lot of insight into why those of us who report on it all have such a powerful love-hate relationship with the Middle East. There is much to deplore. But there is also much to love. This is true of all societies, but few have such passionate, unruly extremes.

I am left with profound regret — that in moving on to create his new life with Ban, Hussein Sumaida must vanish from ours for his own security.

I want to give full credit to my friend and colleague Janet Rosenstock, who acted as assistant author, editor, midwife and nanny to this book, as she did for my previous volume on the Iranian revolution. Over these two demanding but rewarding efforts, Janet and I have become as tightly knit as lobster mitts. We both thank Dennis Adair, who did some of the work and put up with us.

Thanks are also due to my editor at Stoddart Publishing, Donald G. Bastian, who is living proof that a good businessman can be a nice guy as well. If only there were more with his gentle ways and good judgment, the world might not be such a mess.

Maryan Gibson did a copy edit that was a work of art instead of a massacre.

And I am grateful to my superiors at the Canadian Broadcasting Corporation who gave me leave from "Sunday Morning" to write. And to all my CBC colleagues for the loyalty and support they have shown me not just in this, but in some other very trying times as well.

Last and most important, my love and gratitude to my wonderful family, without whose unfailing strength I could not have written one word; indeed I might long ago have given up altogether.

CAROLE JEROME

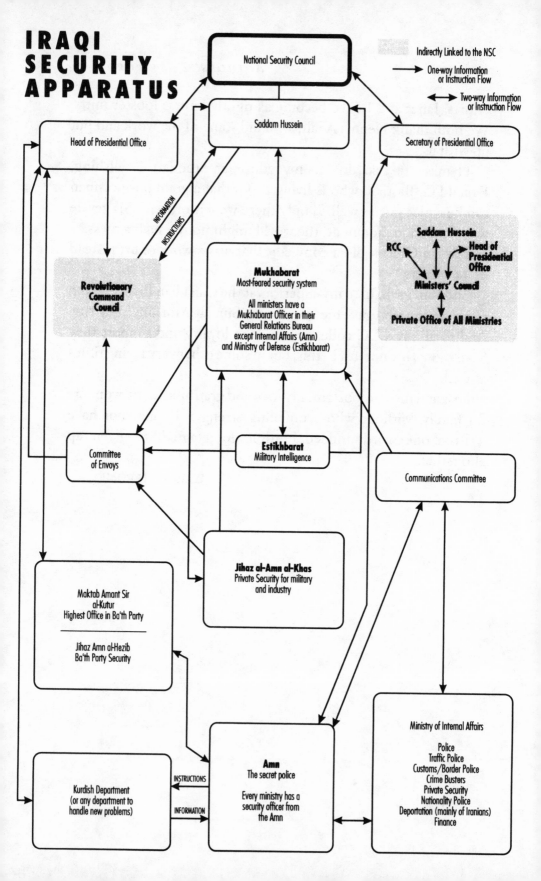

1

VICTIM OF HATE

I CAN RUN MY HAND OVER THE scar on my face and feel my father's signature in my flesh. I was barely two years old when in a fit of temper he jammed my head in the doorway and closed the lower bolt across my face, just above my right eye. According to my mother who feared my father greatly, I cried and bled for hours. My mother told me that I was less than two months old when he beat me for the first time.

I know that when I was small I was an innocent victim of my father's hate. Later, perhaps in order to preserve my sanity, I learned to respond to him with wisecracks, argument and sarcasm. He would fly into a temper, but then at least I could say why he was angry. I also know that if my father had been a normal human being, it is unlikely I would be writing this story today.

For me, for my family, it seemed my father set the deadly pattern of our lives. There was a time when I thought that perhaps I just didn't understand him — though now I find it hard to imagine that understanding would have changed the course of events. Even if you understand pathological violence and fanaticism, surviving it unscathed is unlikely. Humans are not unlike objects in that sense. Whenever my father got angry, he would hurl the crystal ashtrays and porcelain dishes against the wall, so that there was never a complete set of dishes in our house. I withdrew into books and into my imagination, and I began to nurture a hatred for my father that persists to this day. Worst of all, for many years I could not trust enough to love.

My father's horrible temper flared at trivial things — a meal ten minutes late, or a reply from me that didn't show adequate respect for my commander-in-chief. It was virtually impossible for me to meet his neo-military standards because by the time I began to talk, I stuttered, thanks to the constant terror in which I lived. This only made my father more malicious. I was an embarrassment to him, his son who couldn't even speak properly. As I struggled to express myself, he would become so enraged that he would pick me up and hurl me on the floor or into a piece of furniture.

Soon after my sisters and brother were born, they, too, learned to fear him. One sister, Dina, and my brother, Saif, were near to me in age, born in the late sixties. Another little sister, Dalia, was born much later, in 1980. They all were subject to his blows, but I received the brunt of his anger.

My father's favorite weapon was a big blue clog shoe that he wielded like a hammer against our soft skin. We were terrified of it. One day, when I was about seven, Saif and I got up our courage and put it in someone else's garbage. That night when our father came home, he began hunting for the clog. He bellowed furiously for us to confess. Then he lashed out, hitting all of us in a frenzy of evil frustration.

My mother was, and still is, a quiet, gentle person who loves her children. How she endured my father, I shall never know. At least he never hit her, because in some strange way he regarded her as his good-luck charm.

My father's full name is Ali Mahmoud Sumaida. When I grew into my teens, I took to calling him Sumaida, even to his face. He is short, stocky and ugly. He has swarthy skin, a big nose and black hair. My mother, by contrast, is small and frail, with light brown hair and pale skin. Like her name, Suhaila, she is beautiful. They met at university, where he was head of the student underground movement of the Ba'th Party and she was studying social sciences. Everyone who knew them then said she was the most beautiful girl at the University of Baghdad.

When my father took her as his bride, it was like the ancient Egyptian sacrifice of a virgin to placate the angry God of the Nile. My mother, tears filling her eyes, would tell us how unlucky she was to have met him, and to have to live with such a man. If only she had realized in time. Sometimes she would discipline us, too, and then repent if she thought she had acted too much like our father. Violence is contagious. Even the most peaceful people can become so accustomed to violence that without realizing it they first adapt to it, then adopt it.

In spite of everything, my mother somehow retained her peace and kindness. Without her love, we children most certainly would have been lost souls. I, in fact, might well have been killed. While my father constantly attacked me, she constantly defended me, drawing a lot of his fire.

Why he hated me more than the others, I cannot say. I know that later, when he ordered me and my siblings to jump to attention and obey a command, they would instantly obey. I would delay, or refuse altogether. If he told us to get out of the room, they would march out immediately. I would stay put, courting disaster. Whether I was insolent because I had learned to hate him, or whether he hated me because I was insolent, I don't know. But I do know I could not have hit him back or been insolent when he first struck me in my infancy. One day, I would. . . .

Such was life in our family home on Felastin Street. (Felastin is an actual transliteration from the Arabic alphabet, while Palestine is a translation. They have exactly the same meaning.) We lived in one of Baghdad's new, posher neighborhoods in a roomy house with three bedrooms, two salons, a huge kitchen and dining room. It was designed in the style of any modern western house, with all the appliances. The only eastern touches were the archways between rooms. The house was looked after by my mother and my maternal grandmother, with the help of a maid and a cook. Like most Iraqi children, we called our grandma Bibi. She was like my mother, small and sweet and gentle. Two nightingales in the nest of a pterodactyl.

If material wealth meant happiness, then I should have been the luckiest kid alive. We had everything that money could buy. I eventually found out why, and that did not make me any happier. The source of all the wealth was my father's politics, and politics were my father's raison d'être.

Apart from using me as a punching bag, my father barely acknowledged my existence. My quarters were a closet he had made into a room for me. He never talked to me, never gave me toys or gifts, even on my birthday. When I was at school he didn't seem to know or care what grade I was in, what I was learning or how well I was doing.

It is true that in the Middle East fathers do not have the same kind of relationship with their children that they are ideally supposed to have in the West, but even for the Middle East my father was an unusually remote and hateful parent.

When I was six or seven, he took a kettle from the stove and poured boiling water on me, shouting abuse. All I recall is the searing pain, not the cause of this atrocity. The burn spread across my thighs and my little private parts, in large painful blisters that made every movement agony. On this, and every other such occasion, my father refused to allow anyone to call a doctor for me. Instead, my mother would sneak out at 5 a.m., go and get me an appointment, then come back and take me to the clinic herself.

When I was about ten, I became friends with a boy who had a father who talked to him, played cards with him, who was his friend. I always envied that boy.

What I have recounted here is virtually all I remember of my father from my childhood. He flared in my life like an occasional violent thunderstorm. And yet that was enough to make him the driving force of my growing-up years.

Rebellion and revenge dictated almost everything I did in future years. He is like a turbulent shadow, looming over my shoulder. And so he remains in this telling of my tale. But if he remained a distant and awful enigma, the greater power that he represented became clearer to me over the years. My father was the embodiment of the brutal Ba'thist regime of Saddam Hussein. And I turned my hatred of him into hatred of Iraq's rulers.

Ironically at school I found I was privileged, precisely because of my horrible father. Unlike most Iraqi schoolchildren, I was taken to class in a chauffeur-driven limousine. From my first kindergarten class at a small private school when I was five, I discovered that the way was cleared for me. Exams, grades, discipline, rows with other kids, were all smoothed over because of my status. I soon learned that my driver was also my personal bodyguard. One of his duties was to supply the teacher with a gift every two or three months. The gifts and the pressure my father's status could exert meant, for example, that I was excused from oral examinations, which with my stutter I surely would have failed.

A child soon learns the uses of privilege. When I was six or seven I would stuff my pockets with chocolates and other goodies that we, unlike most other Iraqis, always had in the house. I'd learned that the other kids would exchange friendship for chocolate. If one of them displeased me or threatened me, I could have him taken care of by my bodyguard. A big, likable fellow from Tikrit, in the north, he would happily do anything I ordered. At least he was likable to me. I was still too young to know the real meaning of being a Tikriti, as well as the real reason behind all the special treatment of which I so innocently took advantage.

I was special because of my father. I wasn't just little Hussein. I was "Ali Sumaida's son." Those three words, used by so many of the people I came into contact with, were enough to chill any fun I might be having. I hated them. My father was one of the most powerful men in the ruling Ba'thist regime. The privilege came from terror, the tool of raw political power. The special treatment was for my father's benefit, not mine. It denoted his status, not mine. If my father had really cared about me, he would have seen I was placed in speech-therapy classes, rather than bullying and bribing my teachers.

But such actions would have required my father to acknowledge his shameful, stupid son. At all costs a facade of perfection and success had to be preserved. Just like the whole school system, just like the whole society. Success and promotion were earned by corruption and cheating, and so the country was all just a facade. Behind the facade was rot.

In 1969 my father was made head of the Department of Censorship, but each high-ranking Ba'thist Party member held two key jobs. Father's civil job, as censor, was public knowledge. His party job, as one of the high-ranking officers in Saddam's Bureau of General Relations, was secret. He also served as chief censor of the French-language Ba'th newspaper.

No book or film was allowed to be distributed or sold without his approval. The Ba'thists were determined to control people by beating their bodies and starving their minds. Ironically, because my father was the watchdog at the closed gates of learning, I was able to pass through those gates with impunity. Our home had a huge library, a warm, snug room lined with all the forbidden books my father had seized and decided unfit for Iraqi consumption. Since I was not allowed to have any of my friends over and had few toys, that library became my playroom. When my father wasn't home, I would hole up for hours with one of the illicit books. This way I would enter the outside world and learn of its people and its stories. Most of the volumes were Arabic editions.

There was everything from American novels and biographies to treatises on communism and economics.

My favorite discovery was a book about the life of Eli Cohen, the Israeli spy. After establishing a cover identity in South America as a Syrian emigré, Cohen went to Damascus and worked as an Israeli mole inside the highest echelons of the Syrian political and military system. As a guest of senior ranking figures, he even toured the Syrian fortifications facing Israeli on the Golan Heights. Cohen's information was a vital factor in Israel's eventual victory in the 1967 Six Day War. But he never tasted the fruit of his labor. In 1965, within days of his being invited to take a high post in the Syrian Ministry of Defense, he was discovered at his radio set sending messages to Tel Aviv. He was hanged in a public square in Damascus before a cheering crowd.

In my father's world, the 1967 defeat of Arab forces by the Israelis was a festering sore, a deep wound that demanded revenge. It was partly avenged in 1973, when Egyptian forces struck back and wrung a few concessions from the Israelis after a desultory war. But what I read in the pages of Cohen's story was very different. It was there that I began to learn what it was like for Israel to live surrounded by hostile Arab nations. (Later, when I was in the West and could separate the propaganda of both sides from the facts, I learned about what the Zionists did to earn much of that hostility.) But in school in Iraq we didn't learn what the Jews had gone through at the hands of the Nazis. Instead we learned of the Jewish Conspiracy, and the virtues of Hitler and his Reich. Both were greatly admired by my father and his friend Saddam.

Eli Cohen became my personal hero. I almost wished he had been my father. It is hard to convey to non-Arabs just how heinous these thoughts of mine were. What unimaginable treason. Devil-worship. For my father and millions like him, Israel is the archenemy, especially loathed for its usurping of Arab land. And at that level the hatred is valid and comprehensible. But this hatred of Israel is almost pathological, something beyond reason. It marks every moment of our political life and is the foundation of my own story.

To make matters worse at home, as I approached adolescence I became insolent, and my insolence began to take the form of political rebellion. It was not so much that I cared about politics, or even cared about my country's problems. It was simply that I had figured out that my father's politics were where he lived. If I zeroed in on that, I could make an impact. Hurt him, rile him, anything to strike back. Without giving away the secret of my sources, I began to challenge my father on history and politics.

He always described the Ba'th Party to us as "the friend of the people." One night I said, "You and Saddam and the rest talk a lot about the rights of the people. Then all you do is kill people or treat them like slaves!"

"That's the only way to treat them if they insist on going against us!" he shouted back. "They're like stupid fucking donkeys that have to be beaten with a big stick to make them go where they should. You want to have goddamn donkeys running things?"

He always used foul language around the house, the worst of it on me. Especially when I provoked him.

"How do you know they're donkeys if they never get to say what they think?" I replied, knowing it would make him even angrier.

"What would you know about it, you little bastard? The only way to run a country is to have control, and the only way to have control is to make damn sure everybody is afraid to argue. You have to use all the force you've got. Anybody fights you and zzzztt — " he illustrated by drawing an imaginary knife across my throat " — you're dead."

"Pretty swell revolution you have going. Is this what you all had in mind when you were talking about the rights of the people and overthrowing the corrupt old regimes?"

He moved as though to hit me and I backed away quickly.

"Maybe you should take over from Saddam," I taunted. "You know all about how to do everything. You really believe in Saddam?" I knew this would be the last straw for him. My father's loyalty to the party was rapidly being replaced by an even narrower and fanatic loyalty to Saddam Hussein. And Saddam was moving closer to snatching power from his cousin Hasan al-Bakr.

"Get out of here, you fucking little bastard! You're lucky I don't have you killed, too!"

I retired to my closet-room, with its few amusements. Unlike my brother and sister, I was given very few toys, none by my father, and my mother would get me what she could sneak by him.

* * *

My father was born in Tunisia in 1935. His father, part of a large landowning family, had three or four wives, so none of us was ever certain how many of them he actually had at the same time. There was a confusion of children.

The driving force of my father's life was his uncle, Yousef al-Rwaissy, who was closely associated with Habib Ibn Ali Bourguiba, Tunisia's tyrannical president at the time. Bourguiba came to power after France granted Tunisia independence and, taking a page from the lessons of successful dictators, killed almost all of those who had brought him to power. In an oversight, he missed my father's uncle. Yousef escaped to Egypt, where he became acquainted with Gamal Abdul Nasser, whose Arab nationalism was galvanizing long-dormant Arab aspirations of self-government after centuries of colonial rule. Nasser intervened personally with Bourguiba on Yousef's behalf, and he was able to return finally to Tunisia.

My father was mightily impressed by this heroic uncle with the dramatic life, and he immediately began to work in the Tunisian underground movement against Bourguiba. My father was eventually arrested during a protest demonstration and sentenced to death. He never told us exactly how, but he managed to escape. He boarded a ferry to Marseilles in the south of France and eventually made his way to Syria. It was in Syria that my father came into contact with the fateful influence of Michel 'Aflaq, founder of Ba'thism.

The Ba'thist Party was founded in Damascus in 1943 by 'Aflaq and Salah al-Din al-Bitar. In English, Ba'thist translates to Arab Socialist Renaissance Party. The Ba'thist Party has been most important in Iraq and Syria, but it has adherents in all Middle Eastern nations. The party began with reasonably moderate nationalist views, but after Israel defeated the Arabs in 1948, the party grew larger and more radical. Ideologically Ba'thism is a mix of Arab nationalism, national socialism and Marxist rhetoric. In practice the Ba'thist regimes of both Syria and Iraq are nothing more than ruthless dictatorships.

Michel 'Aflaq was a French-Syrian political philosopher who had studied in Paris. His new ideology only added to the confusion of religions, ideologies, warlords and political systems that had plagued the Middle East for centuries. Ba'thism became just another excuse for a bunch of power-hungry men to take over a country "for the good of the people" and run it for the good of themselves, making sure that any people who didn't agree with their plans were crushed — for the good of the people. This unoriginal scheme was wrapped in a hodgepodge of dogma. The Arabs were to throw off their chains — and forge new ones.

So, all fired up with enthusiasm for this new cause, my father joined the Syrian Ba'thist Party. But soon he ran into problems following a couple of run-ins with the Syrian police, perhaps due to various splits among factions in the party. In 1957, my father moved to Iraq. To enter the country with as many advantages as possible, he pretended to be an Algerian. At the time Iraq was heavily backing Algeria in its war for independence from France.

Since my father's papers were mainly in French, it was fairly easy to make them look as if he was from Algeria. It was also easy for him to give the impression that he worked for the revolutionary force, Le Front de la Liberacion Nationale, commonly known as the FLN.

The Iraqis were happy to welcome a combatant from the FLN, and my father established himself with ease at the University of Baghdad where, naturally, he started to work underground for the Iraqi branch of the Ba'th Party.

As far as I know, that was when my father first met Saddam Hussein, another young Ba'thist who was already known as something of a thug. Saddam had been expelled from school at one point for beating up a teacher. Brute force was Saddam's only debating tactic.

* * *

Saddam Hussein came from a dirt-poor family whose hometown was Tikrit, in northern Iraq. Like my father, Saddam had been heavily influenced by a grim uncle who instilled in him both politics and brutality. Saddam was a model student of both.

He was two years younger than my father. The two spent long hours in discussion with their fellow conspirators in the smoky cafés and cafeterias where men whiled away the hours playing backgammon. On occasion such men attended innocent-looking picnics in the parks. There, they plotted revolution. The first major action of these Iraqi Ba'thists was an attempted assassination of General 'Abd al-Karim Qassem in 1959. General Qassem had come to power in a coup the previous year, when he and a group of officers overthrew the monarchy of King Faisal II. Kassem was perhaps the first ruler since Nebuchadnezzar who was genuinely popular with his people. Both Saddam and my father were among the group assigned to hit Qassem himself. They failed, and most of the plotters were rounded up. Saddam, slightly wounded in the fiasco, managed to escape to Syria. My father was never even suspected. Since he wasn't Iraqi, but an Algerian (who was really a Tunisian), it never occurred to the police to drag him in.

After the attempted assassination, the party put my father in charge of its underground activities at the university, while he continued his studies in the history department.

In 1963 the Ba'thists made their first real grab for power in Iraq. My father led the unit assigned to seize radio and television stations. It was a bloody fight, and this time the Ba'th won. Qassem was killed, and his body was displayed horribly on television by the new rulers. They called it a revolution, but it was really a coup d'état. When they succeeded, Saddam Hussein came back from exile in Egypt to join them. My father was rewarded for his part with honorary Iraqi citizenship and the directorship of Iraqi television.

Saddam was given something more to his particular tastes: he was made chief interrogator at the main prison. Once the palace of King Faisal, it was appropriately called Qasr al Nihayyah — Palace of the End — because King Faisal and his family were slaughtered there. It soon became the end for hundreds of unfortunate Iraqis, as well, who fell into Saddam's hands. It was here that Saddam was able to display his full talents as a torturer, using electric wires and prods, nail rippers, chairs with pointed iron stakes and other utensils of the torturer's kitchen. Survivors later testified to Saddam's personal participation in their agonies.

Saddam did not enjoy his new job for long. In Tishrin al Thanni (November) 1963, they were all overthrown again by 'Abd al-Salaam 'Aref, and Ba'thist rivals in the army.

Already the Ba'thist ideology was split into factions within factions. Saddam and my father both went to jail, where they reflected on the reasons for the deterioration of the Ba'th into rival groups and decided it was all the fault of ambitious military officers. Saddam liked to pretend he had genuine military training and rank, but in fact he had none. Deep down he nursed a murderous envy of talented military officers. The decimation of military rivals was to be the hallmark of Saddam's own cannibalistic rule. My father, who was stripped of his citizenship, made a perfect assistant. He was not a part of the military, which automatically made him less of a threat. The two grew closer. Though in jail, Saddam wasn't in as much immediate danger as my father, who was scheduled to be deported. Fortunately for my father, he had a friend in the military police who destroyed the file on him. Another friend, Hammid Alwan, who eventually became the deputy minister of foreign affairs, helped him escape after only three days in jail. Then my father simply took on his Tunisian identity and used his old papers. The Iraqi-Algerian the authorities were looking high and low for was back in business as a Tunisian.

Saddam spent another two years in jail.

My father was despondent. He had lost everything. And now he had a wife, the beautiful Suhaila, whom he had met in university. On January 20, 1965, she gave birth to me.

Since my father could hardly go to the usual police desk to register the birth and didn't want to risk contact with the Tunisians, he had a friend register me at the Tunisian Embassy. Years later, this action would take on great significance.

In spite of all the setbacks, my father stuck with the Ba'thist Party, and in 1968 it paid off. On July 17, they staged another coup, and this time they held on to the reins of power.

I recall a photograph in our home. It shows all twelve coup leaders standing on the balcony of the palace. My father is one of them. From the time of the coup on, the guest list at our house was a who's who of Iraq's rulers.

Ba'th founder Michel 'Aflaq used to visit with his wife and three sons. When he did, our street would be cordoned off and sentries posted all over the neighborhood. My father hated that because it made his house a conspicuous target for would-be assassins. 'Aflaq was to Ba'thism what Marx was to Marxism. Although he was the mental giant behind it, he held no political position and wielded no power. Ironically, while his theories had spawned a killing machine called the Ba'thist Party, 'Aflaq himself was a gentle old soul who looked like Albert Einstein. Everything about him was calm and peaceful, especially his clear bright eyes. While he and my father worked inside, I would play with his sons outside in the garden. We children never paid any attention to politics. We just played our games, oblivious to the fact that our homes were at the eye of a political hurricane.

Father preferred to go to 'Aflaq's, which we did far more often than he came to our house. It was more discreet.

On all these visits, my father was on his best behavior toward his children. The face he presented was of a contented family man with a contented family. These brief interludes of civility gave me glimpses of what a father ought to be, and made me long even more for the real thing. But in my father's heart, the Ba'th took priority over his offspring.

The other chief party ideologist, Dr. Alyas Farah, would also visit with his two sons. He and my father would immerse themselves in arcane discussions about books of political thought. Later, a debonair man named Tariq Aziz came by often, always with a cigar jammed in his mouth. Aziz was the only one who showed any human warmth at all — 'Aflaq was pleasant, but remote — and sometimes he was actually friendly. He remembered me when our paths crossed years later. At one point he had been a journalist, and I always thought of him as one of the few decent human beings in Saddam's circle. It was a mystery why Saddam tolerated someone so intelligent, and it was equally a mystery why someone basically humane could stomach Saddam.

But money and power are strong aphrodisiacs. He became foreign minister by dint of being the perfect yes-man.

I also recall Taha Yasin Ramadhan, a roughhewn character who eventually became the number-three man in the country. He could scarcely string together a coherent sentence, but he and my father used to confer long hours over "election" strategy within the party. I already had begun to understand that elections were won with knives and threats. That was the nature of the men and the party that had just taken over my country.

The coup in 1968 was led by General Ahmad Hasan al-Bakr, who was now secretary general of the party, and became head of the new Revolutionary Command Council. Like Saddam, he was from the northern town of Tikrit.

The Tikriti men all called each other cousin and were as closeknit as shrunken wool. The coup that reinstated my father and Saddam was the beginning of the domination of Iraq by these fierce, unpitying tribesmen. At first Saddam depended on subordinates who were from small, insignificant families from all parts of the country, while he brought his Tikriti clansmen up through the ranks as quickly as possible to replace everyone in any position of power. Eventually people would say that if you were from Tikrit, you didn't claim Iraqi nationality, you claimed Tikriti nationality, which was far more important.

Saddam was given the task he enjoyed most: head of internal security. He turned the savage but inefficient system of the prisons into the savage and efficient system of a police state. In 1963 he formed a unit called the Jihaz Haneen, which translates badly as "Instrument of Yearning" — a typical Ba'thist phrase. Saddam then got busy in earnest and set up the General Relations Bureau. This was the innocuous-sounding name for an apparatus of political surveillance that steadily hunted down and killed everyone who so much as expressed the slightest dislike of the regime. My father was one of its senior officers. Eventually the bureau evolved into the complex system Saddam has today. The Mukhabarat is at its heart.

Mukhabarat is the Arab word for "intelligence," but in Iraq it has acquired a definition of its own. A whisper of the word is enough to create an aura of evil power. The Mukhabarat has limitless powers and is answerable to no one but Saddam. It began systematically to place the country under lock and key, controlling everything from commerce to espionage. One word from a Mukhabarat officer could mean someone's death. People were arrested for vague crimes against the revolution, and simply disappeared.

Saddam quickly gained full control of the reins of terror. He had discovered the ultimate weapon: fear. Fear now ruled every man, woman and child, every nook and every cranny of Iraq.

2

GROWING UP IRAQI

FATHER DID SUCH A GOOD JOB as censor he was put in charge of the Party Preparatory School, as well. It was a factory for turning out ideal Ba'thists. Oddly he never managed to turn his own children into little Ba'thist sausages. Perhaps we were too insignificant in his eyes, or perhaps he thought we would automatically want to emulate our lord and master. Aside from his natural brutality, I never knew what made him such a devotee of the party line. He seemed to need absolute authority in every walk of life. Most of all, he seemed to need someone to control him as much as he needed to control others. He could only function within a tyrannical state. I don't know why. If I could answer the question of what makes people capable of the unspeakable violence that breaks out so regularly in the history of human conflict, I would be answering the darkest mystery of the human race.

Maybe in the act of brainwashing others in his elite school of robots, my father had brainwashed himself, too. Any last vestige of ability to think independently vanished. He became even more domineering at home. Every word he said was an order. There was never a conversation. We children used to count the minutes until he left for the day. Sometimes he traveled outside the country on missions to places like Paris. We didn't know the purpose of these mysterious trips, nor did we really care. We were just glad he was gone.

At school we were subjected to the full blast of Ba'thist propaganda. Sprinklings of math and geography were given together with huge chunks of dogma forced down our little throats. We learned history as seen through Ba'thist eyes. We learned all about the great King Nebuchadnezzar, ruler of the Babylonians. As soon as we could understand the words, we were taught his greatest claim to fame: not the Seventh Wonder of the World, the Hanging Gardens of Babylon; that was insignificant beside his victory over the most evil enemy of them all, the Israelis. It didn't matter that this conquest happened in the fifth century B.C.

In our lessons, the Israelis were horrible people who consorted with demons. We were taught always to be on our guard against these evil people who would try to take away our homes and kill our parents. The Israelis were all forms of the Devil himself.

Nebuchadnezzar was reputed to have captured the Jews and enslaved them, which made him the brightest star in our Ba'thist history books. After Nebuchadnezzar and on through the triumph of Islam in the seventh century A.D., we learned more of our glorious past.

It is true that Baghdad and its people were once a shining light and it is equally true that westerners are largely ignorant of, or choose to ignore, the accomplishments of Arab culture after the first century. Admittedly there has always been a western romance with ancient Egypt and the Fertile Crescent. But it is forgotten that, while the ancestors of those living in many of today's highly industrialized nations were just emerging from the tribal warfare that followed the fall of the Roman Empire, Arab scholars were translating, preserving and adding to the knowledge of ancient Greece, India and the civilizations of antiquity.

Baghdad's Golden Period came in the eighth and ninth centuries during the reign of the 'Abbasid Caliphates. Haroun al Rashid, the fifth of the 'Abbasids, is associated with *A Thousand and One Nights* and the beginning of the Golden Period. Later Caliphs continued his Bayt-al Hikmah — the House of Wisdom — in Baghdad. Here, Arabo-Islamic culture achieved great heights in the fields of mathematics, medicine, philosophy, astronomy, theology, literature and poetry. The greatest thoughts of the Greeks and other ancient civilizations were translated into Arabic. Among the Arabs' many great accomplishments were medicine and mathematics. Ibn Sina, better known in the West as Avicenna, compiled *The Canon of Medicine*. Sixteenth- century doctors like Rabelais are known to have depended on Avicenna's work, which described every phase of treatment for every known disease. *The Canon of Medicine* was the most used medical work between the twelfth and seventeenth centuries. A great hospital was built in Baghdad, where Muslim doctors performed extremely complex operations, including cranial and vascular surgery, as well as operations for cancer. These doctors were the first to use anesthetics, and many drugs were developed for medicinal use. The Arabs gave the West all of this, as well as their numerals, the decimal point, and the concept of zero, without which most modern technology would have been impossible.

Educating us in our past glories was fine as far as it went, but we learned almost nothing about the down side of Iraqi history. The defeats and the cruel tyrants were ignored. I was able to learn about them in my father's library of forbidden fruits.

In 1258, Hulagu, son of Ghengis Khan, captured Baghdad. Eight hundred thousand citizens perished. In 1401, Timur the Lame, better known as Tamerlane, besieged Baghdad with his huge slingshots called mangonels. After six weeks of terrified resistance, the siege ended. Tamerlane built 120 towers around the wall of Baghdad, using the severed heads of 100,000 victims as bricks.

It is ironic that almost six hundred years after Tamerlane, Baghdad would again face an overwhelming military force, the most powerful the world has ever seen: the Americans and their allies in 1991. For the first time, Baghdad faced an army that had come to liberate, to repel an aggression rather than to initiate one. With their cruise missiles, F-15s and unimaginable arsenal of high technology, they would kill fewer people and shed less blood than the swords and mangonels of the Huns and Monguls.

This history of carnage and violence haunted me as I walked through the old parts of Baghdad. In the narrow alleys where dark doorways open into cramped, dank houses, you can almost feel the ghosts, hear the screams and the roar of fire, smell the acrid odor of burning flesh. As a student I looked down when I walked, and thought, perhaps a mother and her children were savaged and murdered right here, their blood flowing over these same ancient stones.

But in school much was skipped. We moved from our glories to the eighteenth century with ease. From 1534, when Suleyman the Magnificent entered Baghdad, till the British took possession, in March 1918, we were a part of the Ottoman Empire (though some parts of modern-day Iraq were independent at various times during that period).

Turkey sided with Germany during World War I, and following the war, Britain was to mandate the area that is now Iraq. The three provinces — Mosul, Baghdad and Basra — were merged into one political entity that now forms modern Iraq. The new borders brought diverse ethnic and religious groups into one state, but they did not change the essentially tribal nature of the society. In 1920 the emir, Faisal I, led an Arab revolt. He established a government in Damascus and was proclaimed King of Syria. A group of Iraqi nationalists met in Syria to proclaim his brother, 'Abdul Allah, King of Iraq. Nationalist agitation spread out from Syria, and by the summer of 1920 the revolt engulfed all of Iraq, except the larger cities where British garrisons were stationed.

The French, who had been given a mandate over Lebanon and Syria in April, were determined to enforce it. They ousted Faisal from power and expelled him from Syria. Faisal went to London to complain about the French. At the same time, the British wanted out of "Mesopotamia" and out of further commitments. They offered Faisal the throne of Iraq and an Arab government under British mandate. Faisal wanted the throne if it was offered by the people, and he also insisted on a Treaty of Alliance rather than a mandate. His proposals were accepted, and on July 11, 1921, Faisal was declared King of Iraq, providing his government "shall be constitutional, representative and democratic." A plebiscite followed the proclamation. The treaty tied Iraq to Britain, at which point various nationalist groups began to work to end the influence of Britain.

The British soon opted for less influence. Iraq became an independent nation — with membership in the League of Nations — in 1932. King Faisal remained on the throne and was succeeded by his son, Faisal II.

It was this king whose overthrow and murder cleared the way for the eventual rise of the Ba'th and Saddam Hussein.

According to my teachers our glorious revolution was going to defeat the Jews once and for all, and Iraq would lead the Arab world into a sunlit future of socialism, Ba'th-style. That meant eternal vigilance, tracking the devils from within. We children were taught the virtue of informing our teachers if we heard anyone say anything against the government, or expressed belief in things we'd been taught were wrong. We were to tell on our friends, our brothers and sisters, and especially on our parents. The least whisper of discontent was to be reported.

This was the horrible foundation of the new police state and its children of the damned. A diabolical refinement of the old rule of divide and conquer, it meant that even the most intimate and private moments were invaded by Big Brother, in the form of little children who knew no better. (In my case, of course, the dynamic was a bit different. I would have loved to turn in my father, but he was one of the Thought Police. And all the nail pullers and hot spikes in the dungeons wouldn't have made me do anything against my mother.)

As you might guess, this atmosphere caused many to leave. Iraq began to deteriorate from within as more and more of the intelligentsia fled to Europe and North America. Thousands of our best-skilled people left, to be replaced by loyal party cadres whose main qualification for the job was an ability to parrot the current dogma.

My family, though, enjoyed the pampered life of the party elite. Every year we went on trips abroad paid for by the party, which meant paid for by the people whom the party was bleeding dry, and by oil revenues. In all, we traveled to more than two dozen countries by the time I was sixteen, including most of Europe, North Africa and the Middle East. We went to a beautiful spa in Czechoslovakia not far from Prague and lived in the lap of luxury while my parents "took the waters." Then, all healthy and rested, we packed up and journeyed to Paris, where we stayed at the exclusive Hotel George V, just off the Champs Elysées. I loved Paris, so much that I kept hoping my parents would leave me there. Paris was a narcotic for me, the stores, the movies, the cafés bright and full of life, and the people all dressed like peacocks.

After a time I began to realize that my father used different names and passports. On the Paris trip he was Jabar Saleh al-Ali, and the occupation listed on his passport was "editor." Even in those early years, I was starting to see that my father was involved in more than just censorship and party propaganda. But I did not learn the full extent of his power until I was his intended victim much later.

After Paris we moved on to Beirut, where my father had a friend in the Arab Liberation Front, an Iraqi-supported militia, working with one of the Lebanese Palestinian factions. Later this militia would form the basis of Saddam's contribution to international terrorism. These were people with whom I would come in contact later in my life.

The Beirut of my youth was still the Paris of the Orient. For me, a nine-year-old child on our first trip, it was an eastern Disneyland, a place of vast fun. For my parents, I suppose, it was like Switzerland: a major banking center, a cosmopolitan center of trade and culture at the crossroads of East and West. It was a glorious city, where so far Christian and Muslim and Druze and even some Jews lived in harmony. There was always a mixed group of children for me to play with on the beautiful beaches in front of the luxury hotels where we stayed. My parents and their friends no doubt preferred their nights in the garish Casino. The Beirut Casino featured near-nude dancers, painted in gilt and silver, descending onto the stage on a huge golden chandelier. By the time I learned about this and was old enough to enjoy it, Beirut, of course, had been reduced to a wilderness of rubble and marauding militias.

But when we were there again in the summer of 1973, we were still able to enjoy much that Beirut had to offer. Then news came from Baghdad that someone had tried to kill Saddam Hussein. Saddam was still officially the number-two man in the country, after Bakr. But everyone knew Saddam as the Strongman of Iraq. Already, he was the one who counted. Without hesitation, my father packed us all up and whisked us back to Baghdad to be by the side of his leader. He was betting on the future, and the future was clearly Saddam.

Saddam was unhurt, and we began to spend our leisure time in Baghdad at the Baghdad Hunt Club, where my playmates were Oday and Kusai, Saddam's sons. Saddam himself used to sit off to one side by the pool with his wife, Sadjidah. She was so colorless she managed to achieve total anonymity. This was a safe policy in a Mideastern nation. Flashy wives like Sadat's Jihan and the Shah's Farah eventually aroused the anger of the reactionary male population, and a lot of the female population, for that matter. So Mrs. Saddam Hussein kept a very low profile, raising it only in innocuous pursuits like women's fashions. Later he took a second wife, a showy blond from the "aristocracy" named Samira Shahbander. It was essentially an attempt at social climbing. He might be one of the rulers of Iraq, but for the upper echelons of the old society, he was a jumped-up hired hand. Not even a real soldier.

Saddam used to keep to himself or quietly talk to party members who approached him. Almost everyone who mattered in the party could be found at the Hunt Club on Fridays, the Muslim sabbath. In addition to the pool there was a fine restaurant, a bar, a cinema, a golf course, tennis courts, a playground and even horseback riding.

I never saw Saddam have anything to do with his sons. He was remote and austere. But then, so was my father in public; he kept his temper in check and acted the noble patriarch. Oday and Kusai and I would play cops and robbers in the playground, scrambling over the "mountain" built for our fun.

One day they became really interested in me when they saw me in a corner reading a Batman comic. "Can you get us some of those?" they pleaded, much to my surprise. With the money and power they had, I had assumed they could get their hands on more than I could. So I kept them supplied with Batman, Superman and other contraband comics. Maybe it was the comics that helped give Oday the idea he could stand up to his father later in life.

That summer Baghdad was being terrorized by a more mundane criminal, a homicidal maniac who broke into homes and murdered the occupants with a huge knife. My father was out of the country on one of his working trips, and my mother was frightened out of her wits. So she arranged with the party office to have round-the-clock guards at the house. I found crates full of their ammunition in the garage. When my father returned home, he blew his stack.

"What the hell is all this!" he yelled. When my mother explained he only became angrier. "Are you crazy? I don't want people looking at guards and things and wondering who the hell lives here! You stupid woman! You want to lead assassins here?"

My mother cried and begged for forgiveness. I was so angry I felt like putting a sign out front inviting assassins into my father's den. Instead I skulked back to the library as soon as he left the house. There I read more of the things he wanted to keep from us.

As I grew older, I liked to look through all the newspapers with the holes cut in them, trying to figure out what had been censored. Then when we traveled outside Iraq, I would find out exactly what had been cut from those papers. The censored material was always either critical of Iraq, or favorable to Israel or America.

The more I read, the more I began to develop my own ideas about Israelis and Arabs. First I figured out that we Iraqis were exposed to only one side of the story. It's as if you are given only one-half of a great painting and asked to judge the whole thing. Then I learned that while we were taught to hate Israelis, many of them were taught to hate us, setting up a vicious circle. It was like a fixed equation: $a + b = x$. Israelis plus Arabs equals hate. Voices of moderation, tolerance and coexistence on both sides were smothered by the more strident voices of hate. It seemed to me that the Israelis had a right to exist. So did the Palestinians. And the fanatics on both sides were making sure that neither of them existed in peace.

Our education regarding America was slim. Basically the moral was that the Americans were power-hungry imperialists who got what they deserved in Vietnam. The only other salient fact was that America was the ally of Israel and was therefore the enemy. Period.

The Soviets were discussed a bit more favorably, because Moscow was currently arming Saddam. Moscow had signed the Iraqi-Soviet Pact in 1972, a very loose mutual alliance of the kind the USSR held with so many Third World nations as a foot in the door. Or rather a boot. It was the usual treaty providing Soviet military aid and Iraqi cooperation. So later, when the Soviets invaded Afghanistan, a fellow Muslim nation, our government officially condemned the act. But it was empty rhetoric. Iraq did nothing to help the Afghans or hinder the Soviets. Not a word about the conflict was ever reported on the state-run radio and television, or its press. The Afghans were furious, and a deep and lasting grudge was born.

But a clear line was drawn between the Soviets outside Iraq and the communists inside. While the Kremlin was busy arming Saddam, Saddam was busy wiping out the Iraqi communist party in a vicious internal campaign of terror.

My father's work took him to the center of this strange relationship with the Soviet Union. In 1976 he was appointed Ambassador to Poland for a four-year term. I was eleven at the time. We moved into an enormous old house in Warsaw, designated by the local authorities. It wasn't quite up to my parents' standards, but they had no choice. Our furniture from Italy and France, carpets from China and crystal from Austria managed to turn the house into a lavish mausoleum. It had three stories, with huge salons and countless bedrooms. We had three maids, a cook and a wolfhound named Auran, who roamed the halls frightening the staff. We lived a life of kings in this poor struggling country. While the Poles lined up for bread and other food in short supply, we dined on imported delicacies from Denmark and drank expensive French cognac. Cognac, in fact, was the local black-market currency. It could buy anything.

This was several years before the Solidarity movement of Lech Walesa gained momentum, and Poland was securely in the grip of the Kremlin. My father had to tread carefully. His main task, I learned later, was to find Iraqi communists and have them kidnapped and shipped home to the waiting hands of the secret police. His predecessors in the post had set up an efficient network of informers inside almost every facet of political life in Poland. With enough money, or even just parties and drinks, it was easy. The embassy was always throwing huge parties with sumptuous banquets and free-flowing liquor. Even a minor informer was guaranteed a place at the trough, and in a country like communist Poland, such treats were rare treasures.

All my father had to do was keep the operation going, putting Iraqis in Poland under surveillance and snatching the key figures who might pose a threat to Saddam. That meant, by and large, communists. Since the Soviet-Iraqi pact, many Iraqis came to the Soviet bloc for studies, and many of them became active in the clandestine communist movement aimed at turning Iraq into a Marxist paradise.

In Poland I was put in the Iraqi school in Warsaw to finish elementary grades. When I was thirteen, I was sent home to Baghdad for a special exam. For the first time, I was at home without my parents. Only my grandmother, Bibi, was there. I felt free for the first time in my life. My reaction was to try to build a bomb. I got hold of one of the books in the forbidden library and found a section on how to build homemade bombs from nitride and glycerine. I carefully mixed up the concoction and put it in a tin can with a rag wick. It was a bit like a Molotov cocktail. I invited a couple of friends over to watch the results. We lit it just outside the door of the house and ran for cover. Nothing happened. My friends laughed like hyenas at me, and I was crushed. It was the end of my career as a bomber. I decided I would have to turn my energy in another direction.

I took up girl-chasing with gusto. I'd been first infatuated when I was ten with a pretty girl in my class. I'd ordered my bodyguard and servant, Salah, to find out all about her — her family, what her father did, everything. In a short time he gave me all the details. I mapped out my campaign and soon had won her ten-year-old heart. I still remember her name and phone number.

As a teenager, I was insatiable. I became a typical hormonal male, lusting after girls, whom I treated with superior contempt. I was awful. And I was even worse after I lost my virginity, thanks to our Polish maid in Warsaw. She was an older woman who taught me what every young man wants to know.

In Baghdad, when I was in my early teens, my pals and I loafed around smoking and playing chess. We also went to the Hunt Club where the party elite and other rich folks cavorted on the tennis courts or sat by the pool and drank expensive liquor. Such was the glorious Ba'thist revolution. Our family still went on costly holidays abroad — to the Riviera, Turkey, Egypt — all paid for by the state.

From Warsaw we went to Spain. We traveled through the south, the land once ruled by the Muslim Moors. My father declaimed the whole time on the glories of the old Muslim civilization, whose culture and treasures had been brought to this primitive land. At the Alhambra, the magnificent palace of the

Moors in Grenada, he was like an American at the Statue of Liberty.

"This is what we brought to the world in the past and what we will return to with our revolution. You'll see," he said, turning to his children. "We will conquer the world. Just like the kings who lived here."

My cynical friends and I had a saying: The Englishman leans on a golf stick; the Frenchman leans on a pretty woman; we Arabs lean on the glories of the past. And blame others for our failures.

3

IN THE PAMPERED ELITE

WHEN I WAS GROWING UP, we didn't go to the mosque very often. In Islam, the home serves as well as the mosque for the five daily devotions. Mother tried her best to get her children to be good little Muslims and say our pre-sunrise, noon, afternoon, sunset and evening prayers. Each of these devotions were intoned while bowing toward Mecca.

She wrote the prayer out for me: *Allahu Akbar, Allahu Akbar, La illa ha il'allah* — God is great, God is great, there is but one God, Allah. She taught me how to wash my face and hands out of respect before these representations to Allah.

"If you love and respect Allah, he will love and respect you," she would say.

But already when I was twelve years old the prayers were irksome, all day interrupting everything I did. Besides, as far as I could see, the mullahs of the mosque were no better than any of the politicians my father brought home. They were always taking from people. If you wanted prayers said for so-and-so, there was a cost. Sometimes the fee was money, sometimes food, jewelry, or for the peasants, livestock. If you didn't want the mullah to report you for some transgression, he was deaf and blind for a small consideration. I believed in Allah, Muhammad and heaven and hell, but I could not accept the mullahs and all their oppressive rules.

Every few months we would visit the great shrines of Karbala and Najaf. I can still remember how they looked to me when I was little: huge and shining and frightening. Karbala and Najaf are the two most sacred centers of the Shi'a. Only a minority of Iraqis belong to the Sunni sect of Islam; about two-thirds are Shi'a. My mother is Shi'a. My father, Sunni.

The easiest way to explain the Shi'a and Sunni branches of Islam is to compare them with Catholics and Protestants; as in those branches of Christianity, the God is the same and the basic story is the same, but the prophets and the rites are treated differently. All sects of Islam trace their beliefs to the Prophet Muhammad. The foundation of the faith is the Koran, the written record of the series of divine revelations Muhammad received from God. All of this was about eight hundred years after Christ, who is regarded by Muslims as the last significant prophet before Muhammad himself. Islam honors all the prophets of the Old Testament and many of the teachings of Christ. It just doesn't regard Jesus as the Son of God.

The Islamic schism occurred with Muhammad's death. Since Muhammad had no male children, there was a dispute over his successor. The ancestors of today's Sunnis decided Muhammad was to be succeeded by a Caliph (a leader something like a pope) who would be appointed by the followers of the prophet. The ancestors of the Shi'a stuck with Ali, the adopted son-in-law of the prophet, who married Muhammad's daughter, Fatima.

Both Ali and his son and heir, Hussein, were killed in power struggles with the armies of successive Caliphs. Ali was assassinated at Kufa, near Najaf. Hussein was enticed into a trap, and he and his small army were massacred by the Caliph Yazid and his men. The tombs of Ali and Hussein are inside the awesomely beautiful mosques in Najaf and Karbala.

The Shi'a commemorate the martyrdom of Hussein every year at the time of Ashura, when the men bare their backs and in a frenzy lash themselves with whips. Thirteen hundred years later, the Shi'a are still the underdogs of Islam, and they still talk of revenge.

Clutching my mother's hand, I would follow her trembling through the magnificent archway at Karbala into the sunlit courtyard. Underneath the soaring golden domes and the brilliant turquoise-and-gold pillars, people would be crying and screaming, or just sitting in groups in niches in the outer wall. Terrified of the noise and the babble, I would cower further into my mother's *ab'a*, the long robe that covered her from head to foot. Normally she wore western-style street clothes, but no women were allowed inside these sacred precincts without this drapery of humility, and perhaps that strangeness added to my anxieties. In spite of in my childish fear, I felt there was a power and aura about the place. I would walk in as straight a line as possible, afraid to touch anything. It was like the western children's game, "Don't step on a crack, you'll break your mother's back." I would try not to step where I might break this unseen spirit. Inside the shrine itself, in the center of the courtyard, I would understand even less of the things people said and did, but gradually, the more I went, I grew less afraid and felt a kind of belonging there.

According to my mother, the Shi'a were peaceful, loving, civilized and oppressed. Since she was all of these things, we believed her. For her, Shi'ism was her relationship with God. It was in no way political. She avoided all politics.

I was fourteen when Ayatollah Khomeini overthrew the powerful Shah of Iran in a full-scale popular Islamic revolution. We all whooped for joy. I'll always remember the date Khomeini returned to Iran from exile — February 1, 1979. It changed our world. Suddenly one of the main pillars of the existing power structure of our region had simply vanished. As a result, it seemed inevitable that something else was bound to collapse, too. None of us had much love for the Shah. The Persians (Iranians) are traditional enemies of Arab Iraq. Worse, the Shah had been an ally of Israel, furnishing it with oil in exchange, basically, for military hardware. So even Sunni Arab Iraq was celebrating. But not for long.

Within months, Iraq and Iran were back in their old stance of mortal enemies. In Iraq, the Strong Man finally took over absolutely. Saddam and his fellow Tikritis already ruled the country through the vicious police and security apparatus they had created. They controlled the economy by controlling virtually every product and service, from the oil industry to horse races, from car parts to camels. Patronage, which had always been a plague, now became the heart of the system that fed the elite and starved the dispossessed.

Ahmad Hasan al-Bakr was only nominally the head of state; Saddam controlled the regime and the country. He had first signaled this with a crackdown on dissidents, and by a slaughter of both communists and Jews. The public execution of seventeen members of a supposed Zionist spy ring in early 1969 was followed by a witch hunt for communists, who suffered similar fates after being tortured to reveal their comrades. All of this was just a prelude to the main business of eliminating rivals within the party itself.

The first to go was Bakr himself. He was put under enormous pressure from Saddam and his powerful allies to resign. His departure allowed Saddam to take over for "the good of the party." The implied threat to Bakr was not even thinly veiled. Saddam ascended to the seat of power on July 17, 1979.

The first thing he did was to purge the party.

I was spending summer vacation with my parents, so we were all in Poland when Saddam took over. One day my father came home in a state of great agitation. We were ordered to pack immediately for home. He told us there was a grave situation in Baghdad. A telex had come from the ministry saying a major plot to overthrow the government had been discovered. Father talked wildly of traitors and spies and was in a perfect fury.

"These traitors will be punished!" he yelled. "They will regret their mothers ever gave them life! They will die, all of them! They are garbage!"

We were accustomed to his ranting about minor infractions the regime saw as mutiny. But we could tell this time it was far more serious. When we returned to Baghdad he stormed off to the ministry, leaving us at home to glean what we could from the television news given by the government. What we saw was an elaborately staged purge of Saddam's rivals. This was carried out in a bizarre meeting of about a thousand party members. It was initiated by a "confession" of treason from a Shi'ite member, who then read out a list of his fellow conspirators. As he read the name of one, the camera focused on the man in question, who appeared ready to faint. The confessor then said, "But he refused to join us," and the man went limp with relief. By now all the men in the assembly were either weeping or shouting, "Long live Saddam! Let me die for you!"

This irrational and hysterical behavior is less of a puzzle for us Iraqis than it is for westerners, some of whom also saw the video. This offer to die for the great leader, whoever he is, is a common declaration of loyalty in the Middle Eastern political arena. Tears and other emotional outbursts that would be seen as evidence for need of psychiatric help in the West are part and parcel of men of power in our culture. It's sort of a hysterical form of male bonding.

Then Saddam harangued the gathering about party loyalty and betrayal. In this emotionally charged atmosphere, other members began rising to accuse others. Executions were demanded. There was sobbing and crying and applause. Then more cries of "Long live Saddam!"

The traitors were to be executed by their fellow party members. The senior party officials lined up in firing squads at Abu Ghareb prison the next day and shot their colleagues. This was not on television. I knew about it because my own father was one of the executioners. It was the kind of work he enjoyed. At home, he was tense and said nothing, but it was clear he derived great satisfaction from the bloodletting.

The "plot" against him gave Saddam a perfect cover for the elimination of others he believed might be rivals. He was especially interested in the armed forces. Though he had assumed a military title and rank, and commanded the armed forces, Saddam still had a deeply rooted fear and hatred of genuine military officers. In a few years, it was a wonder there was anyone left in the military competent enough to clean a rifle, let alone command an army.

Iron rule backed up by firing squads now settled over Iraq.

My family was still part of the pampered elite. In addition to the perks I normally got because of my father's position, I was able to go into business in a small way. Whenever we traveled, I would buy videotapes, small tape recorders, cassettes and, last but not least, pornographic magazines. Beforehand, I had sneaked a look at my father's papers to find out his telex number, as well as that of the Ministry of Foreign Affairs. I would send a telex to the ministry in my father's name, telling them to have someone at the airport to meet me and shepherd me through customs. Father usually stayed abroad longer. I would then sell my contraband at huge profits to my schoolmates. At the tender age of fifteen, I had moved on from chocolate to more serious stuff.

My father had arranged for me to go to an elite secondary school for rising young Ba'thists, but as usual he was not around to supervise, and I simply went to the school of my choice. He never knew. Carrying on my activities at the school I'd chosen was relatively easy. We only had classes three mornings and three afternoons during the week, and there was no discipline whatsoever. The place was rough, complete with fistfights in the halls, but one of the best academically. In exchange for cassettes, a couple of the toughs handled any fights for me. The porn was a big hit. This wasn't *Playboy* or any of the other tame, sanitized sex with the coy-looking pussycat girls. This was the real stuff from Amsterdam. And in our society, where the real thing was pretty much kept under wraps, it was powerful stuff. Some of the fellows managed to get their girlfriends into bed, but at that time, I still held back for fear of the consequences. I knew where babies came from. The Polish maid had been a brief introduction, then prudence took over. We Iraqi teens had blue jeans, the Beatles, the Rolling Stones, and all the other paraphernalia of the sixties, a bit late, but in any event we had it all except freedom.

I had already developed a taste for secrecy and intrigue. Even in my little black market, I kept everything compartmentalized so no one knew who else was buying; sometimes I didn't deal directly but instead went through a middle man. I wanted to minimize the risk and knew that the best way was to tell everyone a slightly different story, keep them all apart, with no one knowing the whole truth of my operation. In a small way I was like the FLN in Algiers, where none of the revolutionaries knew the command structure, in case they were caught. Some didn't even know the FLN controlled them.

That was how I learned to survive in Saddam's Iraq. Iraqis are a very passionate people, drastically so. If we love someone, we'll give him our heart, our eyes, our lives. But if we hate someone, only God knows what will happen. When Saddam's all-seeing state was imposed over people with such strong emotions, it meant that people didn't even trust their own dreams, let alone other people. Even in sleep, we feared we might say something that would displease the beast. I learned early how to live in the shadows.

I also discovered that the revolution next door in Iran wasn't the great liberation of the people we had originally thought. Every day we heard of more killings and people put in jail. We heard how the mullahs were turning out to be even worse than the Shah and his famous secret police, SAVAK. Political opposition to the clerical party of Khomeini's mullahs was banned, books were burned, and the universities were turned into centers of Islamic dogma. Women were persecuted and forced back into the Middle Ages. They were segregated, shrouded in kerchiefs and long robes, forbidden to wear makeup or to be caught in public with any male who was not a relative. The *pasdars*, or revolutionary guards, roamed the streets of every Iranian town and city, savagely enforcing the new orders. It was a long way from the sunny, tolerant Shi'ism my mother had taught me. Khomeini ruled a lot like other warrior priests of Islam of the past, with blood and brimstone.

Then they took the hostages.

On November 4, 1979, a motley group calling itself the Student Followers of the Imam's Line seized the American embassy in Tehran and proceeded to hold the staff hostage for more than a year. That crisis ended what little power the more moderate

Iranian revolutionaries had, and left the radical clergy firmly in charge.

The Koran, like the Bible, is a revelation, but it is also a poetic record, written by mere mortals. As such, it is very clear and precise in some parts, and very vague and open to interpretation in others. The verses, called *suras*, have been used by ambitious political leaders and religious pretenders ever since the death of Muhammad. Politicians drape themselves in all kinds of piousness, making sure television cameras record them at prayer, and power-hungry mullahs issue *fatwas*, declarations of holy law, bending the Koran to their interpretation of the *suras*. The Middle East is fertile ground for religious pretenders, since its people are always looking for a supreme religious leader. Why they are, I'm not sure. Perhaps it comes from living in what the West calls the Biblical lands, where every acre reeks of the history of the prophets and other holies.

Islam, I was beginning to discover, was not necessarily by nature tolerant. In fact, its original followers were ordered to conquer the infidels, and either convert them or kill them. Khomeini and his men were well within tradition.

And as far as Khomeini was concerned, Saddam was one of the infidels. Khomeini had been preaching Islamic Revolution from the safety of the mosque in Najaf — he'd been exiled by the Shah years before and taken refuge in Iraq — and when the Shah asked Saddam to muzzle him or throw him out, Saddam obliged. Saddam, after all, had no love for Khomeini. The imam was stirring up Iraq's own enormous Shi'a population. The Iranian mullahs preached revolution and broadcast their sermons into Iraqi territory. The cassette recordings of Khomeini's own exhortations, which had been smuggled into Iran with such deadly effect, were now being smuggled into Iraqi mosques and passed around.

The Iranian clergy backed a fanatic group of Shi'a fundamentalists in Iraq called the Da'wah. The Da'wah were busy fomenting Islamic revolution in Saddam's own backyard. Determined to wipe them out, Saddam arrested their leader, Ayatollah Muhammad Bakr Sadr, and his sister. He had them horribly tortured and finally murdered.

Then Saddam went to war against Khomeini himself. Saddam launched his armies across the Iranian border in September 1980 proclaiming that Allah was on his side and predicting victory in a few days. His stated objective was the reclaiming of a bit of oil-rich border territory Iraq had lost in a long-ago war with the Persians. Instead, the war became a long-drawn-out mortal combat. Khomeini's men screamed out slogans against Saddam, calling him Saddam Yazid, after the murderer of their great martyr Hussein, son of Ali.

While the Iranians and Iraqis were at it, the Soviets decided to take over Afghanistan in December. Their puppet regime there was on its last legs, so the Kremlin propped it up with 400,000 soldiers and helicopter gunships in a war that became as equally mired as the Iran-Iraq conflict, and equally impossible to win.

At school we were bombarded with propaganda of how the Americans were getting what they deserved in Iran, but that the Iranians, too, were the enemies of Arab Iraq and the True Faith of Sunni Islam. On television, we still had the same old litany of American disaster films, such as *Towering Inferno* or *Apocalypse Now*. We also watched films of cowboys and Indians killing each other, and ones about people fighting terminal diseases and losing. Then there were the films about the oppression of the blacks, plus the endless run of drugs and murder cop stories. You would have thought the United States was one big catastrophe.

In spite of this concentrated effort to turn everyone into America-haters, everyone continued to love American clothes, hamburgers, blue jeans, music and the rest of the outer shell of American culture. At the same time, deep down, many had a genuine hatred of American global power. The reason for this can be explained in one word: Israel. It is a measure of the depth of the Arabs' hatred for Israel that, even though they loved so much about American pop culture, when it came down to brass tacks, they viewed America as the enemy. America meant Israel. Anyone who fails to understand this will not understand why the "situation in the Middle East" cannot be solved. Because America is so intimately allied with Israel, and Israel is seen as the root of all evil in the Arab world, then whenever anything bad happens in the Arab world, it is the fault of the Americans. I don't say this as a theory, but as a fact. For in our unique system of logic, a theory believed is a fact. There is no intermediary analytical thought. My theory is my belief, therefore a fact.

You can have a war between Iran and Iraq, with Iraq using Soviet weapons and with Americans held hostage in Iran, in which both the Iranian and the Iraqi people will tell you unequivocally that the Americans are Behind It All. The Americans are the enemy. It doesn't matter that the Iraqis are flying Soviet MiGs. Iranians announced that America is bombing Iran. And Iraqis announced that America is behind Iran's missiles hitting Iraq.

In 1980, America became a lot easier to hate. Jimmy Carter, who seemed like a nice guy, was replaced by Ronald Reagan, who, with his talk of "evil empires," was a caricature of the Ugly American.

The Soviets, on the other hand, were officially our friends. But as I had already figured out while watching my father at work in Poland, that friendship didn't go very far in either direction. As far as Afghanistan was concerned, it was decided that the best policy was total silence. It was as if the Afghan war were an embarrassing relative, to be kept locked in the room upstairs.

At home things remained pretty much the same: my father yelling at us, my mother trying to defend us. I was afraid of him, but something always made me defy him. I hated the way he used his power inside our home, like using a cannon against a hummingbird. He always acted as if the slightest disagreement with him was an attempted assassination. I came to realize that my father was psychotic. I also realized that he was precisely the type that functioned well in Saddam's dangerously insane regime.

I finally went beyond the pale when I stole the car.

During the war with Iran we had two cars, one with an even-numbered license plate, one with an odd-numbered plate. That was because in this oil-rich country, gasoline was rationed during the war. Even-numbered plates could go out on the roads some days of the week, odd-numbered on alternate days. We could go out every day of the week. One of the cars was a Mercedes 250 that I decided to "borrow" when I was fifteen. I thought it was time I learned how to drive.

Father came home one day for a long nap and I took the opportunity to steal the keys from his pocket to go joyriding. I was feeling terrific until I crashed. Not a bad crash, but the road was muddy and when I turned, the car skidded into a roadside barrier, denting the rear. No problem. I hammered the spot a bit from the underside, and everything looked normal.

I was taken aback the next day when my father came in ranting about the car. I had forgotten the gas gage. My obsessive father kept a check on the gas gage.

He used an extra big belt and hit me as hard as he could. For the first time in my life, I hit him back. I was big now, and strong, and in my fury and hatred, I really slugged him. My mother came running in screaming and trying to pull us apart.

I wasn't afraid of him anymore. I knew he was just an empty

bully. So I made a copy of the car keys, and kept on borrowing the Mercedes. Furious, my father actually sold the car. If he could have, he would have sold me instead.

The wonder was that he took me along when the family moved to Zimbabwe. In 1982, he was appointed first Iraqi ambassador to this former British colony. To do things in style, the Iraqi government had bought a magnificent piece of land with an enormous and luxurious home for the meager sum of $100,000 U.S. Probably the former estate of a well-to-do family of English Rhodesians, long since gone. The house was L-shaped, with spacious rooms and expensive antiques from Europe, inlaid cabinets from Hong Kong, Czechoslovakian crystal. A kidney-shaped pool graced one side of the gardens, and a tennis court was set out on the other. There were garages with rooms above for our bodyguards, maids and cooks. With this Shangri-la as his base, my father's job was to handle Iraqi relations with virtually the entire African continent. I was soon to begin to be aware of the real nature of my father's work as a "diplomat."

But at seventeen, I was still too young to be fully aware of just what Father's job was. My relationship with my father was as always: nonexistent save for his customary outbursts of irrational fury. If he did speak to me other than in anger, it was in the manner of a master to a servant.

"We are going to a luncheon at (so and so's) this afternoon. The family is expected. You will be ready at noon."

My mother, resigned to this hollow home life, performed her role as ambassador's wife in a perfunctory but dutiful way. And she was still the one warm refuge of love and affection in my life. I was far more intent on having fun. During the year I was in Zimbabwe, my friends were the sons, and daughters, of other diplomats who attended the same elite school as I. My pals and I didn't talk about politics; we talked about cars and girls.

In my sixth and last year of high school there, I passed my exams, as well as the special test administered by the Iraqi Ministry of Education for university entrance. My first choice was to join the elite air force — so that I could eventually take one of the MiG's or Mirages and defect to Israel like Munir Rouffa, an Iraqi pilot who had delivered his state-of-the-art jet fighter to the Israelis in 1966 when he flew over the rainbow. Saddam's anathema was my hero. Along with Eli Cohen.

My father must have suspected something devious, because he refused to even consider the air force. He wanted me to be a doctor. Not so that I could actually be a doctor. So that he could have his son, the doctor. I applied to Inglewood in Los Angeles for electronics and avionics and was accepted. Father said no. Finally my mother was able to make him relent enough to let me go to England, at her expense, to study computer electronics.

So I was off to England and to a whole new world of freedom.

4

INTO THE LION'S DEN

I WONDER IF THE BRITISH KNOW that Mideastern spies, conspirators and assassins regard their country as the world's biggest playground. And not just in London. The provincial towns have been hotbeds of activity, too. I ended up in Manchester and it was no exception.

I loved England. For the first time in my life I was truly on my own. I was seventeen. It was easy to get to know other students because most of us lived in the comfortable university residences. I had my own room, a big bedsitter, with a sink and one of those incredibly old-fashioned English heaters that have to be fed with coins. Eight of us shared the one bathroom on the floor. Among those on my floor were a Norwegian, an Italian, a Malaysian and a Spaniard. We were a hodgepodge of nationalities.

I could have taken meals at the residence, but I preferred to go out so I could practice my English. I had done well in English at school and had taken private lessons in Poland. I wanted to become truly fluent.

Everyone told me, "If you want to learn English really well, get an English girlfriend." I took their advice and began my pursuit enthusiastically. The pill and western culture removed all constraints. I discovered that many English girls harbored the myth of the romantic desert sheikh, and I seemed to be considered more talented in bed than their own chaps. Or maybe I was perceived as a bit of a cave man, which some girls found a turn-on. Anyway, I was happy to oblige. Until I settled down with a steady girlfriend named Sue. And I was happy. It wasn't just the sex. It was being able to have a normal friendship with the girls, with or without sex, instead of the old-fashioned and artificial codes of my own country.

We went to private parties held in rented discos, and I made money on the side selling tickets to these wild nights. In return for the odd free ticket, a few of my fellow students helped me through some of the courses and labs.

Among the other Arab students, especially the Iraqis, I said nothing about my father. The last thing I wanted was for his reputation to follow me here. I invented a story about his being in the paper business.

All my life people had called me "Ali's son" or "Sumaida's son," and here I could be me, plain old Hussein. It was exhilarating. I was free of him. But then I realized I was not free of his shadow, and his imprint was deep in my soul.

Ironically, now that I was free, I wanted to strike out at him more than ever. Politics had always been the surest way to score a direct hit, and now that I was grown I was in a position finally to take full advantage of that knowledge.

I decided I wanted to join one of the Iraqi groups in England that was working against the regime of Saddam. This meant I had basically two choices: the communists, or the Da'wah. I ruled out the former without even checking them out. Communism hadn't a chance in Iraq, and in any case what I'd seen of Marxism made me believe it was just another form of tyranny. Why have it replace Ba'thist tyranny? That left the Da'wah, the Shi'a Islamic movement. I began to feel them out.

At that time, I still believed that Shi'ism might really be as my mother described. I thought that perhaps the Iranians had just got it all wrong and used this ancient Arab faith for their own perfidious Persian ends. The Persians had been conquered by Muslim armies and had been forced to accept Islam, but then had turned it on its head: they embraced Shi'ism, which was the avowed enemy of the Arab Caliphs. I held out a last hope that the Shi'a movement would be my answer — until I met the Da'wah face-to-face.

During lunch or after classes some Iraqi students would get together and talk of home. A frequent topic was the war between Iran and Iraq. This inevitably brought the conversation around to Shi'ism.

When I mentioned that my mother was Shi'a, the boys in the Da'wah took an interest. The fact that I'd been named after the two great Shi'a martyrs, Hussein and Ali, further reassured them. Assuming that I would automatically be sympathetic, they'd rant on about how wonderful Khomeini was and how when he won the war, Iraq would become a new Shi'a Islamic republic, just like Iran.

These were Iraqi students like me talking, but it seemed they wanted Iraq to become a province of Khomeini's Iran. I held my tongue and listened. I was both fascinated and appalled. I pretended to agree, not sure of what I was doing, or of what I planned to do.

I got to know one of their number, Noman. It turned out he was the head of the Da'wah cells in Manchester. The cells had thirty or so members. Small, but terrorists and guerrillas don't need numbers. They need dedication.

Noman was fairly tall, yet pudgy. He had the sort of scruffy beard the Da'wah fellows all affected, and short hair. He always wore a military-type khaki fatigue jacket. Noman had been trained in Lebanon, where he had relatives. There, he and his fellow recruits were taught basic military skills, as well as the specialized skills used by the radical Lebanese Shi'a militia, the Hezbollah, which means Party of God. At the time, the world had barely heard of the Hezbollah, or its radical core, Islamic Jihad, both of which were supported and in part controlled by Tehran. But in a few years they would grab global headlines as the terrorist kidnappers of westerners in Lebanon. What they demanded for the release of those hostages was the release of several Iraqi Da'wah guerrillas held in prison in Kuwait after they bombed the American and French embassies there. This was the sort of thing the Da'wah trained for; they learned about explosives.

In 1982, before I went to England, they had bombed the Iraqi Embassy in Beirut, killing about thirty people. Noman was particularly proud of this exploit, giving the impression he had been part of the overall planning. He talked about how he and his men were waging a *jihad*, a holy war against Saddam the infidel. The taking of western hostages, the Israeli invasion of Lebanon, the bombing of the Marines and the American Embassy, all made headlines in the western press, but this bit of inter-Arab violence essentially went unreported in the West.

The Da'wah was one of two main religious movements in Iraq. The other drew its members from Sunni Muslims. It was strictly political, without a military wing, since it didn't have a foreign sponsor to pay for arms. It was patterned after the Ikhwan el Muslemmin, the Muslim Brotherhood, which was founded in Egypt and boasted such alumni as Yasser Arafat. In Iraq it was called the Brotherhood, and at the time it supported Saddam as the least of several possible evils.

The Da'wah was the movement that Saddam was doing everything in his power to wipe from the face of the earth. This militant Shi'a group has both a political and military arm, and is backed mainly by the Iranians. After Saddam killed its leader, Bakr Sadr, it was led by Ayatollah Muhammad Bakr al-Hakim (no relation). Under his leadership, the military arm grew more radical and more daring. Bombings became a daily occurrence in the cities of Iraq. They hit everything from the television station to pipelines and marketplaces.

The Hakim family controlled the other rival Shi'a faction, as well. It was called the Monathema al-Beit, meaning Organization of the Descendants of the House of Muhammad, and was run by Bakr al-Hakim's brother, Mehdi al-Hakim. The idea was for the family to control all factions and eventually unite them all to take over from Saddam when the moment was ripe.

Saddam wanted to make sure that moment never came. When a Da'wah suicide bomber drove an ambulance loaded with explosives into the headquarters of the air force, the Iraqi regime went to new lengths to identify the perpetrator. To foil pursuit, a Da'wah bomber always commits his final act of glory carrying no identification of any kind. In this case, the bomber was blown into bits and pieces. Undaunted, Saddam's men gathered them up, sewed them all together and presented this grim reincarnation on television. They offered a reward to anyone who recognized it. When the corpse was finally identified, they killed the man's entire family.

Unlike party and army people, whom Saddam dispatched with quickly and neatly by firing squad, the Da'wah merited the special attention of Amn torturers. Information about Da'wah cells, their members and plots were wrung from those suspected. A favorite method was to force a glass bottle up the rectum and threaten to smash it inside and then twist it. If this didn't work, the captive might have his hands tied tightly behind his back and then be strung up by his arms with ropes passed through his elbows to a heavy rotating ceiling fan. The agony as the shoulders slowly separated from the body can only be compared with descriptions of the excruciating pain of crucifixion. Few survived it.

Saddam also deported thousands of Shi'ites to Iran, as well as Iraqis of Iranian origin. Among the deportees he included agents of his own to work inside Iran against the ayatollahs. These deportations also provided him with another way to get rid of dangerously talented military officers.

As it turned out, the Shi'a who were deported early on were the lucky ones. Until the war with Iran, whole families were evicted from their homes, their property and businesses confiscated, and they were taken in trucks and dumped at the Iranian border. Later, during the war with Iran, the government thugs would keep the men of military age (fifteen to fifty) in Iraq. We knew of one poor Shi'a woman who had seven sons, and when she and her father were deported, her sons were held in Abu Ghareb prison in Iraq. Two were executed, and no one knows about the other five. She and her daughter finally left for Syria. She was always asking, "Where are my sons?" and crying.

Once Saddam began to move against the Da'wah, all the detainees disappeared. A special secret department was formed for the job of getting rid of any Shi'a who didn't show sufficient support for the regime. Some were sent to walk over Iranian mine fields.

By 1984, when I was in England, the Da'wah leadership had been pretty well wiped out inside Iraq. Mehdi al-Hakim was in Tehran. Even the agents that the Da'wah had managed to send in from Iran and Syria were being intercepted, as Iraqi Intelligence had penetrated their networks. Hakim was assassinated in early 1988 in an astonishing operation by the Mukhabarat. Astonishing in that it was so meticulously and elaborately planned and carried out. While al-Hakim was at a conference in the Sudan, two agents came up to him as he sat with two other delegates in the lobby of the hotel where the conference was held. They shot him point-blank, without using silencers. In the ensuing chaos, they escaped to a waiting aircraft at the nearby airport and boarded without any obstacles, as they showed their diplomatic papers.

The Da'wah cells in exile did much the same kind of work that the Iranian revolutionaries did during their years of opposition. They concentrated on recruiting, holding anti-Saddam protest demonstrations in places like Hyde Park and, above all, propagandizing. They had learned from Khomeini to make all the right noises about how they believed in democracy, to woo western journalists and politicians. What they planned, of course, was a theocratic dictatorship as thorough and brutal as Khomeini's. In fact they wanted full union with Iran.

This is what I was involved with in far-off Manchester.

Noman was in his mid-twenties, a perfect specimen of a person whose meaningless life finally took on significance when he became a religious zealot. Powerlessness was replaced by feelings of power. Religion provided the answers to all his questions and provided the explanation and the solution for all problems. The cause of all problems, of course, were the infidel Israelis and Americans; the solution was Islam. Noman was absolutely dedicated to this answer. Islam was not just the answer in politics, but to every aspect of life. At a coffee shop one day he decided to try to bring me further into the fold by persuading me to give up girls and drinking.

"Girls are bad for you, for your life. They should have no part of what is important to you. And drinking! It's against the law of Allah."

I just looked at him. Cynically, I thought, he just wants to have his head clear for the important business of repression and killing. Like Saddam, Khomeini made sure that his version of Islam invaded every moment with a woman, every sip of a drink, every breath in and out — every facet of life.

"Khomeini is a great man, and the savior of our people," he went on. "Saddam," he whispered, as he leaned closer, "is our enemy, the enemy of Islam and of the people. He's in power only for himself. He tries to fool the people into thinking he's a good Muslim. But he's a fake and a tyrant. We're going to deliver him to Khomeini. Then Iraq will be free."

You got the first half right, I thought silently. Saddam was certainly a fake and a tyrant. As the war dragged on, he made greater and greater efforts to appear more Islamic than the mullahs. His propaganda machine had come up with a family tree that traced his roots back to the great martyr Hussein himself, and it was posted in every mosque in the country. On television Saddam was seen at prayer regularly. Meanwhile Khomeini's hordes kept calling him Saddam Yazid, the traitor and murderer.

Noman and his friends began to invite me to their homes. We discussed the latest *fatwa* (declaration of religious law) from Khomeini, what happened in the last battle with our soldiers, and the latest massacre of frenzied teenagers sent into battle with plastic keys to heaven and promises of martyrdom. The discussions were grotesque.

Noman and his friends believed that everything negative that was said about Khomeini was enemy propaganda. Khomeini never killed anyone. People being executed in Iran were being killed by someone who only pretended to be Khomeini. Khomeini was innocent of all the oppression, the rape and torture of young women, the horrible, stupid war. At the same time, they would babble about how the war was justified, that to free Iraq there must be sacrifice for the freedom. What freedom? I thought. Khomeini's? I couldn't believe it. What planet did they live on? But there again was that old mental disease: my theory is my belief, therefore a fact. For these fanatics, the Islamic revolution was paradise.

For me, the Da'wah were a disappointing bunch of lunatics. Khomeini and his Islamic revolution had built the perfect killing machine, and I had no doubt that these boys would do exactly the same in my country, given the chance. It was even conceivable that they would be worse than Saddam, just as Khomeini was worse than the Shah. Iran had turned into a killing field, like Cambodia.

In science we learned that for every action there is an equal and opposite reaction. The Da'wah taught me that for every oppressed Shi'a there is an oppressor of the same stripe. Therefore my equal and opposite reaction to the Da'wah was extreme.

One night in 1984 around Easter, I made a decision. I know now that it was a hasty decision, probably even a stupid one. As I look back, I am amazed and a bit appalled at the way I took so many drastic steps, made life-and-death decisions, in a kind of fit. Whether this impulsiveness is the result of life under my father, or life under Saddam, or both, I don't know. But when I look back, I realize that I was becoming motivated not just by an urge for vengeance on my father, but because I was developing political beliefs of my own. And knowledge. And given what I now knew of the Da'wah and Khomeini's brand of Islam, I could not work for them. That was more important now than my personal vendetta.

On the contrary, I decided I had to do what I could to destroy the Da'wah. I made the decision in spite of the fact that it meant working for the forces that supported Saddam Hussein.

There was another Iraqi student on the campus named Hassan, whom I knew from the Iraqi students union. From bits of talk I overheard, I knew he had something to do with the Ba'th Party. Hassan, who was a bit older than me, was studying for his PhD in nuclear physics. To study such a subject meant he must have had links with security and intelligence in Iraq. Anyone at that level in such a sensitive area had to be cleared by intelligence. I went to him and told him the truth about my father's identity.

I also told him I had learned a great deal about certain of our Shi'a compatriots in the university. Two days later, Hassan brought me to a small lounge above the bar at the university to meet two men from Sheffield who had come at his request. The room was rather dark, with only one window looking out over the quadrangle. The carpet muffled any noise. I looked at the two men and realized I was dealing with Saddam's chosen few. Their aura of power and ruthlessness was unmistakable. The larger of the two was introduced as Auda. Later I realized he was one of two Iraqi agents who had been captured in Iran by the Shah in 1976 and returned to Iraq as part of a friendship-treaty deal. Auda was a senior agent. He listened intently to my story of Noman and his colleagues, then questioned me about my background. My father's name was enough in itself. My bona fides were above suspicion.

"This will be the first time in eight months we've been able to penetrate the Da'wah," Auda said in a deep, slow voice. "You'll be the mole."

It was only then that I fully realized the ramifications of what I had done. My God! I was working for the secret police. That meant that one way or another, I was working for the Mukhabarat itself! In Iraq this is the most powerful arm of the security apparatus.

Auda was with the Jihaz Amn al-Hezib, the Instrument of Party Security. It was in turn controlled by the Maktab Amanat Sir al-Kutur, which translates badly as the National Bureau and Keeper of Secrets. Somehow in English it sounds like something out of a children's book. In Arabic it sounded as grim as it really was.

When the security matter in question was outside Iraq, the

Mukhabarat took over direction of the Jihaz Amn al-Hezib. And here I was joining forces with these dreaded men in a dim room in an English university in Manchester.

Auda instructed me to continue pretending that I was in agreement with my Da'wah friends, to learn everything I could and then to report to him. Each Monday and Thursday, if I had anything to report, I was to go to the library at a specific time and to a specific part of the shelves. Auda would be on the other side of the row of shelves, and I would pass my report to him across the books. If I had nothing to report, I simply wasn't to show up. If there was anything urgent, I was to contact a captain in the Ministry of Defense who was studying English at the university, a man by the name of Sami al-Asadi, and we would meet at his home.

As I became more accepted by the Da'wah group, Noman invited me to attend the sessions they held at the home of another member named Salah. It was a small place, in a neighborhood of row housing just outside Manchester. About six or eight of us would gather in the bedsitting room upstairs, having tea and praising Khomeini. I used to make it a point to arrive exactly on time, which meant a while before the others, who were always late. When Salah went downstairs to let the others in, I would quickly go through the papers on his desk, looking for names, bank accounts, anything.

Even though these fanatics represented a horrible threat, spying on them didn't give me a good feeling. Quite the opposite. I was nervous and frightened. There was no telling what they would do if they discovered me. I tried not to think about it. I just did the job I'd brought down on my own head.

When we were all assembled, Noman would hold forth on the latest *fatwa* from Khomeini, the latest "victory" in the war, and the rest would make noises of praise. They were a motley lot, all with that scruffy beard and variations on the jeans and khaki jacket

Noman liked. Myself, I had always been something of a modish dresser, with a preference for the snazzy styles of the German brand Matinique, carried by exclusive stores worldwide. No blue jeans for me. That should have warned them I wasn't one of them at heart.

Sometimes Noman told his group about agents going into Syria to train before going into Iraq. And though he never revealed the agents' full names, he revealed their route: it was the same route traveled by the Kurdish resistance and ran through Turkey.

My secret-service colleagues helped my credibility by spreading stories about how I was a dangerous anti-Saddam activist. So by day I went around with the Da'wah putting up stickers that said Saddam was a new Hitler, and by night I went around with Saddam's agents taking them down.

Every few days I passed along my reports in the library, giving Auda names, dates of meetings to be held and plans of clandestine activities. I gave him their bank-account numbers and revealed the source of their support. Some money was transferred from Syria and some from Algeria.

I never knew what became of Noman and his Da'wah pals. But they were small fry, and I figured Auda and his bosses simply kept them under long surveillance in order to get to the head of the enemy. In any case, none of my Da'wah gang disappeared right away. For a time I rationalized what I was doing by telling myself I knew what kind of fate the Da'wah would have in store for most of Iraq if they ever got into power. I had Iran to show me in technicolor.

But no matter how I rationalized, I was not happy with what I was doing. I think what bothered me was the realization that, by a horrible twist of fate and politics, I was working for the monster Saddam and his killing machine. And my father. The more I thought about this, the more I tossed and turned in my sleep. One night, a strange idea began to form in the clouds of my mind: Mossad.

My old idea of defecting to Israel, of being an Iraqi Eli Cohen, had always been there, hovering at the edge of my thoughts. I rolled over again and tried to sleep. Mossad. The Israelis.

Maybe I could even the score with my father and his master, Saddam, if I worked for the Mossad. I could get in touch with them somehow. I could offer my services to help them fight Saddam. In the morning, I sat down to write a letter to the Mossad. Since I didn't have their address, I simply wrote on the envelope "Israeli Embassy, London."

I said I was an Iraqi and proposed getting together to fight people we both hated. "If you want to talk," I wrote, "send someone to Manchester, to the Britannia Hotel on the main street." I gave them a time and date, then added, "Have your man wear a red flower in his lapel."

This was authentically stupid. My only excuse is that I was nineteen years old. Half-aware even then of how ridiculous it was, I went to my rendezvous. Of course no one showed up.

Undaunted, I decided to travel to London and go to the Israeli Embassy in person. I felt like Daniel headed for the lions' den.

5

WORKING FOR THE ARCHENEMY

THE ISRAELI EMBASSY IN LONDON is a formidable-looking building located in the district of High Kensington. When I went there, the street on which it sits was barricaded. Unlike the American Embassy, which seemed to be so highly vulnerable to attack at the time, the Israeli Embassy in London, like its missions all over the world, was secured because the worst was always expected.

It was pouring rain when I reached the Israeli fortress. I had barely got to the gate when I was forced through a metal detector and roughly searched.

"Business?" the guard questioned suspiciously.

"I want to see someone in intelligence," I stammered.

The guard's face twisted. "What the hell for?"

I fished out my ID and thrust it at him. "I must see someone in security and intelligence," I repeated.

The guard narrowed his eyes and motioned to another guard, who ambled over. "This jerk wants to see someone in security and intelligence."

The second guard looked at my ID and grinned meanly. "Really," he said sarcastically.

"It's important," I insisted. I knew I must have looked less than reputable. I was soaked. I must have looked like a drowning rat, an Arab rat at that.

The first guard shrugged and phoned. His eyes on my ID, he spoke to someone in rapid Hebrew, and then put the phone down and returned his eyes to me. I only understood one thing in his conversation, and that was my own name, Hussein Ali Sumaida.

"Tomorrow," he instructed, "go to the consulate entrance and ask for Isaac."

I wanted to argue, to insist they see me immediately, but I didn't. I assumed their insistence on tomorrow must have had some purpose. Perhaps they thought I was unbalanced and that such a person would not return for an actual appointment. Perhaps they wanted to do some checking.

It was still raining the next day. What would London be without rain? Jerusalem? This time when I was checked at the gate I was allowed inside after another thorough search and a pass through the metal detector. I was told to follow a winding path past the main embassy building to the consulate on the other side of the inner garden.

Another guard gruffly directed me upstairs through a white door and then through another door on the right. Inside was a small waiting room. Another door led to a well-furnished office. It was there that Isaac was waiting for me.

He was a fat man, a bit taller than me, with spiky gray-black hair. In his gray suit he seemed to me a typical Israeli, businesslike and tough.

He was also angry. "What do you want?" he demanded. "And who sent you?"

"Nobody sent me. I want to work with you," I offered.

"Let me see your passport."

I fished in my pocket and handed it over.

He studied it and scowled. "Does your father know you're here?"

So they had checked. Perhaps they had checked out that stupid letter I'd sent them, too. I shook my head, "No. He knows nothing. It was my idea." Vaguely I wondered if they'd thought about my age. Perhaps they thought this was merely a teenage prank.

"Wait here," Isaac instructed.

I waited as if I was in a trance. Then the door opened and a tall, distinguished-looking man strode in. He was bald, with dark eyes. He spoke to me in Arabic and I noted he had a distinct Palestinian accent.

"I apologize for not coming to the appointment you proposed," he said elegantly. "My name is Yusef."

"It was my fault. It was a ridiculous proposal."

"No, no. We just didn't have anyone to send on such short notice. Now then, tell me more about yourself and why you're here."

I told him the whole story. Everything I could think of about my father and his work, and why I wanted to work for them. Yusef made me feel comfortable and confident. But I knew that whatever he did, it was a deliberate strategy. This was a very clever man I was dealing with, a professional.

He gave me papers to fill out, long questionnaires that asked about virtually every detail of my life and my thoughts. I remember many of them: How many times a day do you drink water? How many cigarettes do you smoke? Do you drink alcohol? Do you take medication? Do you sleep with girls? If so, how many? Who are your friends? How old are they? What are their jobs? What are their politics? How did you meet them? Do you have any Jewish friends? How much pay do you expect? Have you approached anyone else? It went on and on, and took hours to complete. Yusef helped me when I wasn't sure of the question or just how completely to answer. When I finished the question-naires he continued to ask me for more information. I told him all about my father and my abused childhood. And I told him about my one-man black-market operation with computer disks and porn magazines. I thought that since spies have to be willing to work outside the law, my petty crimes might actually serve as a kind of recommendation.

"I'm sure you must be hungry," he said after a while.

I nodded and he picked up the phone and ordered some food. In about fifteen minutes, a secretary brought Kentucky fried chicken, and we went on with our work. He was helpful, gentle-manly and absolutely impossible to read. I had no idea what he was thinking about my responses. I just answered every question as best I could. I was committed. I was going to do everything they wanted, without reservation.

"Would you like a smoke?" he asked.

"No thanks. I only smoke one a day. And I had my cigarette for today."

He leaned back, relaxed and lit up. "What will you do," he asked, drawing on the smoke, "if you see me in the street one day?"

"I say hello, of course, " I replied, thinking maybe they wanted to know if I would admit to knowing Israelis.

"No," he said, "you won't. You walk right on by as if you'd never seen me before in your life. I'm just another stranger on the street. If there's one chance in a million, we take care of that chance. That's why we're still alive. Understand?"

I understood. And I was elated. In my mind these were the pros. These were the men who could enable me to fight back, to right some of the wrong, who could help me take revenge on my father and on the regime of Saddam Hussein.

Yusef told me to return the next Sunday.

* * *

The next Sunday it was raining again. The soggy weather did nothing to help my spirits. I had taken some tranquilizers to calm my nerves though I was more determined than ever to become part of the Mossad, especially now that I felt close to being accepted. Still, any contemplation of what I doing couldn't help but make me agitated.

I was allowed through the black gates. This time I was to go to the main embassy building, not the consulate. I walked up the winding path, and then through the gardens, to be confronted by a huge wooden door.

I was thoroughly checked again by guards with a metal detector and finally allowed inside. The great door was about two feet thick, the biggest door I had ever seen. It was secured by a thick metal bar. Inside, I found myself in a large empty lobby, with a fireplace and a huge black mirror over the mantel. A guard-receptionist checked my passport, then searched me and everything in my pockets.

Discovering my tranquilizers, he said quickly, "What's this?"

"Candies," I lied automatically, and popped one in my mouth. I did not want to be disqualified for a bad case of nerves. Lying, I knew, would not disqualify me.

The guard directed me to an office off a hallway to the right. Yusef, was there, ready for me.

"Good day," he said, unfolding a map of Baghdad and spreading it out on the table.

"I want you to identify some buildings for me."

"Sure," I replied, looking down at the map.

"Point out the Ministry of Defense for me."

"Here," I said, pointing.

"Now show me the presidential palaces, the Amn, the Rashidiya prisoner-of-war camp and the military airport." They were asking me things that I knew they must know already, but I obliged.

"This is a pretty old map," I said. It was, in fact, an old black-and-white map from the fifties. "If you bring me a more recent colored map, I can show you better."

"No. We don't need that," Yusef replied.

"How about an aerial map?"

"No. Not necessary."

"I once wanted to join the air force," I told him suddenly, "and be like Munir Rouffa, the Iraqi pilot who defected to Israel in 1966 with his MiG-21."

"He did us a huge favor," said Yusef, "and we did everything for him so he could start a new life. We'll do the same for you. If you work for us and then want to stop, just tell us, and we'll get you started in a new life."

For the first time, I didn't believe him. In everything else, I trusted him; these people were not going to play games with me, put my life in unnecessary danger. But I was not totally naive. I knew this was a marriage without a divorce clause.

I told Yusef about the reading I did as a child, and how I hero-worshipped Eli Cohen, the Israeli agent who operated on the front lines of the enemy army, bravely finding out everything, down to the last detail of the last soldier's last cigarette. I thought I was going to be a spy like him.

The reality for me was nothing quite as glamorous. Spying, I was to learn, was not so much derring-do as it was banal snooping. I wasn't a trained commando, or a specialist in any sensitive area like weapons. My special talent was people. Talking to them, getting them to talk to me. The Mossad recognized that trait and saw in me an ideal recruiter. I could swim in the sea and hook them a fish. Any kind of fish. If a man is a criminal, then I can act the criminal. If he's religious, I'm more pious than the pope. If he's a gardener, I love flowers. If he's a painter, I've studied Leonardo. Then I can get into his mind and figure out if this man has a weak spot, a grudge, a reason that would make him material for the spy mill.

This talent, I believe, is the natural result of growing up as I did. I was a loner who read a lot. I was well traveled. I became a chameleon because I had to be a chameleon to survive in the many environments into which I was dropped.

* * *

For two years the Iraqi ran a special, very private school in England, near the town of Woking in the hills of Surrey. The entire establishment was rented by the Iraqi Ministry of Defense, and every student there was a cadet under the auspices of the ministry. A new locale in England was found every few years. About one hundred students were sent at a time. They studied English, history, mathematics, physics and other academic subjects under the learned eye of top British teachers. They lived, ate, slept and studied inside the school grounds. The nearby townspeople in Woking were well aware of their Arab neighbors. For, at specific times, the students were allowed the freedom to go into town. They had lots of money to spend, and set about looking for a good meal and a good time. The students always acted within the letter and the spirit of English law. They had strict curfews, though, and were not allowed any overnight guests of the female persuasion. A cadet caught in any misdemeanor would have a lot more than a few English bobbies to deal with. He would be shipped home to Baghdad, which is partly why England was preferable to the United States for this school. Baghdad was only a direct six-hour flight away.

Those who passed their "A" level examinations were placed in universities throughout England, again at the expense of the Iraqi Ministry of Defense. For the most part these students were in high-tech electronics courses or computer science. Most of the cadets were destined for the elaborate weapon-modifications programs developed by Saddam's minions.

The school near Woking was one more illustration of how the English, along with other western powers, helped for years to build up the military machine they would go to war against in 1991. When war broke out in the gulf they arrested almost all the Iraqis in these training programs. After the war, these Iraqis were released — and immediately sued the British government for wrongful arrest.

All this is not to say that every Iraqi student in England was there on His Highness Saddam's service. But it was very difficult for ordinary Iraqi families to send their children abroad to study. A child abroad meant sending money abroad, and this alerted the government to the fact that a son got out. The questions would start. Why did he leave? Did he not pass the government's own security check for a foreign scholarship? Why not?

Some families managed to circumvent Iraqi security by making arrangements with wealthy Iraqis living outside the country who in turn could not send money to their relatives still in Iraq. The rich expatriates in Britain gave pounds sterling to the student, and the student's parents in Iraq gave money to the exile's family. All this subterfuge was necessary because of the absurd lengths to which the Ba'thists went in order to repress any spark of opposition. It probably created more than it prevented.

The security checks on the boys — there were no girls — before they were chosen for the honor of the cadet school in England was incredibly thorough. Political correctness was more important than actual ability. Still, there were enough very bright ones to fill a lot of the places at the elite school. Once they were in Woking, the security and surveillance continued under the eagle eye of Iraqi supervisors like the Major.

My first assignment was to find out everything I could about the Major. I was to assess this Iraqi military man and determine if he could be recruited for the Israelis. I knew two of my old classmates were at the school, and the idea was for me to arrange a visit and wing it from there. Yusef offered no particular advice, and at this point I was given no special training. I assumed that they wanted to see how I would get along on my own before parting with any of their tricks of the trade.

I shook Yusef's hand and walked out into the streets of London. I had done it! I was working for the Mossad! I walked rapidly toward the underground station, a hundred thoughts racing through my mind. My God, the Mossad! I'm an Iraqi working for the "Zionist entity" itself. Ha! Take that, Dad! Fuck you, too! And you, Saddam! After all these years, a whole lifetime so far, of the bastards controlling me, now at last *I* was in control.

* * *

I raced home, packed a few clothes and caught the next train from Waterloo. As it rumbled out of the cavernous old station and rolled south through the grimy outskirts of London, then into the countryside with its high hedgerows and the neat fields, the adrenaline subsided and I sobered up a little.

I was not yet fully under the Mossad umbrella. The Israelis were feeling me out. This assignment was a safe way to see if I could pass muster. They would assess how I handled myself, find out what they wanted to know, and all along I would be on my own hook. I settled down in my seat to plan carefully, to make sure I did everything humanly possible to please them.

I hadn't phoned ahead to my old school friends, deciding

instead simply to arrive on their doorstep. I would tell them I was fed up with Manchester and wanted a holiday so I'd come to see them. Maybe the Mossad wouldn't have agreed, but I knew that was the best way to behave with my people. I don't trust the telephone. On the phone you can't assess reactions because you can't see facial expressions, and people can easily put you off just by hanging up.

* * *

The grounds at the Woking School were spacious. There was a beautiful garden, and the main building was one of those old two-story redbrick English institutions that no amount of modernizing could protect from the drafts. Nonetheless, it had all the modern conveniences including a pool table, a large dining hall and kitchen staffed by English employees. The dormitory rooms were large and comfortable.

My old pals — they were really only acquaintances, but in a foreign country acquaintances look a lot like pals — were glad to see me and invited me to stay. Soon we were having a regular class reunion, talking, drinking beer and shooting pool.

"This place isn't bad at all," I said as I checked out the lay of the table for my next shot. "I wonder if there's any way I could be transferred to the Ministry of Defense and join you here?" I lined up the cue and fired.

"You can always talk to the Major," said one of my mates. Bingo. Right in the pocket.

The Major, a man in his forties, was short in height but long on arrogance. He reeked of the Estikhbarat, the arm of military intelligence for which he worked. I knew that no minor functionary would be sent to keep an eye on cadets as important as these.

The Major lived off campus, but he arrived daily with his wife, whom he left in the car outside the gates as he entered the grounds to check up on things. This daily visit of an hour or two seemed an odd way to keep up surveillance on the school, but the students all figured he had one or two stool pigeons in their midst. These informers would send in reports to the military officer at the embassy, who would then inform the Major.

When he strode into the garden, students would gather around him, flocking like fans around a football hero. In fact, they wanted to be there if anyone said anything that required self-defense. A few days after my arrival, I was in the garden with one of my friends when the Major arrived. My friend introduced me to him and we were left alone to talk when the group dispersed.

"So, where are you from?" he asked curtly.

"I'm studying electronics in Manchester. I'm interested in transferring to the Ministry of Defense courses, if possible . . ."

"I can't do anything from here. Admission is handled in Baghdad. But you should have enough connections to get in, shouldn't you." It was a statement, not a question. He knew who my father was. But he was not unfriendly, and we discussed a few innocuous matters, like the high quality of British teachers. My real source of information about the Major came not from him, but from his students, who had made a close study of him. The most useful fact I gathered was that he cheated on his wife. In a small town, that sort of thing is impossible to keep secret. It made him vulnerable: the Mossad could use women to get to him. "Penetrate" him, in the language of espionage.

In any case, school was about to recess for the summer. By now I had figured out that the Israelis really weren't interested in the students or the Major. The assignment had been a practice run. I knew what the Israelis really needed were Iraqi recruits in high positions. And to acquire them, they needed a rover like me. They had lots of knowledge about what was going on, but their difficulty was in penetrating the Iraqi organizations. They needed to have an agent in place, and day-to-day information on the nitty-gritty inner workings of various groups.

I returned to London and reported my findings, such as they were, to Yusef. He seemed quietly pleased. The Israelis began to pay me, look after my expenses and anything else I told them I needed. Unlike Iraqi agents, who have to have the consent of the highest authority for even a bus token and must account for every penny they spend, I did not have to become a bookkeeper. These fellows gave me twenty or thirty pounds one day and fifty another. I could buy suits or whatever took my fancy. I remember a gray silk shirt I bought and wore to one of the regular Sunday Mossad meetings.

When I arrived at the Israeli Embassy and entered the main hall, I saw a face in the black mirror over the fireplace, watching me from the other side of the glass. All I could make out was a bald head and dark glasses, but it was a face I would never forget, a huge face, watching.

This time I was taken to the other side of the embassy to a lounge with a small kitchen. Inside were four men. Besides Yusef, there was a man they called Mark, who looked like a Wall Street broker and spoke fluent Arabic. Another was a short bald man with thick glasses who was introduced as Morris. The fourth was an old fellow with hollow cheeks who had come, they said, from Israel.

We all sat in armchairs around a low, polished wooden table inlaid with leather. Morris passed around coffee in chipped mugs from the kitchen. Mark opened the conversation, asking if I wanted to hear a joke about Iraqis. I nodded, and he told the one about the backward Iraqi from the hills who becomes a powerful member of the Ba'th Party and is sent to the embassy in London. When he arrives at Heathrow he has to fill out a form that asks for his name, passport number, age and so on. When he comes to the line "Sex: M or F" he checks off both. The immigration officer says, "Hey you, why did you check off both M and F?" The Iraqi replies, "Whatever comes along is all right with me."

I wasn't sure exactly what they expected or wanted from me as they all guffawed, but I thought the joke was sort of funny even if it wasn't the greatest.

"Here," said the old fellow from Israel, offering me a cigarette. "Your one cigarette for today."

If he was trying to impress me, he succeeded. Silently they were saying, "No detail is too small."

"Tell me again just exactly why you have chosen to work with us?" the old man asked. He had a deep raspy voice as if he smoked and drank too much.

"I want to work against Saddam. That leaves me with three choices: Iran, Syria or Israel."

"Ah," he said, with a knowing smile, "Iran. We help them even though they are nothing, they are incompetents. But they're doing us a favor by making war on Saddam. And Syria, ah, Syria is like a woman wearing a chador. Every time there is a little bit of wind, it lifts up the veil and shows everything. So easy for us. And we — " he grew suddenly serious " — we hit your nuclear reactor, didn't we?"

They certainly had. No one in Iraq would ever forget the day in 1981 the Israeli jets streaked out of the western skies and obliterated Saddam's beloved Osirak, as it is known in the West. In Iraq it was known as Tammouz, so named by Saddam. Both "Osirak" and "Tammouz" are versions of the name of the god of the dead of ancient beliefs. The name alone gave lie to Saddam's claim that it was there for peaceful purposes. When I heard the air-raid sirens, I was listening to an Israeli radio station from Jerusalem. But by that time the jets had already been and gone, and soon, the Israelis were announcing the destruction of Iraq's nuclear threat. Later the Iraqi news broadcasts told us that because of the evil Israelis we would not be having any of the promised cheap electricity; Tammouz/Osirak was no more. But nobody was fooled. We knew what the reactor was really about: Saddam's nuclear bomb.

"How did people in Baghdad feel about that?" the old Israeli wanted to know.

"They were frightened and astonished that you could come and go like that, could do anything you wanted, it seemed," I told him.

The old Israeli looked pleased, like a satisfied cat.

"And Saddam was livid," I went on. "The head of that defense area was executed, as were all the others responsible for air defense along the route. But I guess you know that."

He smiled a tight little smile. "Morris will be your control officer. You'll be a good team. If there is anything you need we will take care of it. You will both need code names. Do you have a preference?"

I thought for a moment. "He can be Yusef Akim," I suggested. "Akim is easy for me to say, even if I'm nervous and start to stutter."

"And yourself?"

"Saify. Assad Saify."

"Welcome to the Mossad, Assad Saify," said the old man from Israel.

* * *

Morris was an affable type, with dark blue eyes and a bald head. He was clean shaven and, ironically, looked like a German beer magnate. He could understand Arabic but spoke it poorly, and so we used English. I found myself liking my control officer when we met for our first session. Our meetings now were always outside the embassy, usually in the Churchill Hotel near Marble Arch, where the noisy coffee shop afforded us public privacy.

The first thing Morris told me to do was to stop working inside the Da'wah for Iraqi intelligence. "An unnecessary complication," he told me. I was a bit bewildered, because it seemed to me the Da'wah and all the other Islamic fundamentalist movements posed an even greater threat to Israel now than their old adversaries, the Palestinians. Give the Palestinians a few square miles and they'd be happy, regardless of PLO rhetoric and fringe fanatics. The Da'wah, Khomeini's faithful followers, would settle for nothing less than annihilation of the "Zionist entity."

In fact, it began to look as though the Israelis were making the classic mistake of preparing for the last war, instead of the next one. Maybe they weren't as omniscient and omnipotent as I'd thought. But they were still my best bet for working against Saddam. Maybe they were just testing my obedience and my abilities.

I was to be paid $250 (U.S.) a month plus expenses in pounds sterling and bonuses if I did my work well. But I was to keep at my studies and only do Mossad work on the side, without taking time off from my schoolwork. They were insistent on this. In the long run, it was clear they wanted me to be in a good position for them. Flunking was hardly the way.

Morris then showed me a piece of paper with numbers on it. "This is the telephone number of the embassy," he said, "and this is an extension. If there is anything important, call and ask for this extension and say you want to leave a message. Don't leave your name. If there is nothing, don't call."

Taking the piece of paper, I thanked him and left to walk the streets of London. I was filled with conflicting thoughts as I considered what I had done. It is one thing to think about consequences and another to realize them. And I realized that I was now eligible for execution in Baghdad.

6

"MY SON IS SCUM!"

AT FIRST MORRIS PUT ME through my paces in the most basic of all skills for cops, killers and spies: tailing and shaking tails.

He told me to be at the Cumberland Hotel near Marble Arch at eleven the next morning. "When you see me, say nothing, act as though you don't know me and then follow me. Don't talk to me unless I talk to you."

Anxious to be on time I arrived quite early at the Cumberland, where dozens of visitors milled about in the garish lobby. It was all ersatz velvet and gold leaf. In America such decoration is found only in Las Vegas where gaming casinos emulate this once popular Victorian style.

I had hardly taken a seat on one of the cushioned settees and snapped open a newspaper when a fat, overdressed Arab sat down beside me. He was one of those ostentatiously wealthy types who spend too much money on their clothes and never achieve quite the right effect. Had he been a westerner he would be sneered at as nouveau riche.

"Hello, my brother," he said in Arabic. "You are Arabic, no? I am Tunisian. And where are you from?"

"Iraq," I said, and returned to my newspaper.

"Ah, Iraq. Yes, fine country. Look, I am ashamed to ask, but well, I am in such a situation, and I'm maybe being presumptuous, but I saw you were an Arabic person like me and maybe might help me . . . What part of England are you from?"

"I'm studying in Southampton," I lied, "in the south."

"I'm staying near Oxford," he revealed. "And, well, I don't have the money for the train to go home and . . ."

"I can't help you. I'm just a student and I don't have much money myself. Sorry about that." How flimsy could an approach be? His suit was worth a small fortune.

He muttered apologies and left.

While I was still wondering what that was all about, Morris came into the lobby, looked around and walked out again. I dutifully trotted out and followed him on the opposite side of the street. He strolled around a couple of blocks, then made a loop over to the Churchill Hotel.

I stuck to him like a hound after a hare. This sort of thing was almost second nature to me. Because of my father's background and his own fears of assassination by any one of the numerous anti-Ba'th groups, our whole family was used to looking over its shoulder. For that matter, so was almost the entire population of Iraq. An awareness of prying eyes and ears is simply a daily reality of life in any police state.

I had also by now developed my own system of making sure I was not shadowed. Spending time with the Da'wah for the Jihaz had simply sharpened up my methods. For instance, every time I left the residence in Manchester I took an indirect route. I sometimes took first one cab, had it drop me somewhere fairly uncrowded, the easier to spot anyone following me, and then jumped in a second cab. I did this in London, too, but London had the added advantage of the tube. It wasn't a matter of discovering who the follower was, but only of losing him. Several of the stations I had reconnoitered were ideal for shaking a pursuer. Euston and

Piccadilly were labyrinths of tunnels and connecting platforms. It was easy to jump out of a southbound train and onto another going northwest. I used to have a vision of all kinds of spies and spooks and tails and shadows down there riding all over the place.

So following Morris was child's play. I padded into the bar of the Churchill and, ignoring him while he sat at a corner table, took a seat of my own across the room. After about five minutes, he came over to me.

"Hi," he said casually, sitting opposite me. "Well, that's fine. You're clean." Meaning I hadn't been tailed by the wrong tail. Naturally they had put a tail on me, looking for Iraqi tails.

He ordered a couple of coffees and when they arrived began to speak about the Mossad's immediate plans for me.

"Like we said, forget the Da'wah for now. We're a lot more interested in a Palestinian you told Yusef you knew at Manchester. Name of Haithem."

Haithem was a good-looking character who was taking a post-graduate degree in English at Salford. His thesis was a study of the Shaback, formally known as Shin Bet, the Israeli equivalent of the FBI. Under the auspices of the British university system, Haithem was busy looking for the vulnerable points in the Israeli intelligence armor.

Haithem and I had talked on occasion, and from a few of the subjects discussed, I gathered he was with Fatah, the military arm of the PLO. "He likes to talk about sex," I told Morris. "What he really seems to like is sex with hookers. Steady girlfriends aren't his style."

Morris nodded. "Get close to him. Be his best buddy. Find out everything you can about what he's been up to, who he knows."

Getting close to Haithem was easy. All I had to do was express an interest in his favorite hobby. Already I was learning how often the oldest profession was the best weapon in the espionage arsenal. Soon we could be seen most nights roaring around town in his top-of-the-line Rover, a luxurious navy blue land yacht with a leather interior and enough room in the back to serve as a traveling bordello. Haithem had a lot of money. Whether it was PLO funds, family wealth or whether it came from more insidious sources, I never learned. There were some things we all kept from each other. But Haithem confided in his newfound Iraqi "friend" about a lot of other things.

We caroused around picking up expensive hookers, cheap hookers, gorgeous whores and plain old whores in Manchester's red-light district, near Chinatown. I kind of liked Haithem. He was at least fun to be around. One night it would be the Million-aires Club with a couple of tarts, the next dancing till dawn the night before exams. We were screwing our brains out, and we were hungover to boot, but we managed to pass the exams.

In the middle of all these carryings-on, we would talk about Iraqi politics and Fatah exploits. Since I was Iraqi, he could assume I hated Israel and easily believe I was on the side of Fatah. But as far as I was concerned, Fatah were just another bunch of jumped-up pseudomilitary fanatics who were making life impossible in the whole godforsaken Middle East. I have a lot of sympathy for the Palestinian people, who have been condemned to their own diaspora since the founding of Israel. But I never bought the line that blamed Israel for everything. Maybe I was wrong, but in any case, my war was with Saddam. That meant working with Mossad and that meant working against Israel's enemies, whether they were mine or not. There's an old cliché about the Mideast that I get very tired of hearing pronounced by "experts" on western news broadcasts. It goes, "The enemy of my enemy is my friend." A fatuous oversimplification. Instead I prefer, "The friend of my friend isn't necessarily my friend." The key to the Middle East is understanding that you can never really understand it. It's a bit like the Arab scholar who warned a western student, "Once you have learned Arabic, you will find that you have acquired a magic key — to a vast, empty room."

I am not writing to defend my actions but to record them, for better or worse. And at this point, what I was doing was informing on the PLO. Haithem gave me some small nuggets of information for my new masters.

Haithem was from Nablus, a large town on the West Bank. A Muslim holy place, it is the site of the Temple of Abraham, revered by Jews and Muslims alike. Jewish settlers had come in droves since the Israeli occupation. In the temple itself, the Muslim worshippers had been shoved aside and given only a tiny space by one wall for their prayers. From there they watched the crowds of Jews come into the temple: children in yarmulkas, the very Orthodox with their *payess* (long side curls) and flat hats bobbing and nodding, and Jewish tourists from the United States. As Haithem and his friends watched, they remembered when the temple was theirs alone, and they nursed their hatred.

Fatah was the perfect home for such young Palestinians. In 1972, it was Fatah operatives who shocked the world when they murdered eleven Israeli athletes at the Munich Olympics. Since then, Fatah has attacked Israeli diplomats, embassies, businessmen, aircraft and ordinary civilians from Bangkok to Madrid. They've used mail bombs, among other means. Ironically mail bombs were first used in the early days by Jewish terrorists like the Stern Gang and the Irgun. In their fight against the British and the Palestinians, the latter blew up the King David Hotel in July 1946 and killed ninety-one people. These two groups did not represent all, or even most, Israeli settlers at the time, but the wounds they opened have lasted. Menachem Begin, among others in recent Israeli governments, belonged to those groups.

Into this seething pot of insult, injury and injustice, people like

Haithem were born. Haithem had been one of Fatah's commandos and was proud of it. He had been in on some of the less-spec-
tacular guerrilla attacks and had distributed leaflets inside the
occupied territories calling for resistance and uprising by the
Palestinians in the territories, as well as among those who were
Israeli citizens. As a result of the work done by Haithem and many
others, the now famous *intifada* was born. The *intifada* pitted
stone-throwing Palestinians against Israeli soldiers in the occupied territories. These flames of hatred on the West Bank would
be fanned by the war with the Americans in the gulf, a war in
which the Palestinians would see more of the West's double
standard that permitted Israel to occupy Palestine, but evict Iraq
from Kuwait.

I had the impression Haithem preferred to rest on his laurels
and let others carry on the tradition. Yet I knew he would go into
action again if called upon. However, whooping it up in Manchester, Haithem and I were a long way from the Temple of Abraham.

One night Haithem and I and our ladies of the night went to
an expensive private club. We sat at a secluded table, and while
Haithem and I spoke Arabic, our English doxies chatted about the
champagne. We got to talking about Fatah operations inside
Israel.

"You know how we get the guns through?" Haithem asked, his
arm flung around the shoulder of the lady he'd brought. "*Al
nuktah al meitah*," he said smugly, "the dead spots."

"Dead spots?" I said, looking interested.

"We prearrange a spot where the weapons are to be buried.
Either inside Israel itself, or just across the border in Lebanon.
Our commandos inside Lebanon handle that part. We have hidden routes to slip across into Israel. Then the actual hit team picks
up the stuff for the operation. That way the hit team can cross in
clean from the West Bank or even Jordan through the damn

checkpoints. And they can rebury the guns and leave the same way. Clean as a whistle."

I looked suitably impressed. Israel had established a sixteen-mile-wide zone north of its border in occupied Lebanon to prevent just this sort of thing. Israeli troops inside Lebanon were supposedly assisted by a bought and paid-for local militia led by a cashiered Lebanese army major named Saad Haddad. This militia was touted as Christian, but the Israelis knew as well as everybody else that they were just a hodgepodge of thugs.

Haithem waxed eloquent. "We work right under their noses. One of the spots is just south of Nakura right at the border. They would never find it without directions. You have to be a certain distance south of a certain fig tree, fifty meters from the sea at high tide. Neither group knows anything about the other — I mean the gang who buries the weapons and the pickup gang. The information about the drop is passed through the network on the West Bank."

"Where do the weapons come from?" I asked as my girl nuzzled my neck. "It can't be that easy with the occupation."

"We can easily run them through Lebanon. But the best we buy from Israeli soldiers."

"Israeli soldiers? Sell arms to you guys?" It hardly seemed possible. I was stunned.

"Everybody has a price, my friend. Everybody. It's only the price that varies." And he took a long drink of his champagne.

It was only a few months after this that Fatah killed three Israeli hostages it had kidnapped in Larnaka, Cyprus. And then it carried out more operations in Israel itself. In February 1986, a bus was bombed and another was hit a year later. Fatah's explosives experts tried setting off bombs in Jerusalem, and Fatah's Force 17 group claimed responsibility for the stabbing of an Israeli in a Gaza market.

When I reported all this to Morris, he listened intently and was clearly not happy to hear about Israeli soldiers selling weapons to the enemy. Still, he maintained his poise and pressed me for more details. I could only add what Haithem had said, that everyone had a price.

I continued seeing Haithem for a while, gleaning whatever I could about Fatah contacts in England. I obtained some addresses, but no details on other specific actions. Morris always told me not to pry too obviously in order not to raise suspicion. It was more important to keep myself clean for future work. He left it unsaid, but he could only mean work inside Iraq itself.

"Okay," he told me after my third report, "you can drop Haithem now." It was like playing chess on a lifesize board. We were having a sumptuous luncheon at a window table in one of London's best restaurants in the Strand. As we enjoyed the lobster and Chablis, Morris simply moved Haithem off the chess board. He didn't explain why and I didn't ask. What they did with the information was their business. Their business, I knew, could be terminal. But that was the game Haithem had agreed to play when he took up with Fatah. The same game I agreed to play when I hooked up first with the Jihaz and now with the Mossad. We were all fair targets, and the old rule "If you can't stand the heat, get out of the kitchen" applied in spades. Haithem, as far as I knew, was allowed to carry on in good health. Unlike another of my later targets.

"Forget Haithem," Morris continued. "We have something else for you to do. The summer break is coming up. We want you to go to Brussels for the holiday and stay with your father."

I would rather have jumped into a snake pit for them. "If you say so," I replied without enthusiasm.

"Call me here in London when you get there. We'll have something arranged by then. In the meantime, see what you can find out about security at the Iraqi Embassy in Brussels. Don't do anything more than talk to the people you would ordinarily meet there. We'll go into it in more detail later." And he got up from the table and shook my hand in friendly dismissal.

* * *

I took the boat-train to Brussels and was met at the station by my father's driver in the big black Mercedes diplomats seem to prefer. My first problem was how to phone Morris. I could scarcely do it from the house.

I told the driver I wanted to call my tutor in England but didn't want to use the home phone, because that was paid for by the government and this was my private expense. I told him to pull over when I saw a phone booth. He stuck to me like a bear sticks to honey. He leaned against the booth and kept right on talking until London answered. He had probably been ordered not to let me out of his sight or hearing.

I could hardly use my code name to contact Morris as arranged, and I couldn't use his, so I asked for the mythical tutor, using my real name. The secretary didn't twig and told me there was no such person there, then hung up. Exasperated, I gave up and let the busybody driver take me home.

After a short time we arrived in one of the expensive neighborhoods where the powerful seem to congregate. People like my father, the Iraqi ambassador. It was on the outskirts, not far from where the Battle of Waterloo had been fought. The house was yet another vast and sumptuous establishment.

My mother threw her arms around me when I walked in, talking and remonstrating happily. "You've been away too long! Why don't you visit more? Oh, look at you, you're skin and bones. Don't they feed you anything? You should come home more for a good meal . . ." Mothers must be the same all over the world.

My father, though, was his same old self: the perpetual thundercloud, harbinger of the storm. As usual he was drinking whiskey, which only made matters worse. He barked out an order to get ready for dinner. That was my welcome home from him.

Mama busied herself making a roast chicken dinner, my favorite, and I just stayed in the kitchen with her, talking about my classes and how good the professors were and reassuring her that her investment in my education was worthwhile. I left out any references to girls and to Israelis. She would have been horrorstruck at either one.

It was one of those rare occasions when my brother and sisters and I were all home at the same time. My brother, Saif, was at the International School in Brussels, where he mingled with the children of all the other diplomats and NATO representatives, as well as with the children of Common Market ministers. My older sister, Dina, was studying dentistry in Iraq and was home for the summer. Little Dalia was only four years old, and we all fussed over her like a favorite pet.

Dinner was actually a warm and pleasant affair until it was shattered by father. As usual I was the cause. I said something unwise about the abysmal failure of Saddam's war with Iran. With a roar, father overturned the entire table and stormed off to his study, shouting all manner of curses at his son.

"Scum! My son is scum! A traitor! I won't have it!"

For one terrifying moment I thought he'd guessed the truth. But it was just his usual ranting. If this is what I was betraying, I thought, so much the better. At the same time, I was aware that I was not acting now only for personal revenge but truly for my own growing political beliefs. I was gaining some distance from my awful parent.

At least we had pretty well finished eating. While the maid cleaned up, we children tried to console mama. We brought her hot coffee, and after father was asleep, late at night, I sat up with her while she read the coffee grounds.

"I don't understand," she said in a small voice, peering into the cup. "I see so many abnormal things, things together that normally are not. I can't read them."

I felt a chill. But I patted her shoulder and said, "But, mama, you live in a completely abnormal family, so it's just a picture of the chaos around here. It's probably the dinner table."

"I suppose you must be right. Why does he have to be that way? And why do you have to keep upsetting him? You know what happens. Why can't you try to go along with him instead of always fighting, fighting . . ." She began to cry softly. I felt terrible and selfish and remorseful as I tried to comfort her. But I knew I would do the same again.

The next day I was able to get to a phone at a post office without the nosy driver. I dialed the Israeli embassy in London and said I was Franco calling for Morris. Franco was one of my other code names. Sergio Franco. As a general precaution, I had set up this identity some time before. It had been quite simple. I introduced myself to the people in the office of the student union as Sergio Franco and made a point of visiting them fairly often on student business. When they "knew" me well enough, I asked for some student travel papers, a library card (I "lost" mine), and they issued them all without question. I would just have to stay out of Spain. Sergio Franco couldn't speak a word of Spanish.

"Was that you who called last night?" Morris asked immediately, an angry edge to his usually amiable voice.

"I'm sorry. But somebody was standing right beside me and I had to make something up. It's clear now."

He sounded relieved. "We have everything set for tomorrow. I'll be in on the morning flight. Meet us at the Ramada at noon. The usual precautions."

When I arrived at the Ramada, a planeload of orthodox Jews had just arrived fresh from Israel on El Al. I took a seat by a potted plant and idly glanced at my newspaper, feeling like someone in a bad movie as I watched these strange-looking Jews with their long black coats, *payess* ringlets and wide-brimmed hats. They didn't even seem to be from the same world as Morris and Yusef. Maybe they weren't. Our world of subterfuge and double crossing was light-years away from these tradition-bound men and women, whose right to a country the Mossad was supposed to protect. Not that all, or even most, Israelis are orthodox, but after a time, agencies like the Mossad, the KGB, MI5 or the CIA all seem to develop a life of their own. I was thinking these deep thoughts when I heard someone paging Mr. Franco. I went to the desk.

"There's a call for you, sir."

I picked up the phone in one of the booths by the reception desk. "This is Franco."

"Hello. I'm a friend of Morris. Do exactly as I say. Leave the hotel and take the street that is across the road a little to the right. Walk up and take the first turn right. Follow that street to the end. Turn left and then take the first turn right. Keep walking. I will be there." And he hung up. The Mossad knew by now that, as well as having a photographic memory for things I observed, I remembered instructions verbatim.

The sun was shining as I left the hotel and crossed the street. As I walked the prescribed route, a car passed me full of happy sightseers looking out the windows. It was a gray-and-brown Citroën with French plates. When I turned the corner, it passed me again coming the other way. Then again, as I rounded the next corner.

I willed myself to continue, to ignore it. At the end of the route, I found myself on a blocked-off pedestrian street in the old quarter. It was full of colorful coffee shops and boutiques and restaurants. I was standing there looking around when I saw him. It was the face I had seen watching me in the black glass in the hall of the Israeli Embassy. The dark glasses, the bald head — he had an indefinable something I could never forget.

Just then Morris casually walked up to me with another man.

"Hi," he said. His companion was tall and aristocratic-looking with light brown hair. "This is Daniel," said Morris by way of introduction. "He will be your contact here in Brussels."

When Daniel spoke I recognized his voice as the one who had called me to set up the rendezvous. "I'm inviting you to lunch," he said, "before we all get down to business."

The Mossad almost always did this, preferring to talk about trivialities from food to football scores until after the meal. The habit seemed to prove the notion that food was tremendously important to Jewish culture. During the meal I would give them an account of my expenses and they would pay me with no questions asked, content with a receipt made out on anything handy, a napkin or a match folder.

After our meal, Daniel shepherded us up a small side street to a secluded little hotel. The bald man in the dark glasses stayed outside, visible from the front window. The others said nothing about him. I was never to learn who he was.

We checked in at the desk, then trooped upstairs to a small room. Since we were a patently suspicious-looking bunch of characters, grown men checking into one tiny room, either the hotel was a haven for hookers and pimps or, more likely from its neat appearance, run by one of the thousands of *sayanim*, Jewish sympathizers the Mossad has in every country in the world. (There are so many that a lot of people automatically assume any Jew is a fellow-traveler of the Mossad, which irritates Jews who mind their own business in their home countries.)

"Everything all right?" asked Morris, bringing me back to the business at hand. We were sitting around the coffee table.

"Fine," I said. "I have some of the information you want right here," I added proudly, and handed him notes on what I had learned so far about security at the Iraqi Embassy. It was the basics on who the inside guards chosen by the Mukhabarat were. He turned on me angrily.

"Don't ever do that! Never! Never put anything in writing. Keep it all in here," he hissed, jabbing at my temple with his finger.

I was taken aback and felt my face redden with a mixture of embarrassment and my own anger. And a kind of shock. I had just glimpsed the Mossad side of Morris. And I realized my pal was forged of steel.

"Never mind," said Daniel, interceding, "he can learn step by step. No harm done." It was as though they were acting good cop, bad cop.

I was still digesting this and recovering my poise, when the door opened silently and a large bald man came in carrying a large and obviously heavy suitcase. Not the man I had seen on the street. Another one. My life seemed to be filling up with bald men.

"Ah, hello, doctor," Morris greeted him. "Just in time." Then Morris turned to me. "The doctor here is going to ask you some more questions. Give him your full cooperation. I'll be going back to London now, and while you're in Brussels, you'll work with Daniel here. You'll have to have a contact point. The phone at your father's house is out of the question. Any ideas?"

"There's a sort of bar-restaurant called the Macao about ten minutes' walk from the house," I said after a moment's thought. "I could be there for his calls. Or yours."

"Perfect. Go there every day at six in the evening and stay for an hour. If there's no call from us, just go home."

"Am I Franco?"

"Yes. Use that name here."

Morris and Daniel departed and left me in the hands of the doctor.

"My name is Yusef, " he said, shaking my hand in a friendly manner. I was beginning to think Israelis were called Yusef as often as Arabs were called Ahmed, Ali or Muhammad. Or perhaps he used it because they knew I already liked the Yusef I had met at the embassy. Some sort of psychological tactic?

He settled his bulk on the couch vacated by the other two men and set the large case on the coffee table.

"Well, then," this Yusef began cheerfully, letting out a big breath with the effort, "let's see what we have here." And he snapped open the case and drew out sheaves of papers and envelopes, some pencils and felt markers, as well as a small cassette tape recorder.

"I think we'll do this first," he announced, handing me a big piece of paper and some colored pencils. "I want you to draw me some pictures. A man, a woman and a child."

The Mossad was certainly full of surprises. Now we were going to kindergarten. But I assumed they knew exactly what they were doing, and I obediently started to draw, wondering what my artwork would reveal about my innermost self.

He took a brief look at my pictures, nodded, then dug into one of the envelopes. Pulling out a handful of pieces of cut-up photographs, he instructed me to put them together. I did that, too, in short order. Then he read off a list of numbers and asked me to repeat them. With my memory, it was easy.

"All right now," he continued, holding up a picture of a ship in full sail. "Something is out of place in this picture. What is it?" There was an anchor in the crow's nest.

"And what about this house?"

I peered at the picture. "There's a cat in the doghouse."

He showed me a photograph of a woman sleeping on a couch in very ordinary living room. She was dressed for daytime and there was a letter on the floor. "I want you to tell me what happened just before this picture was taken."

This session went on for hours. A Rorschach test. More questions about my childhood. Memories and associations with certain sounds and smells. We spent a lot of time talking about my father, how he had beaten me and generally made life miserable from the day I was born.

"And how do you think people see you?" Yusef asked suddenly.

The question brought me up short. I wasn't sure anymore how I saw myself, let alone how others saw me. "Nothing special," I said, thinking. "Likable, I suppose. I mean, I seem to be able to get along with everybody, no matter who they are or what they are. Except my father of course. But I've decided he isn't really human. Some kind of mutant. But I like people up to a point, and on a superficial level I have a lot of friends."

"And how do they see you?"

"As an easy-going rich kid, I guess. Maybe a bit of a playboy."

"But you also seem to do well at your studies. Without much effort."

That was true. I had never worked very hard at school. I would party the night before an exam and still walk through it. "I guess I'm fairly smart, but I don't think anyone sees me as an egghead or a genius or anything. Of course, I don't really let anyone know me or get very close to me."

"Why?"

"Habit. Maybe because I've spent a lifetime hiding myself from my father," I answered truthfully, but I couldn't help thinking that this aspect of my personality probably made me good material for the spy's lonely trade.

After six hours of questioning, the doctor thanked me and said that was all we had to do and sent me home.

The next evening, I went as arranged to the Macao at six o'clock. It was one of those "theme" places, all done up to make people think they had walked out of the dreary Brussels weather into, well, Macao. It had real palm trees and murals of sunny beaches. I ordered a piña colada and waited. And waited. Nothing.

7

DOING THINGS MY OWN WAY

Affter three days of piña coladas and endless waiting, Daniel phoned. "Go to the same place we sent you the first time and wait for me — at noon," he said shortly. As I walked to the Ramada, I was fairly sure they must have had someone watching to make sure I was clean.

When he arrived at the Ramada, Daniel looked as aristocratic as ever. There was something about his bearing and the quality of his suit that placed him a cut above the rest. But it was out of the question to ask him about his own background. In this business, I answered questions. I did not ask them. We went to the coffee shop and ordered a simple dinner.

"We want to know everything we can about the Iraqi Embassy here," he said to me in low tones. "Names of all the staff, addresses, family situations, how much they're paid, who the Mukhabarat officer is, the other security people, the telex operators, what kind of telex they use. Naturally we want to know the codes, as well as who has access to them. We also want to know about your father's office, what it looks like, what chance there is of bugging it and where it would be best to place a bug." He paused, then continued, "Make mental note of the cars, the licenses and who drives them. We need everything you can find out about how the embassy operates, and above all, any clandestine operations."

In other words, Daniel wanted the embassy in the palm of his hand. The task was actually fairly easy for me. No one at the embassy knew the real state of affairs between my father and me; to them, I was simply the son of the ambassador. They assumed that being nice to me would put them in his favor; they were just as terrified of him as I was. To be sent to a posting where my father was in charge was the nightmare of everyone in the foreign ministry. In addition to his fearsome personality, they had another reason to be afraid. I was soon to learn what that was.

I began dropping into the embassy from time to time to chat with and get closer to the guards and secretaries. I should add that they were all men. Women were almost never employed. That meant that most Iraqi embassies looked more like police stations than embassies. The guards actually live in flats on the upper floors.

The building in Brussels on the Avenue de la Floride was a very plain, functional brick building, a square block with large windows at the front. The consular section was behind the window to the left, and people could be served from this window without having to come inside. But as the ambassador's son, I had free access and could just sail through the heavy glass front doors. It was a simple matter to let people believe I was merely on holiday and was feeling bored. "I just came to hang around," I'd say casually. Sometimes I'd invite one or two of the men to join me for drinks in a nearby bar. No problem. After all, I was the lazy spoiled rich ambassador's son with nothing much to amuse himself. The unsuspecting embassy staff told me most of what I needed to know.

I even learned about the coding system. It was a complex letter code that was changed every so often by a mechanic who would come from Baghdad and alter the decoding machine by the telex. But it was always a four-letter code. For instance, a message like LONDON OPERATION APPROVED might read AMDH BGYR FKPL.

Daniel seemed happy with this information. And I was able to tell him exactly where all the weapons and ammunition were kept in the embassy. There was a special armaments cupboard on the main floor just behind the guard's post near the consular section. It contained mainly small arms: pistols and AK-47s and the odd RPG-7.

As for clandestine operations, I learned that the main purpose of virtually all our embassies was to hunt down and destroy enemies of Saddam Hussein. That was the raison d'être of the entire intelligence apparatus and, in fact, of the entire Iraqi government; even the basics of running the country came second. My father, I learned, had ruthlessly performed that task in Poland, Cuba and France, and now Brussels.

I had always suspected that my father's activities included a great deal more than orthodox diplomacy. My conversations with the staff gradually made it clear, but one in particular was a graphic confirmation. One day I noticed two of the security men standing in a corner of the embassy's main reception hall enjoying what was obviously a huge joke. I moseyed over and asked them what was so funny.

"See that big box over there?" said one, pointing to a big crate labeled FURNITURE. It was assembled with the rest of the parcels for the diplomatic bag.

"What's so funny about that?" I asked, suspecting the horrible truth.

"It's furniture all right," they said, sniggering. "An armchair, complete with an occupant." At this they doubled up, slapping their thighs.

"Oh," I said knowingly, "one of those. Who's the lucky traveler?" I had heard the stories, but it was still hard to believe.

"One of those Kurdish bastards. He's sound asleep and off to a free vacation in beautiful Baghdad." Then they collapsed with the merriment of it all.

I looked at the crate and thought of its poor unlucky occupant, drugged and tied into his very special airline seat. Would he wake up in the baggage compartment and realize his ghastly fate? Would he struggle and scream in vain up there in the sky? Or would he come to only after they had landed and unloaded him into the waiting arms of the Estikhbarat?

He was a mere fifteen feet away from me. And there was nothing I could do except tell the Israelis. But I knew they would do nothing to save him. That would be the end of their informant — me — and their information. Fifteen feet away, and already he was in Iraq, another grim statistic. Whoever he was. No wonder the embassy staff was so afraid of my father. He directed agents in these kidnapping operations, hunting down opposition to Saddam even outside Iraq.

The Kurds had been a thorn in the side of rulers of our part of the Arab lands for centuries. They were fiercely independent tribes whose native territory was a triangle of land at the borders of Iraq, Iran and Turkey that overlapped into all three countries. They had been alternately persecuted and supported by all three, depending on who was trying to cause problems for whom. Iraq had egged on Kurdish autonomy movements in Iran to cause problems for the Shah, until Tehran and Baghdad made a deal. Now the Kurds again were out of favor and hunted down like deer.

In addition, there were internecine quarrels among the Kurdish fighters, the Peshmarga. Some took bribes of guns and territory from Saddam, and in return agreed to submit to his rule and inform on their less cooperative compatriots.

Saddam decided the best thing would be to wipe out all the

uncontrolled elements. At first it was done piecemeal, by harass-
ment and arrest inside Iraq, by operations like my father's abroad,
and the infamous diplomatic crates. But eventually Saddam found
this much too slow and inefficient. Much like Hitler, who wanted
a faster, cheaper way than bullets to wipe out the Jews, Saddam
wanted a faster, cheaper way to eliminate the Kurds, and then any
leftover enemies. He, too, ordered a Final Solution. Orders were
given to the Estikhbarat to coordinate the project with army
training and testing divisions.

And so they began working in earnest on chemical- and biological-weapons research and development. The Kurds were to be
the first to experience the hideous results a few years later.

The unfortunate victim in the armchair would travel first to the
Hague where the crate would duly be stamped as a diplomatic
shipment. Then to Amsterdam, since there was no direct flight
from Brussels to Baghdad (the diplomatic bag always went via
Holland). In Amsterdam, he would be put on board the Iraqi
Airways flight to home, torture and, probably, death. All along the
way, customs inspectors and airport security would wave him on
through, because he was "protected" by his diplomatic status.

This gruesome use of the diplomatic bag was stopped, albeit
briefly, in the West. One of these crated-up travelers woke up on
the baggage wagon at London's Heathrow Airport on his way to
the cargo hold of the plane. The handlers heard muffled screams
coming from their cart and took it back to be opened. I would love
to have seen the faces of the British customs and security officers
when they saw the FURNITURE. There was the usual strain on
bilateral relations for a while after that, but then it was business
as usual again between Saddam and the British. The western
governments know perfectly well about these horrific goings-on,
but seem to accept them as just part of the way the world turns. I
wonder if the people they presumably represent would be so

acquiescent if they knew what goes on behind all the veils of diplomacy.

It's common knowledge that all embassies, whether American, Israeli, Iraqi or whatever, harbor spies of one kind or another. In Brussels the Mukhabarat agent in charge at the embassy was a debonair fellow by the name of Muhammad Salman. Captain Muhammad Salman. His office was a very ordinary one on the ground floor opposite the main entrance. Salman was a graduate of the French department at Baghdad University and along with the language had acquired French tastes in food and clothing. He was given to stroking his mustache and raising one eyebrow when contemplating anyone who sat on the other side of his desk. But despite his fondness for drink and the good life, Salman absolutely could not be recruited by an intelligence agency of another country. He was one of those whose needs were so well taken care of by his position in the Ba'th regime that he had no need to look elsewhere. He was also totally loyal to Saddam by nature, being one of those whose sophisticated exterior is only a thin veneer over a primitive tribal heart.

I also furnished Daniel with a few extra tidbits from the annual July 17 party celebrating the 1968 Ba'th Revolution. It was the usual formal affair, held at the Meridian Hotel. My mother, dressed in an expensive gown of chiffon over a silk sheath, dutifully joined my father in the receiving line and greeted the guests, a collection of diplomats, journalists, EEC ministers and members of the Belgian foreign ministry. I bribed the embassy photographer to give me copies of the official photos and later, going over them with Daniel, was able to give him a full who's who. In particular, the liberal sprinkling of arms dealers.

One of the most important was a dealer by the name of Gerald Bull. Bull was a Canadian with American citizenship. He had distinguished himself by designing modifications for both artillery and artillery shells that would dramatically increase their range. But he'd had a falling-out with his North American sponsors, including the U.S. Army. When he was charged with breaking trade embargoes by supplying South Africa, they'd hung him out to dry. He was sent to jail for four months. So Bull had turned to working for Saddam Hussein, among others.

Saddam's first interest was Bull's modification of the 155-mm Howitzer called the GC-45, a gun with double the normal range. After initial run-ins with other dealers, about four hundred of Bull's artillery pieces were supplied through South Africa and Austria. When he got out of jail in 1981, Bull was based in Brussels — the arms center of the world. As one pundit put it, "All guns point from Brussels."

That constituted the other main part of my father's work, the work of any Iraqi ambassador in Belgium. Arms. Buying and brokering. And looking after Gerald Bull. When my father left the post in 1985, a senior Estikhbarat officer named Zaid Haider was appointed to replace him. By then Gerald Bull was the main priority of the Brussels post. Gerald Bull's big guns had become the key to Saddam's dream of the conquest of Israel — and perhaps more. The guns opened up a lot of possibilities, from Kuwait to Cairo.

Bull also was working on something that promised even more for Saddam: the Supergun. Its barrel was three feet in diameter and one hundred feet long. He claimed that it could shoot accurately to a range of a thousand miles. Granted enough money to develop further refinements, he said its shot could go as far as six thousand miles. (Bull had taken old plans from World War II archives of Nazi papers, which showed the design for the V-3, a supergun with the range of a rocket. The Germans had been defeated, and the V-3 prototype destroyed before they could build the real thing. Its main design advance was the use of a sectioned barrel to handle the acceleration of the projectile.)

The Americans had rejected the whole idea years earlier, but now Baghdad footed the bill. They began to build the Supergun at a plant near Mosul, a city in northern Iraq. Bull kept it secret by ordering different parts from different companies and countries. Parts came from Italy, Greece, Germany, England and Belgium, so nobody had the full picture. Except the Mossad.

The Mossad had had Gerald Bull's number for a long time. In March 1990 he was allegedly assassinated by Mossad agents in Brussels.

* * *

How I went about getting the desired information on the Iraqi Embassy in Brussels had been left up to me. The only proviso Daniel had made was that I was not to take foolish chances. Therefore the only information I did not supply was the information a search of my father's office might have provided. I had decided that any effort to get into his office would be foolhardy. A man who noticed a few gallons of gas gone from his Mercedes at home would notice the tiniest thing amiss in his office.

Daniel was pleased with what I had produced for him. Pleased beyond measure. Iraq had always been the most difficult country in the Mideast to penetrate, and I must have been like manna to them. Still, the Mossad couldn't seem to overcome their preoccupation with the Palestinians.

"We need you to find out what you can about the PLO representative here. He and his family seem to have some Iraqi friends, so there should be a way for you to connect."

The previous PLO representative in Brussels had been Naim

Khadar, a young intellectual. He had been a breath of fresh air, a voice of moderation and negotiation, who had been on the verge of a real breakthrough in finding a settlement with the Israelis when he had been assassinated in 1981. Some thought it was the work of extremists within the PLO who did not want any settlement short of the annihilation of Israel. Others inside the network believed it was, in fact, the work of the Mossad, for equal and opposite reasons.

And now I was ordered to track his successor, a man we called al-Arabeh.

It wasn't a job I enjoyed, but it was just that: a job. And so I did it. I stayed at arm's length but learned about him through mutual friends, pretending to be an admirer. In truth, I had no feelings one way or the other about him. Maybe he was a fine fellow, maybe he was another PLO thug. I told myself that judging him wasn't part of the job. My job was to deliver information about his habits, his usual routes to and from home and friends' homes, the kind of thing useful for relay shadows and worse. I didn't think about what I was doing, simply handed over the information. There is nothing particularly glamorous, admirable or moral about spying, though at the time I didn't fully realize that. I was still caught up in my need for revenge on my father and Saddam. In my mind they had merged into one all-important enemy. If others fell in my path, so be it. It would be a long time before I began to realize how insidiously we become like the enemy we fight.

* * *

In autumn 1984 it was time for me to go back to England for my next year of engineering studies. My mother, totally unaware that her son was not quite what he seemed, said good-bye with a brave effort to keep from crying. My father wasn't around. He was at the embassy, preparing to move to New York. He was being transferred to the prestigious post of ambassador to the United Nations. Perhaps this posting was a reward for the number of crates of furniture he had sent home as gifts to his master.

Soon after I arrived back in England, I met with Morris at one of the restaurants we both favored in Soho. He told me the Mossad were content with my work so far. Nothing was ever said about the deductions made by the doctor from my drawings and inkblot tests.

As Morris dug into his rich pastry, he said, "There's a Syrian in London we want to know about. He's at the Imperial College in nuclear physics. This one is an important target. It's a kind of make-or-break time for you, too. If you make it, you can rise in our ranks. If not, well, you may just stay where you are."

At least the Mossad had turned its attention to a more current danger than the Palestinians, even if it wasn't Iraq, which I still thought was worthy of more effort. My personal view was that the Da'wah needed to be penetrated, since not much is known of it. But the Mossad was turning toward Syria. Syria's Ba'thist president Hafiz al-Assad and Saddam Hussein were now locked in a battle to the death for supremacy in the Arab world. They loathed each other.

Syria under Hafiz al-Assad deserved a prominent place in anybody's rogues' gallery. Especially a Syria that had nuclear ambitions.

"Can you get to him?" Morris asked of the Syrian he had mentioned.

"Sure. I have friends at the college. No problem."

I shall call the Syrian Rifaat Khaddam, which is not his real name. He was a nice fellow from Halab, in northern Syria. He was also a brilliant scholar, but a bit of a country lad and naive. In addition, he was a climber with big ambitions and dreams of castles in the air. That made him vulnerable, and I zeroed in.

It was easy to strike up an acquaintance with Rifaat when I dropped in on friends at the college and joined them for lunch in the dining hall. My friends, too, were in the elite sciences, and it was inevitable that they often sat with the fellow Arab doing his PhD in nuclear physics. Rifaat was good-looking, with a resemblance to Saudi Arabia's Sheikh Zaki Yamani, the famous energy minister, but nonetheless had no luck getting girls.

"You should have seen the one we saw at the disco the other night," said one of my friends with a salacious look as we swallowed down the awful English institutional food. "Could she move!" He wriggled his shoulders and hips. "Hassan here couldn't begin to keep up with her. Not a hope!"

"I don't seem to have the right moves for the girls here," moaned Rifaat. "They all act as though I'm a dirty old man or something."

"'Or something' is right. Or another horny Arab!" a friend piped up.

Rifaat just looked miserable while we laughed.

"Never mind," I reassured him. "I can introduce you to girls. I have lots to spare." I was playing the original macho creep. In all truth, I hated the idea of introducing him to any of the girls I knew. Not that I was possessive; I just didn't want to get any of them even marginally involved in this deadly caper. Fortunately none of them took to poor old Rifaat at all, which was all to the good. Trying to find him a girl made me his buddy, though he still hankered after his dreams. And that meant money. At least with money he could buy a woman or two, and some decent clothes. He always looked a bit tacky, even if he did have a face like Sheikh Yamani.

So I showed him a good time, from the Playboy Club to Covent Garden, all on my now unlimited Mossad expense account. I told him that a friend of my father was a wealthy businessman who paid me a lot of money for doing bits of work for his office in England.

While I developed Rifaat's taste for the good life, I gradually learned about his work and where he fitted into the plans of his sponsors, the government in Damascus. Like Iraq, Syria paid for scholars overseas and had very definite long-range plans for them.

Syria's plans, I learned, were nuclear weapons. What Rifaat Khaddam revealed was dynamite. Or rather atomic. Syria had just begun to build its own nuclear reactor. The hardware was coming from the Soviet Union; some technological help was coming from Germany; and Syrian scientists like Rifaat were being trained by the British school system. He reported regularly to the Syrian Embassy. They kept a tight rein on him and wanted to know what he was learning day by day, plus anything else he was able to pick up from fellow students and teachers. The British school system was like the United Nations, a rich potential source of contacts and information.

It did not take a genius to figure out that Hafiz al-Assad was not building a nuclear reactor to lower his people's electricity bills. Like Saddam, he was going into the bomb business.

When I reported this to Morris, he looked stricken. It seemed that the Israelis had not known this was actually under way, though in its earliest stages. Why they should have been surprised, I don't know. Arab leaders have always made a point, if they can, of having as good or better weapons than Israel. And Israel has nuclear weapons. The fact that the Soviets were aiding and abetting Assad was hardly shocking, either, given that Syria was at the moment a client state of the Kremlin. (We can only hope that the Soviets were supplying better material and technology than what they'd used to build Chernobyl. The devastating effects of the accident and explosion at the Soviet reactor near Kiev still resound all these years later.)

After a time, Rifaat was thoroughly hooked on the good life, and he openly expressed envy of my relationship with my father's generous "friend." He wanted to meet him. So I arranged to meet Morris in the restaurant at the Churchill to tell him this. He was delighted and dug into his breakfast with enthusiasm.

"Tell him your father's friend is coming to visit this weekend, and you're having dinner with him. Ask Rifaat to come along if he likes."

Then to my horror, as we walked out together I saw the "penniless" Arab from Tunisia who had accosted me before in the Cumberland. Was he an agent, then, following me? He was sitting at a large table with half a dozen other Arabs. Out of the corner of my eye I noticed that Morris averted his face. But he offered no explanation. Then I decided the Arab might be almost anyone's agent, hanging around hotels, picking up what information he could from fellow Arabs like me. But who did he work for?

Morris changed our meeting place to another hotel near Piccadilly. I was constantly on edge now, and over the past weeks I'd begun to lose my hair, until all I had were a few wisps. I told my friends I'd had to take some strong medicine for a medical problem and left them to make wisecracks about social diseases. I had a social disease all right. Espionage. My hair eventually grew back but I was seeing the toll this cloak-and-dagger life was having on me, even though on the surface it seemed so innocuous, so mundane. The mysterious Arab reminded me that I was playing at the ultimate high-stakes table, where a wrong bet could mean a knife in the ribs or a bullet between the eyes.

The meeting between Rifaat and my father's "friend" went like clockwork. Morris called himself Mark for the occasion.

The three of us met for a costly lunch at one of the better small restaurants on Charlotte Street, near Oxford Circus. At a nearby table were others I recognized from the Israeli Embassy, seemingly minding their business. Which they were. Our business.

It was fascinating watching Morris in action. He controlled the conversation completely and deftly maneuvered Rifaat into position, without really giving away a single fact about himself and his masters. As far as Rifaat knew, "Mark" was a German businessman living in London. His company had extensive business interests in the Middle East and wanted to expand into Syria, but needed some inside information on potential contracts in order to give it a competitive edge. Mark even had business cards. Rifaat didn't really care who Mark was, as long as he was sure of being paid as handsomely as I apparently was. So Morris had a relatively easy job reassuring Rifaat that he would not need to take risks, just pass on information that was easily accessible. That was the bait of course, and once the hook was firmly in his mouth, he would be asked for a great deal more.

So Rifaat had a new job, as a "consultant" to a German technological firm, selling Syrian nuclear secrets to the Mossad. I saw him a couple of years later, looking very well off and something of a fat cat.

Morris gave me two hundred pounds and a new sound system. That was nice, but material reward was not the reason I was in this game. I still wanted to get my teeth into Saddam. Morris left me to concentrate on my studies for a while. In the winter of 1985 he arranged to meet me again at the Soho Restaurant.

"We want you to try to get someone else for us," Morris said. This time he was accompanied by another of his colleagues, who was introduced to me only vaguely and who said nothing before, during or after the entire meal. I assumed it was part of the Mossad's vetting procedure.

"Are you aware of the pilot-training program your government runs in the north of England?" Morris continued.

I had to confess I wasn't.

"It's outside Carlisle, just south of the Scottish border. They train military pilots, and as far as we know it's mainly on helicopter gunships just now. The head of it is an Iraqi Air Force major. We want him. But first we want to know everything we can about him."

It seemed that as far as the Mossad was concerned, I still didn't need any real training at this point. The little tailing exercise and a couple of other equally minor sessions were the sum total of my schooling for spydom. They were leaving the tactics on these missions completely up to me, probably because they had worked so far.

The following weekend, after five days of classes to which I'd barely paid attention, I boarded the train to Carlisle. British Rail was in the throes of another strike, and so my trip was a dead-slow milk run, ambling along through the chilly countryside near Oxford, winding around the Yorkshire Dales, through the gray mists of the Lake District and on at last to Carlisle.

Carlisle was cold and dreary. With alternating snow and rainfall, it was even drearier, a panorama of mud and dirty slush. An Austin Mini served as a local taxi, and when I got in I told the driver to take me to the pilot school but to please, please wait for me. It was beginning to snow in earnest and I had no desire to be stranded in a place like this.

"I don't have the exact directions," I told the driver.

"No need, no need, my lad," he replied cheerfully. "Everybody in town knows where you chaps are." He seemed friendly enough and I figured that the school was probably the economic mainstay of the dismal little town.

He took me to a tiny airport on the outskirts and settled down to wait while I went inside to find my major. Like any small airport, there was the usual cluster of squat buildings and huts, and a hangar. Either the aircraft were out on winter training or they were all in the hangar, because I saw none around. I went into what looked like the main office building, in reality just a shack.

A young Englishman behind a counter greeted me. "What can I do for you?" he asked.

I had decided to fall back on my diplomatic connection, my dear father. "I'm from the Iraqi Embassy," I told him, showing him my diplomatic ID, "and I've come to look up a friend." I gave him a false name.

One of the officers came in as I was speaking and now greeted me in Arabic. "Never heard of your friend here," he told me affably, "but he might be with one of the other groups. Let's go over to the officers lounge and see if anyone else knows him. The second-in-command is there, I think. Unfortunately the major is at the embassy in London today."

He steered me across the yard toward the gray bulk of a barracks building, just visible through the heavy snowfall. Inside we stamped the wet snow off our boots and joined four other officers in a comfortable lounge — comfortable, that is, by military standards. They all greeted me in a friendly enough fashion, including the second-in-command, a classic military type, ramrod straight and with a brisk way of speaking. Of course he had not heard of my friend. But he invited me to join them for tea.

The major's absence was a stroke of luck. It was always easier and faster to find out about someone from others. Furthermore, the second-in-command turned out to have a grudge against his superior; he had ambitions above his rank of captain that the major was thwarting. In fact they all jumped in to complain about the boss with no prompting at all from me.

"I wish you would report our problem to the embassy," said the number-two man. "It's hopeless here."

"The major is a boozer and a womanizer, and nothing gets done properly around here," chimed in another. "The boys are doing half the work they should. This is no way to train an air force."

"I thought the major was a big hero," I offered.

"Was. Now he's a has-been." The major, Morris had told me, had been shot down in combat over Iran and had walked five days through the desert to get back to Iraq. As a reward, he had been posted to the safety of Carlisle.

"I'll be glad to get out of this place," said a lieutenant old enough to be a major general. "What I would do for a bit of sunshine!"

"We'll be going home in a couple of weeks from this session. But someone ought to tell them to straighten out the major," the captain persisted.

"Does it really matter?" I said. "After all, I thought the British flight instructors handled the work that really matters here."

"Without the Brits, we wouldn't have a damn thing going," another muttered.

In a way, nothing had changed from the days of Lawrence of Arabia, when everything from the Persian Gulf to Constantinople was Britain's private domain. The armies of what are now Saudi Arabia and Iraq were then virtually British divisions, armed and trained by Her Majesty's men.

Saddam was simply carrying on a time-honored tradition, though for his own interests, rather than those of Westminster. Once again, I wondered why the British, the Americans and the rest of the western powers were so short-sighted. We have a saying in the Middle East: "Don't despise snakes just because they don't have dragon's horns." It means don't underestimate them, because if you do they will grow up to be dragons, complete with horns and breath of fire. Couldn't the western nations see they were helping the Iraqi snake grow up to be a very large dragon, complete with horns and an air-force escort?

It was no wonder many in the Arab world, and for that matter western critics, felt that a totally cynical partnership existed between governments and the arms industry. The arms industry made huge profits keeping the conflicts raging in the Mideast. The Americans, Soviets, British, Germans, French and even the Chinese kept stoking the fires already burning in the so-called Holy Lands. The hostilities and rivalries were our own, home grown for centuries. The firepower came from meddling superpowers and arms merchants, who then added their own global ambitions to our regional ones.

Israel was in there, too. And Israel, just like the rest, played the game strictly for its own interests. Right now Israel's interest was to find out everything it could about Iraqi air power. It could learn all it needed to know about the Saudi forces through their American allies. Syria was well penetrated, and had pretty much tipped its hand in the war in Lebanon in 1982. But Iraq remained a closed book. Morris and his masters wanted a mole in the Iraqi Air Force at any price. They wanted someone high up in the ranks. The major would have been perfect, a war hero, privy to more than the average major, and because of his drinking and taste for hookers, he was vulnerable. But they told me he was going on leave almost immediately. Too soon for a safe recruiting operation right now.

I was disappointed. Recruiting the major would have been a clean shot at Saddam's war machine. But it looked like his position was none too secure, to judge from his colleagues' hostility.

When I got back to London and reported to Morris, he was crestfallen but philosophical. "Forget it. Don't go back, it would look too suspicious. We don't want you to blow your cover, and besides, we have another assignment for you."

We were talking over lunch at the restaurant in Soho again, this time in the company of yet another silent colleague of Morris's.

"Your assignment is a man named Kamal Khatib," Morris continued. "He is a very big fish. Right now he's at Loughborough University, near Nottingham. He's a senior structural engineer on one of Syria's important pet projects."

Syria again. Not Iraq. I was disappointed.

"He's involved in the construction of underground hangars for Assad's fighters and bombers," Morris finished with a bit of a flourish.

I felt a shiver slide up my spine. Anyone involved in such a high-priority sensitive military project would be no cakewalk. Khatib would be savvy and no doubt ruthless. And yet the Mossad still gave me no special instruction, apparently content to let me handle things in my own way. They must still have thought, after all, he's an Arab and should know the enemy better. For the first time, I felt afraid. The underground bunkers for aircraft had been whispered about in Iraq, too. Syria's Hafiz al-Assad wasn't the only one building them. Saddam was, too.

The underground hangars for military aircraft were the result of Saddam's imagination and his engineers' ingenuity, plus a great deal in the way of European materials and technology. They were like subterranean aircraft carriers, with several parking levels and hydraulic lifts to raise and lower the jets. The Iraqis were also ironing out the wrinkles on underground runways, which would allow a jet to do the first part of its takeoff without being exposed above ground.

The reason for all this burrowing was simple: every Arab leader had a vivid memory of how the Israelis had destroyed the Egyptian air force while it was still on the ground in 1967, and the humiliation still burned. For Saddam, it had become more important to protect his squadrons than actually use them. The symbolism was what mattered.

Of course any enemy power would seek first to destroy its foe's air power, as that was the key to controlling a battlefield in modern warfare. So finding out exactly how those hangars were built and what their weak points were was an extremely high priority for the Israelis.

I sat, full of foreboding, in the train to Loughborough. This time I felt acutely out of my depth. But there was nothing for it but to forge ahead.

Loughborough was a small, clean, modern little city, with an old train station that featured a footbridge over the rail lines. I crossed and found a taxi to take me to the best hotel the place had to offer. I checked in and, after a light meal, went to my room and called Morris. Then I spent a restless, nervous night. In the morning I took a taxi to the university.

The campus was huge, with a variety of modern buildings. I took a deep breath and walked through the main doors of the administration building. I told the woman at the registrar's office that I was looking for a fellow Arab, a friend of mine named Kamal Khatib. Checking her computer list, she told me he wasn't an undergraduate but I might find him in postgraduate studies. She sent me to another building.

When I asked at the desk, Khatib was indeed listed. He was doing a doctorate in structural engineering. As the secretary checked his file for me, I saw his ID card. Something was wrong. If he had handed in his ID it meant he was leaving, but it was only midterm.

"He may be down in the laboratory," the secretary said brightly. "It's just down the hall there."

I quickly located the large lab where they did work on structural stresses and on prestressing concrete. At one end I found a genial Englishman checking some specifications at a drafting table.

"Kamal isn't here just now," he said in answer to my inquiry. "Great fellow, great fellow. Superb engineer. You must be family, I suppose. Well, you can be proud of his work here."

He chatted on a bit, assuming, the way westerners do, that someone looking for someone is a friend, not an enemy. He gave me Khatib's address.

I went back to the hotel and phoned Morris, hoping he would call the whole thing off.

"Go and see him tonight," he instructed.

Night had fallen by the time I drove up to the small housing development on Durham Road where Khatib lived. I left the taxi some distance from the house and walked up to his gate. It was bitterly cold. Then, not far down the block, I saw two men sitting in a blue Toyota. Its headlights were off, and I couldn't hear the engine running.

I stopped, paralyzed. There was a bench on the sidewalk nearby, and I crossed to it and sat down in the falling snow to try to pull myself together. I wanted to run as fast as I could, but to turn back, I decided, would look even more suspicious than to go in. So, my heart beating about two hundred times a minute, I opened the garden gate and walked up to the door. As I pressed the doorbell and waited, I asked myself why Khatib's house was being watched. Then I heard footsteps inside. The door opened, and there he was. A big man, Khatib managed to look fearsome even in his pajamas and wool robe.

"Sorry to bother you," I stammered. "Mr. Khatib?"

"Yes?" he snapped.

"My name is Hussein, and a mutual friend suggested I come and see you."

Standing back, he told me to come in out of the cold and led me up a few stairs to a small vestibule off his living room. I was both relieved at my success so far and more terrified than ever at the thought of being discovered. Already I could see myself in a large armchair . . .

The mutual friend, of course, was a figment of my imagination. I called him Jabir and had written a letter to Khatib from him, saying he hoped his old friend Khatib would help his young friend Hussein get settled in Loughborough. Jabir was made out to be someone fairly important in the Amn, and I was banking on Khatib's having the usual Arab arrogance that would not allow him to admit he didn't know any Jabir. It was the sort of thing that would have worked just fine with a lesser power than Khatib.

"I don't know anyone named Jabir," he said, his eyes narrowing as he opened my letter. As he scanned it, I could almost hear his mental gears changing. "I don't know anything about this, or about you," he said as he finished. He folded the letter and kept it in his huge hand.

I prayed for the ground to open up and swallow me. "I must have come to the wrong place, then. It must be another Khatib," I said lamely. "I'm sorry to disturb you. I'll be going now . . ."

I backed out of the room, down the steps and out the front door, trying to move slowly and nonchalantly but wanting to break into a run. Would he signal the men in the car to apprehend me? Or were they Mossad, keeping an eye on my escapade?

Whoever they were, they were gone when I emerged from the house. I looked up and down the street and saw no one. Nor could I see a taxi to take me away from this unlucky place. I walked rapidly through the snow till I finally saw a pub. I went in to have a drink. Somewhat restored, I made my way to the station and managed to get the last train to London.

Back in my hotel room there at last, I had a hot shower and tried to quell the case of nerves that made my stomach feel like a bag of cats. I slept badly and the next day wandered the streets in a fog of worry. In the early evening I went to an Iranian restaurant I liked called the Abadan. There I ate a solitary meal, still thinking of Khatib and the awful risk I was running. Before, my risk had been kind of theoretical. Now it seemed much too real.

I went to the cinema and sat through a double feature without hearing a single word or seeing a single frame. The next morning I went to meet Morris. I was early, and stopped for Kentucky Fried Chicken on Oxford Street. I was just ordering at the counter when a policeman rushed in and ordered everybody out. There was a bomb threat next door. From time to time London was still being rocked by explosions, bombs set by everyone from the IRA to Libyan terrorists. It was not a good day.

8

"SOMEBODY IS COMING
FROM BAGHDAD"

I FELT THAT THE MOSSAD WAS constantly testing me while at the same time keeping me in reserve for something bigger. It seemed likely that as the son of a highly placed Iraqi diplomat I was intended to be a mole, one who could be activated whenever I became most valuable to them.

I had already told the Mossad that my father was about to be transferred from Brussels to the Iraqi mission at the United Nations. He would serve as Iraq's ambassador to the U.N., a prestigious position. Morris, my Mossad contact, made it clear that they did not want me to work for them in the United States. On that point he was adamant, even though I suggested I could probably find out useful information inside the Iraqi U.N. mission. "No," he said. "You can go there for holidays, and maybe one of us will see you for dinner, but absolutely *no* operations. We're not allowed to work inside the United States."

This conversation took place just before Jonathan Jay Pollard, a civilian employee of the U.S. Naval Investigative Service, was caught working for the Mossad. Looking back, I think either Morris was being disingenuous, or such highly dubious operations were known only by a top few in the Mossad, while those below believed in the U.S.-Israeli special relationship.

Soon after the Khatib fiasco I met with Morris. "We may invite you to Israel," Morris said enigmatically. "But right now, we have another idea. Just go back to your studies for now, and concentrate on them. Then we want you to go to Brussels again for the summer vacation." He paused, then added, "See if your father can get you a job in the London Embassy. Nothing big — filing or something."

I didn't say anything but I was appalled by the idea. A sudden request to my father from his anti-Ba'thist son to work among Saddam's faithful drones was certain to make him deeply suspicious. In spite of all that Morris, Yusef, the doctor and the rest of those in Mossad knew about my relationship with my father, they did not seem to grasp just how out of character such a request would be. Perhaps they thought I had exaggerated. Perhaps they had no experience of such a murderous father-son conflict.

"My father doesn't trust me. He'd be suspicious if I asked to work in the London Embassy — even if I only asked to scrub floors."

Morris didn't look put off at all. "Look, you're to remain in England to finish your degree. We need to have you with a foot in the door of the Iraqi London Embassy. We've been having one hell of a time penetrating the London operation of Saddam's diplomats." He paused again. "Maybe your mother will intervene on your behalf. Look, just try . . ."

I thought the Mossad had been careless in the Khatib affair, or at the very least the plan to recruit Khatib was hastily prepared. This new assignment suggested the Mossad had become even more careless. Clearly they did not understand the enemy as well as I originally thought they did. This proposal was fraught with risk, and almost guaranteed to expose me. But I so wanted to get even with my father and see Saddam toppled that I nodded, knowing that my reluctant agreement was emotional, not intellectual. Somewhere, my rational voice screamed, "No!" even as another voice argued that my job was to do what they asked. Torn, I agreed, nodding once again.

In the midst of this emotional turmoil, it was a wonder I even remembered to write my exams, let alone find the presence of mind to pass them. In the end, I passed all but one, in electrical circuits and waveforms, which I would have to repeat in September.

I packed for Brussels with a heavy heart. On the boat-train to the continent, I met a beautiful Italian girl who helped keep my thoughts from the approaching reunion with my father. But inside my head I kept hearing the lyrics of a current popular song by the Eurythmics about rain falling on my head. . . .

* * *

The house in Brussels where my parents lived had a glass-enclosed room that overlooked the pool and the garden. The fine bamboo furniture and green plants made the room a tropical oasis in the Belgian northland. It was here that I met with my parents.

An ordinary son meeting with an ordinary father might have been relaxed in this paradise, but I was no ordinary son. My father was no average father. The solarium was an artificial garden; for me it was a psychological hothouse.

My father was angry. He used a tone I knew and feared. "Why the hell do you want to work in the embassy all of a sudden?" he demanded.

"I need more money," I blurted out. "England's expensive."

"I give you more than enough goddamn money!" he exploded.

"It would be good for me. The people at the embassy would appreciate it." I was babbling.

My father just stared at me. His expression suddenly changed. I stopped talking. My father's anger had become something cold and calculating, which was much more menacing. He turned and walked out, but I knew his leaving meant there was worse to come.

My mother sat still. She looked at me anxiously.

"Will you talk to him for me?" I asked.

I could tell she wasn't any happier than my father about my wanting a job in London. But her reasons were different. Mother disapproved of the way I lived. She assumed I *did* want more money, and she assumed I wanted it to live the life of a playboy in the western world.

"Why do you have to live *that* kind of life, anyway?" she said. "You run all over the place with your dreadful girlfriends."

Poor mama, she didn't understand. Still, she went to my father and spoke to him on my behalf. They had a major argument. A few days later she approached me on the subject. "Why do you want to work in the embassy?" she asked. "Is it really to work, or for something else?"

I knew my father had put her up to questioning me this time, but I let her continue. "You've always fought with your father about the Ba'th, about Saddam, about the car, about your clothes, everything!"

She was distraught. But there was nothing I could say.

"And always just to provoke him. Now, I don't know what you're doing, whether this is to provoke him, too, but it's always the same old fight . . ." She hesitated, then began to cry. "I believe you have done nothing wrong, but he suspects you have."

Then her voice became a near whisper. Her eyes filled with fear for me. "He's been going through your clothes, your room, your papers!"

I felt the blood drain from my face. I had left a book with phone numbers in my dresser. The numbers were in code, but only a simple code.

My poor mother was almost hysterical even though I hid my fear and she knew absolutely nothing of my activities. "Please," she begged, "tell me you aren't working for the Iranians! Tell me you're not working for the Iranians!"

I almost laughed in relief. This was an accusation I could deny without lying. "No, no, mama, of course not. Why would I do such a crazy thing? There, there, your worry is all over nothing."

My relief was short-lived. Her next words turned my blood to ice.

"Your father says somebody is coming from Baghdad. They're coming to see you."

* * *

Unable to sleep, I sat in the darkness in my room all night. I couldn't even lie down. I was afraid to close my eyes. My mind was paralyzed. All I could think was, what is coming from Baghdad? What is coming from Baghdad? What fate lay ahead for me? And what agent of that fate? An assassin? The Estikhbarat? A carpenter maybe, to build me a crate?

And what rough beast, its hour come round at last,
Slouches towards Bethlehem to be born?

Those lines by W. B. Yeats, from "The Second Coming," refer to the devil taking the place of the Christ child, and they are among the most chilling lines in the English language. I felt they might have been written for that night I spent in the darkness, feeling the beast draw nearer, its hot breath on my neck.

I had to think. I had to formulate some kind of plan.

By morning I knew I had three choices. I could try to run for it and inevitably be caught. I could contact my Mossad colleagues and ask for help. But I knew that if I was truly exposed, I would be of no further use to them, so their help would be unlikely. Or, I could try something as outrageous as it was dangerous. I chose it.

I called the driver and had him take me to the Iraqi Embassy. I went straight to the office of the Mukhabarat officer, Salman. "I have something to tell you," I said without preamble. "I want you to send it directly to Baghdad without telling my father."

Salman looked at me with mild interest, but as I continued, his expression changed to one of astonishment. And when I confessed unblinkingly, "I've been working with the Mossad," his face went dead white. For a full three minutes he could not speak.

"I was introduced to these two guys by a girlfriend," I went on. "I didn't know they were Israeli, let alone working for the Mossad." This was a lie, but some of what I told him was basically true. "They asked me to find out some things about the embassy — it was all small stuff, meaningless, really. They wanted to know about salaries and who the telex operators were. They paid me well."

Salman still remained silent and pale. "I figured out before long who they were," I continued, "but by then I was hooked by the money and the girls that went with it. Besides, by then they had me by the short ones, didn't they?"

It was a stupid story. But I knew my people. I knew that my only chance was to go to them before they got to me. A sort of preemptive strike. I had to brazen it out.

Salman pulled himself together enough to ask for details. He hardly knew where to start or what to ask. "You just tell it," he stammered.

I decided to tell him everything. I gave him names and places. I started with the Fatah drop spots and the Syrian nuclear physicist, and finished with Khatib and the underground aircraft bunkers. This was my neck on the line now. As for Morris and Daniel, my Mossad contacts, I knew those weren't their real names, anyway. Only God and the Mossad knew who they really were.

I had to give Baghdad everything, as accurately as I could. The Mossad could take care of itself. Every word I said, every phrase, every thought in my head, could seal my fate. One mistake and I was a dead man.

"I want to get out," I said desperately. It was the simple truth. My visions of being another Eli Cohen were gone with the wind of suspicion I knew my request for a job in the London embassy had caused. Down deep I knew I didn't have Cohen's nerve or his professionalism or whatever it took to play this deadly game to its bitter end.

It is hard for outsiders to comprehend the enormity of my crime in Saddam's world and the punishment that would await me. As strong as the English phrase "high treason" is, it doesn't come close to describing what I had done. An Iraqi working for the Mossad was akin to a Jew working for the Gestapo, perhaps worse. To Iraqis, Israelis had attained a status of evil beyond that of such mere mortals as Gestapo agents. To Saddam and his cohorts, Israel had become almost mythic. Part of the myth was its modern invincibility; part of it was the much older spirit of Masada. At Masada, a thousand Jewish zealots, led by Eleazar ben Jair, held off a Roman force of 15,000 for two full years. When the Romans finally took Masada, they found that rather than face enslavement, the defenders had taken their own lives. Only seven women and children survived to tell the tale. In a strange way Saddam absorbed this bit of mythic history and made it part of his compact with his god: he would fight Israel, even if it meant fighting to the death of the last Iraqi.

As I continued my "confession" I could see that Salman was badly shaken. His world was crumbling. In this regime, heads like his could roll as a result of this sort of catastrophe. Salman would be seen as having harbored the devil in his post.

"This will all go to Baghdad," he said hoarsely.

* * *

The next day was July 17 and time for the annual celebration by the embassy of the glorious Ba'th Revolution of 1968. Dressed in their finery, the usual collection of diplomats, journalists and politicians gathered in the Meridian Hotel. I would have preferred to stay shut in my room, but the ambassador's son had to show up, or the ambassador would get a black mark on his report card. I found myself a corner by the buffet table and munched on caviar, wishing for the evening to end. One of the younger fellows from the embassy joined me. He wanted to talk about who was who.

"See that one over there," he said, pointing to a tall blond man by the door. "He just came from Baghdad." Then he leaned closer and whispered dramatically in my ear, "Mukhabarat!"

Poor Salman and the man from Baghdad stood quietly talking by the doorway.

There is a Bedouin tribe in northwest Iraq who are blond and Aryan-looking. They can pass so well as westerners that many of their number serve as Mukhabarat agents. They are among the most loyal of Saddam's followers. In their region they control everything from smuggling guns across the Syrian border for the Islamic militants to running mushroom farms and construction companies.

This man was one of these. As I looked across the room I knew he had come for me. But the whole picture had changed now. His mission had been thrown off course by my confession. I caught him looking my way once or twice. He did not approach.

The following day Salman informed me that he had received instructions that I was to go to Baghdad and handed me a ticket made out in a false name. This was not a good sign. It meant that the Mukhabarat did not want a record of my travel to show up on the flight manifests. They could get away with it because at all ticket or passport control checkpoints, my separate diplomatic ID was my laissez-passer. With that ID I could board any airplane without having to show anyone a ticket. Eventually the ticket would be collected, but no questions would be asked.

When I gave my mother the news that I was going back to Iraq she was upset. Salman quickly assured her I had done something wonderful and that certain powers in Baghdad wanted to thank me personally. Her mood quickly turned to relief, and she bustled about helping me get ready, happy to send me home with a packet of letters for her friends. (The Iraqi post office was regarded with great suspicion by most. No doubt the heavy load of work opening up everyone's mail slowed down the service.)

When I told my father I had been summoned to Baghdad he was angry and perplexed. Usually he was the first to know every-thing, but clearly he was being kept in the dark. He pressed me for an explanation. "Why do they want you in Baghdad?"

"Something to do with the party," I answered vaguely. "Salman can explain." I had no idea what story Salman would give him. Thanks to my confession, Salman's position was none too good.

On July 19 my father and Salman accompanied me to the airport. My father remained silent for the whole trip. I knew he was scared for himself. Always himself, I thought bitterly. I was scared, too. Scared for my life. My father, on the other hand, was afraid of losing his position and prestige.

At the airport he made a show of being solicitous. The perfor-mance was for Salman. My father asked if I had everything I needed and even offered me money. To me his act was transparent; all he was really doing was trying to find out what awful thing had happened and how it was going to affect him. Living under the Ba'th regime, my father always assumed that whatever happened was for the worst. Despite my fear for myself, I actually found myself laughing inside at his desperate antics.

They both stayed to see that I actually boarded the plane, a Sabena Airlines flight to Amsterdam. From there I transferred to the Iraqi Airways plane to Baghdad. My ticket was economy class. Thanks to the procedures I'd followed, no one save my parents and Salman knew I'd left Brussels. I was virtually nonexistent. I might as well have been in one of the diplomatic crates.

* * *

Once the plane entered Iraqi airspace we were ordered to pull down all the window shades in order to black out the aircraft because of the danger of Iranian attack. Steeped in the anxiety of my own drama, I had almost forgotten the war with Iran, which had raged for five years now. Five years of senseless slaughter.

We landed at Saddam Airport. I blotted out all thought. I was just a moving dummy, following the other passengers through the bureaucratic maze. I told myself it was all out of my hands now and meekly waited for my escort. Strangely no one appeared. Still fearful, I glanced about and forced myself forward. My whole plan hinged on my voluntary confession and return.

Then I saw two security types, wearing safari shirts and light slacks. Their guns, Makarov automatic pistols, were stuck casually in the backs of their belts, and they were both smoking cigarettes. They were the Mideast version of gunslingers. Their job was to meet and greet other gunslingers — arms dealers — coming into the country from around the world. They had a lot of work these days. I walked up to them and asked if they knew the whereabouts of the guys from the Mukhabarat who were supposed to meet me.

They informed me curtly that they were Estikhbarat. "The Mukhabarat is downstairs."

So I set off to find the Mukhabarat agents, but I got lost. Saddam Airport had been built while I was away. A modern, shining new tribute to our great leader, it was all glass and chrome and vast empty spaces.

Downstairs I finally found a man with a badge and asked if he had seen the Mukhabarat agents anywhere, or if anybody could show me the way. I couldn't believe it. Here I was searching high and low for my jailers. He began to ask me who I was and why I wanted the Mukhabarat.

Suddenly someone behind barked, "Get out of here!" and the man snapped to attention, said "Yes sir!" and turned away.

I whirled around and there behind me was the blond Mukhabarat agent who had come for me in Brussels.

"Hello," he said. "Have a nice trip?" Without waiting for an answer to this absurdly out-of-place question, he told me to put away my passport. Then he escorted me through passport control.

"I'm Khaled," he introduced himself as we walked along.

He was about my height, five foot ten, and dressed casually in a striped shirt and trousers. He had an airport security pass clipped on one pocket. We went to the baggage area to claim my luggage, a black Samsonite case filled mainly with food. It contained my favorite things like mayonnaise and canned goods that couldn't be found in Iraq.

Then another young man joined us. A really good-looking guy with jet black hair, he looked like an American movie star. He was dressed in a beige suit, and had an easy, engaging manner.

"Hi," he said. "I'm Jamal. Nice to meet you."

I opened my case for the customs guard, but he told me to close it and gestured me on.

Outside at the curb we got into a small Mitsubishi-made car. Jamal drove, and Khaled sat up front with him. I sat in the back. They put their airport badges away and Khaled took my passport. Officially I had never left Brussels, and now I had no passport. Nervous as I was, my companions' friendly manner consoled me.

The drive from the airport into the city had a surreal quality. So much was new to me; so much had changed in Baghdad since my departure with my family for Zimbabwe in 1982 when I was sixteen. (I had gone straight to England from Zimbabwe in 1983.)

A concrete wall stretched along the right side of the airport road. Feeling like a tourist, I asked what it was.

"It's a private place for His Excellency Saddam Hussein," Khaled replied.

It was in fact Saddam's palace, Saddam's bunker and Saddam's lake. I later learned that the whole extraordinary compound had been built as an ultrafortified redoubt to which Saddam could repair either for leisure or for a last ditch stand in war — nuclear or otherwise. Its walls were three or four meters thick, and much of the palace was under ground, even under the man-made lake. The complex, designed to withstand virtually anything, was in the shape of a ship's anchor, making it impossible for any enemy planes to hit it completely in one fly-over. I never saw inside it, but the stories about the place had already reached mythic proportions.

As we turned toward the Mansour neighborhood, a modern, high-class district in the center of the city on the west side of the Tigris, I noticed all kinds of new enterprises. There were even fast-food outlets, rather like McDonald's, lighting the night with brand-new neon signs. I badgered Jamal and Khaled with endless inane questions. Their answers were polite, but no more, no less.

We dropped Khaled off at the Mukhabarat headquarters. People give this compound, with its iron bars and high walls, a wide berth, and if they have to pass by it in their cars, conversation becomes hushed. In the dark, it was difficult to see much of this place that seemed to be Khaled's home, just the ghostly shape of a large white building in the rear. Khaled got out and told me he would see me in the morning. As he strode up the walk, then vanished inside, only his blond hair was palely visible in the moonlight.

I got into the front seat, and Jamal told me he would drive me to my family's home. Should I have been surprised that they were taking me there? My nerves were stretched taut, and I was exhausted. What were they going to do with me? Was this some kind of psychological cat-and-mouse game?

On the way Jamal chatted about intelligence services around the world, comparing them, indulging in some shoptalk for my benefit. "All the world's intelligence agencies are the same," he said. "Some may have more high-tech equipment, but basically we're all the same. The contest comes down to who can out-think the other."

He told me he was an officer who taught at the National Security College. He was happy to work in such an elite institution. I knew only a little about the college, which was the training ground for the best of the Mukhabarat, the ones who became officers. But right now I didn't want to hear about the Mukhabarat. My fear had begun to recede when I hadn't been taken me to Mukhabarat headquarters, and weariness had taken its place. When we drew up to my family's house I leapt out and ran up the steps to the door and banged on it loudly, shouting, "Bibi! Bibi!"

There was no answer. I decided my grandmother must be sleeping on the roof, which is the custom on hot nights. On the roof one can be under the cool night sky.

I ran out into the garden and called Bibi again. Finally she came down and opened the door, her black braids falling over the shoulders of her nightie. Her thin little face lit up when she saw me.

"Oh, my! Is it really you? How did you get here? Are you here to stay? Oh, come in, come in . . ."

Jamal edged himself into the house, too. He was polite to my grandmother. He called her "Hajjiya" in deference to the fact that she had made the pilgrimage to Mecca. Nonetheless he barged in without invitation. He was, after all, an officer in the Mukhabarat. Regardless of how chatty he had been he was now discreetly doing a check. For what I didn't know.

After five minutes or so, he left.

"I'll pick you up at up at 9 a.m."

It was now 3 a.m. I was home in Baghdad, back in the dragon's lair.

Bibi had a hundred questions. Why had I come home? Was there trouble with my studies? My father? Was I staying for good? But I was too tired to answer, even for Bibi. I begged to be excused and went straight to bed.

9

"YOU ARE IN THE CIRCLE NOW"

THE NEXT MORNING, JAMAL picked me up. Because he was dressed in a gray suit, I decided this was an official appearance. It was, after all, the middle of summer, and most people chose cooler, less formal wear. I was dressed in my usual natty Matinique style — black pants and black T-shirt, as if I was going to my own funeral, but forever fashionable.

Jamal was just as chatty as he'd been the night before. This time, as we drove along Felastin Street toward the Mukhabarat head-quarters, he talked about hookers, drugs and gays. He acted as if we were drinking buddies who had an understanding about such things. I knew he was testing me, looking and watching for my reactions.

"We caught one of the air-force pilots with a small boy," he confided. "We think he's probably doing things to other boys, too. But we're not sure what to do about him."

"What do you mean?" I asked, exasperated with this crude technique. "Why the hell would you let a man molest small boys?"

It went on like that until we reached the Mukhabarat com-pound. At the main gate, he stopped the car, flashed his ID and the gate opened. I looked around, curious in spite of the fear I once again felt creeping around the edges of my mind. There was a small stream running through the compound and, on the other side, rows of houses, as in any neighborhood. But the streets were closed. Then I realized that it once *had* been a neighborhood, and that it had been taken over lock, stock and barrel by the Mukhabarat. The only inhabitants were the agents and officers at their desks, or those at work on more brutal activities.

There were armed men everywhere, carrying everything from machine guns to RPGs. Jamal parked in a small lot to our right. He told me to stay in the car while he went into the guardhouse. When he returned he pinned a small white badge on me. It featured an odd-looking eight-sided green star. I had no idea what it signified, and I wondered vaguely if it was like the Star of David the Nazis had forced the Jews to wear, the star that later marked them for extermination.

We drove farther into the compound toward the big white building I had glimpsed the previous night. I noted now its huge glass windows. We walked up the long path leading to it, and at the end were made to walk through a metal detector. Then a guard searched us. When that was finished I looked up and saw Khaled. Jamal left me there with him.

Giving the guard a phony name for me, Khaled led me down the main hallway. I could see a large conference room on the right, and similar but smaller rooms on the left, each with a couch, two chairs, a table and a chair behind the table. We entered one of the smaller rooms and waited in silence for five minutes, during which I grew more apprehensive. I had a past, I feared for my future, but I had no present. Officially I wasn't there. Not even the guard knew my real name.

Suddenly the door opened and Khaled leapt to attention and saluted. A short, bald, ugly gorillalike man strode in. My heart sank. I thought, Oh, shit! What am I going to face today?

The Gorilla did not shake my hand. "Are you Hussein?" he roared.

"Yes, sir."

"Sit there."

He clapped his huge hands once, loudly. A servant scurried in. "Three teas!"

Somehow he even made ordering three teas sound menacing. He sat behind the table, staring at me without blinking, until the tea arrived in three small clear glasses on a tray, as is the Middle Eastern custom. Khaled was still standing. The Gorilla told him to sit down, then he fixed his gaze on me again.

"We did not want to end with you like this," he said evenly. "But it has happened."

I was paralyzed. What did he mean?

"But you came to us before we came to you," he continued. "Now you will cooperate with us."

Did he mean it was easier to kill me if they caught me first? Did he mean now that I had confessed they might consider some other course? That was my desperate hope when I'd taken the rash step of approaching Salman.

The Gorilla's name was Radhi. Though he was not in uniform, just wearing summer civvies, he was clearly high up in the ranks of the Mukhabarat. He was just as clearly from the Israeli desk. Only the really tough ones took on Israel.

He turned to Khaled and said, "You are a *rafiq* —" Arabic for comrade "— so you will interrogate him. And you," he added, swiveling his gaze back toward me, "will answer him. Then we will see what we will do with you."

He left without returning Khaled's salute.

I let out my breath, but my relief was short-lived. Khaled began to ask me questions, going over the same ground I had covered with Salman in Brussels. I knew that Salman had recorded everything, so I had to get it all exactly the same. Khaled wanted to know about the Mossad in every minute detail: what routes I took, how they handled surveillance, how they handled tailing and being tailed, what the officers looked like, what they acted like, every small reaction in a situation, what cars they used, did they leave the car engine running when keeping a house under surveillance? He wanted to know all my feelings and observations and judgments, and how the Israelis make an agent feel like one of them. The interrogation went on for eight hours without rest or food for either of us.

I said only one thing that was a mistake. I said I thought Morris was a very clever man.

"Why? Do you mean you like him?"

I could have bitten off my tongue. One thing an Iraqi must never do is say anything positive about the Zionist enemy. The Israelis are to be despised; they are lower than worms.

Internally I shuddered. If the Mukhabarat ever discovered that I had not been trapped but had willingly gone to the Israelis, that I actually admired certain of their abilities, I would most certainly die — and not quickly.

I was protected by the completely unbelievable quality of the act I'd committed, I thought as I again tried to push fear from my mind. Any Iraqi would believe I was seduced by money, women and life in the fast lane. No Iraqi would believe I'd actually volunteered my services to an enemy held to be so heinous.

* * *

The next day Jamal picked me up again and took me to headquarters and the same room. Then he began asking all the same questions as Khaled had.

Perversely I found this reassuring. If they were going to kill me, surely they wouldn't waste all this time. And even more perversely

I had a sneaking suspicion that because of my experience with the Israelis, they felt deep inside that I had more skills than they did, and so they wanted to pick my brain. I could see it in their eyes when they asked things like, "How did they do it?" But of course they would never admit to any admiration of the Israelis. Even if the enemy is formidable, you don't admit it. This attitude is the cause of many a military defeat.

At the end of the day Khaled arrived. "We've worn you out with all this," he said sympathetically. "Now you're invited out as our guest."

Of all unexpected events, the three of us went out for a night on the town. They took me to a cabaret club called The 1001 Nights, in the swank Al Rashid Hotel, a palace of white marble built for an international fair that never took place because of the war with Iran. Men could not get into The 1001 Nights without a female companion, but we were not mere men. We were Mukhabarat. My escorts flashed their IDs and the three of us waltzed in.

The floor show featured musicians playing a combination of old Iraqi tunes, disco for the customers who wanted to dance, then new Iraqi tunes like "Hella bi Fares al-Bedda" — "Welcome to the Desert Knight" — all in praise of Saddam.

The Mukhabarat actually owned some nightclubs. One was the Khan Murjan, in an ancient renovated prison. Its revenue was given to the family of one of Auday's bodyguards, after Auday, Saddam's son, killed the bodyguard in a fit of pique.

As the music blared on, Khaled and Jamal tried their drinking-buddy act on me. They spoke about their days of being trained for the Mukhabarat overseas, in Rome and Geneva. Jamal said he liked Geneva, but Rome did not appeal to him much.

Just what they were fishing for I don't know. It was a bizarre evening. As he drove me home, Jamal turned the conversation to military matters, talking about how Mukhabarat officers used cocktail parties to contact arms merchants or middle men to obtain embargoed items like TOW missiles that bring down jet fighters and bombers.

I just looked at him. In Iraq, any eight-year-old knows that the U.S.-made TOWs are anti-tank, ground-to-ground missiles, not ground-to-air missiles like the U.S. Hawk or the Russian SA-9. I said so and Jamal just laughed indulgently.

What a ridiculous way to find out what I knew.

The next day Jamal took me on tour of the city. It seemed he wanted to see how much I could observe and retain. "Remember the license-plate number of that car," he directed once, pointing ahead of us. Then twenty minutes later I noticed the same car in the traffic. When I told him I saw it, he set off after it. Drawing up alongside, he shouted "Stop! Stop!" to the two girls inside.

They were typical middle-class Iraqi girls, all made up and dressed to the nines, red nails and all, male bait. Typical Mukhabarat girls. Not agents, but Mukhabarat just the same.

"Hi," said Jamal, getting out of our car and ordering me to follow.

"Hi," said the girls.

"Whatcha doing?" said Jamal, in an imitation of western-style girl-chasing. He told them he was an engineer in some innocuous business, and I was his buddy who was studying in Manchester, England.

"Oh, say, I have a brother in Manchester," one of the girls gushed.

Oh, say, I thought. What a coincidence.

"C'mon and join us for a ride," the other girl invited. Their car was nicer than ours.

"No, thanks," I said even though I know that in the Mukhabarat, they decide everything for you. They decide when you eat, when you sleep and whom you sleep with. Just the same I went home in a taxi, and surprisingly Jamal didn't object.

Back in the refuge of my room, I realized what I had been doing. I had been thinking of Khaled and Jamal and myself as *us*, the Mukhabarat. Is that what was happening? Was I being brought into the circle?

I was finishing dinner when Khaled phoned. "You have something to do," he said. "I'll be right there."

I put on my trendy lace-up shirt and new trousers and wondered what treat they had in store for me. I was less worried now. I was even growing confident. We drove to the Mukhabarat headquarters, but once inside the gates this time we transferred to a white Cutlass sedan and drove around to the other side of the compound. There were surveillance cameras everywhere, on every post, every building corner. We walked up to the door of a large modern building, and Khaled stood before it and said, "Hussein Ali!" He'd used my given names as an *Open sesame!* The door swung silently open.

Inside, all the doors were glass and the floors marble. The guard was festooned with a Kalashnikov rifle, cartridges and walkie-talkie.

"Good evening, *ustath*," he said, using a term of respect that means "master."

I turned around to see who he was referring to. He was referring to me.

We went into a room full of TV monitors, the other end of the cameras outside. The men there stood up and shook hands with me, and were generally very friendly. Oh, my God, I thought, they're expecting someone else. We continued on to another room. Two men were standing in front of a large three-part painting of sea and mountains — a copy, though, not the real thing. Khaled snapped to attention and saluted the men. One was

Radhi, the Gorilla. The other was a professorial-looking man of about fifty, wearing glasses.

The Professor talked as Radhi and Khaled listened in silence, watching my face. "You made a mistake," the Professor said abruptly. "Why did you say this Israeli agent, Morris, is clever?"

I went cold all over.

"Are you a traitor?" he asked, then continued without pausing for a response. The questions were all rhetorical. "Yes, you are. Did you work with the enemy? Did you try to destroy the government of His Excellency? Yes, you did. Have people been killed for doing this? Yes, many have already been killed for less than this. Your turn will come."

His voice droned on as he pronounced the sentence. For the first time in my adult life, I cried.

I hated crying. But I could not stop myself. They were going to kill me. It didn't matter which of their methods they used, but they were going to kill me. The seeming friendliness, the night-clubbing, had all been a cruel joke.

"I have never seen a case like this in my life," continued the Professor angrily. "But," he added, "your father is one of us, so we cannot make the final decision here. We'll refer it to His Excellency, Saddam."

A reprieve! I couldn't believe my ears! Because of my father's status, that final judgment had not been made.

My accusers were clearly furious, though, furious that I had preempted their own attack and had forced them into this position. Because of my "confession and repentance," and above all my father's position, they were actually granting grace to a Mossad agent. The Professor almost choked on every word.

"We are giving you a chance no one has ever been given before," he said through gritted teeth. "You will return to England. You will be contacted there."

He did not actually say the words "double agent," but I realized my big chance could mean nothing else.

"You are in the circle now," said Radhi with cold menace. He leaned over me, with his knuckles on the table. "And someone who enters never leaves."

* * *

At seven the next morning, Khaled took me to the airport. Once again we bypassed passport control. He actually escorted me on board the plane, then left at the last moment. The Iraqi Airways flight took me to Paris's Orly airport. From there I had to transfer to the city's other airport, Le Bourget. But to do so I needed a transit visa, and the name on my ticket was not my real name. As far as my passport and my tickets were concerned, Hussein Ali Sumaida had simply vanished into nowhere for five days. There was a stamp out of Belgium on the nineteenth, but no stamp of entry anywhere for the past five days.

To add to the confusion, I had some diplomatic papers from Brussels in yet a different spelling of my name. I gave the French official an apologetic explanation about how Arabic names got spelled differently everywhere, and how sometimes it was the first name and sometimes the middle name. Finally he just gave up, said okay and waved me on. I took the bus to Le Bourget and from there flew on to Brussels. Once again, I had managed to lie to avoid trouble. I contemplated the fact that people seemed to believe me, especially when I tell outrageous lies. Exactly why this is true, I'm not sure. Women tell me it's my soft brown eyes. Certainly it's not my father's big nose.

I was surprised to find my father at the airport waiting for me. He was standing there at the passenger exit, looking both curious and happy. I had never seen him look the way he looked then, and he had never, ever before met any flight of mine.

"What happened?" he growled once we were in the car. "Who did you meet?"

I told him I was not allowed to say, on orders of the Amn — the secret police. We lapsed into silence.

At home my mother was busy packing everything for the big move to the United Nations in New York. She, too, was curious about my doings, but asked no questions. She was just happy I was back.

Then we were off to the United States for the holidays. My new masters at the Mukhabarat had told me to go with my father when he was transferred and then, when it was time, return to school in England. "We'll contact you there," they had promised.

* * *

Manhattan overwhelmed me right from the moment our plane entered the infamous stack of planes that circled above the city waiting to land. I had traveled a great deal, but Manhattan was unique — and ugly. I wondered how on earth people could live and work in this crowd of skyscrapers. It took me time to appreciate the energy of New York.

We were cocooned, as always, by money and staying in a luxury flat in the Waldorf Astoria that must have cost $2,000 a day. There was more than enough room for all of us, my parents, my sister and brother, and the nanny.

If I needed anything special done there was always Yassin.

A staff member of the Iraqi mission to the United Nations, he was our "fixer." And he could fix anything, from an American passport to a green card, from automatic rifles to cocaine for a party. A green card would cost $7,000. I wanted a driver's license, without taking the practical exam. That cost me $300. Pocket money.

Naturally, Yassin was Mukhabarat, a man with a totally inscrutable face. He also took care of any "envoys" from Baghdad who arrived unbeknownst to the American authorities for special assignments. But not long after our arrival, Yassin's cozy career was abruptly interrupted when his brother got into trouble with the security people back home, and he was summoned back to Baghdad. Knowing the regime's habit of ruining not just the offender but all his near relatives as well, Yassin begged my father to help him stay at his post, but my father was a stone wall. Yassin simply didn't show up at the mission the next day, and that was the last we saw of him. He was rumored to have gone underground somewhere in the States. Yassin should have known better than to ask my father for help. A man who will not help his own son certainly won't help a servant.

In all this time, since I left Morris in early July to go to Brussels, I had been completely out of touch with the Mossad. They had known that I was scheduled to go with the family to New York, and so had not expected any contact for a while. Since they did not want me to work in the United States for them, I assumed they were waiting until I returned to England to repeat my failed exam. But they knew nothing, I hoped, of what I now thought of as the Five Missing Days — the days I was a guest of the Mukhabarat in Baghdad.

It was mid-August when my father was summoned to Baghdad. At the same time I returned to England. The exam was the least of my worries. Given how cluttered my mind was with my situation, how I managed to pass I don't know, but I did.

First there was the problem of my work inside the Da'wah for Auda Sultan and the Amn al Hezb, the party security. As I was racking my brains over how to squirm out of that, Auda Sultan contacted me. When he came to my room in the Student Village, he solved my problem for me: he had been contacted by Baghdad and told that he'd been taken off my case. I would be handed over to a new control later. My new control was called Razzouki. I supposed the Mukhabarat had contacted him.

With that complication out of the way, my big problem now was what to do about the Mossad. It was obvious Baghdad expected me to continue working inside the Mossad as a double agent. But I simply couldn't work against the Israelis. Besides, if I was caught, they would kill me.

The other obvious possibility was to work as a triple agent for the Mossad. The mere idea was breathtaking: work for the Mossad as an agent in the Mukhabarat working as a double agent against the Mossad. It would be an almost unrepeatable chance to penetrate the Mukhabarat for the Mossad and feed disinformation to my Iraqi masters about the Mossad. A spy's field day. Also probably his last day.

It was a young man's fantasy — but I was growing up. Even if I'd had the courage — and a death wish — I was certain it was out of the question. The Israelis would never accept me in this delicate role. They could never afford to believe I was what I claimed. They would be far safer, all things considered, to cut their losses and silence me.

On the other hand I could hardly just refuse an order from my new bosses in Baghdad. Somehow I had to fix it so that I could *not* stay in England, and therefore not serve them by working against the Mossad. That was the least I could do for Morris and Yusef and my own self-esteem. As usual, I came up with a half-baked plan: I got myself arrested by the British police.

It was fairly simple. I arranged for a friend to steal his girlfriend's Visa card and give it to me. Then I waited a few days until she notified the company and the police. As soon as I was certain the authorities knew about the theft, I went to an expensive menswear store and tried to make a huge purchase with her card.

Like police all over the world, the British who collared me were rough. They took me to a rundown old police station and searched me. They were turning out my pockets when I remembered a phony ID I had with me. (It was easy for Iraqi students to collect phony IDs for various purposes. Someone who was leaving the country would sell his bits of identification to a fellow country-man.) But if the police found the false ID now, my whole game plan would be blown. I'd be put up for considerably more than petty theft. While the police were busy going through the papers I had taken out of my trouser pockets and spread on a table, I slipped the ID into a hidden inner pocket of my jacket. In retrospect, it's unbelievable that they didn't notice.

After a time I was put in a dungeonlike cell with a heavy door. I looked around frantically for somewhere to dispose of the incriminating ID. I found only smooth stone. Then I saw a small crack along the doorjamb. I tore the paper into tiny bits and painstakingly stuffed them into the crack.

A woman came to my cell to interrogate me. She asked about my means of support and the like. I lied and told her my family sent $200 a month — which was far too little to live on. But since I had prepared in advance to leave the country, I had a lot of cash on me, and of course she wondered why. In the end, after a lot of double-talk on my part, they let me go. I was to return for a hearing September 28. The papers they served me with said that if I was convicted, I would be deported.

The papers were my salvation. They would convince the Mukhabarat that I could not live in England and work inside the Mossad for them. Naturally I never went to the hearing.

10

THE LAW OF THE JUNGLE

WHEN I PHONED MY FATHER in New York to tell him I had to leave England for good because of a problem with the police, he was furious. If he could have jumped out of the telephone receiver and strangled me he would have. By now, he knew everything the Mukhabarat knew.

"You goddamn fucking little bastard! You were told to stay in England!" he yelled. Then he smashed the phone down.

He was at home when I arrived, and he greeted me with stony silence. The next day he asked my mother to send everyone else out of the house: servants, children, everyone. He demanded to be left alone with his treacherous son.

"So, you are trying to destroy me?" he began, then gathered momentum. "What the hell do you think you're doing? After they told you to go to England, and now you fuck it up! Who the hell do you think you are? I'll see *you* destroyed before you destroy me, *K'athar*! You scum!"

Five days later I received a presidential order, which I still have, saying my studies were to be transferred to Baghdad. It was brought by the foreign minister, Tariq Aziz, himself, who was visiting the United Nations for a session on the Iran-Iraq war.

It was October 1985, and the war was now five years old. Iraq had been trying to end the conflict ever since Saddam realized more than four years before that it was a lost cause.

I was to return on Aziz's private government plane, a Boeing 747 named *Al Qadisiya*, after a famous battle of ancient times when we defeated the Persians.

When the time came, my father took me to the plane. *Al Qadisiya* was flying from New York's Kennedy Airport to Washington first, then on to Baghdad. Since it was a diplomatic flight, the only security we had to pass was Iraqi. Everyone on such flights enters and leaves the United States without visas or other American formalities. The plane was parked on a special area of the tarmac. We could simply drive in through the gates and up to the aircraft. Several large boxes were loaded into the cargo hold, and I wondered what, or who, might be in them. Our own agents guarded the aircraft with the usual array of weapons.

The first-class cabin was ultra first-class, with enormous armchairs and the best food and liquor. The center section had been converted into a spacious conference room, while the back portion was set up like the economy section of any commercial flight.

On the way to Washington I sat up front with some of Tariq Aziz's delegation. They discussed their shopping coups, not the war, and watched American TV shows picked up on the front screen by satellite. Tariq Aziz himself had gone to Washington earlier by land, and so we were, in effect, simply following him.

We landed at Andrews Air Force Base outside Washington. Once again there was no American security for us to pass. While Aziz met with Ronald Reagan's Secretary of State, George Schultz, some of us went shopping in the limousines provided, then spent the night at the luxurious Hay Adams Hotel, where a whole floor had been blocked off for the Iraqi delegation. Our security boys were everywhere, in the kitchen, at the reception —

I expected to find them in the bathrooms. After a room-service meal I strolled down the hall to pay my respects to Aziz.

He was much as I remembered him from those frequent visits to our home when I'd been growing up. A Havana cigar was forever between his lips and he wore the *dishdasha* gown that he preferred in private indoors.

Aziz was something of an enigma, a Christian from the Chaldean Catholic sect, yet in a seemingly powerful position. But in reality, when it came down to essentials, he was powerless, as were all Saddam's men. As many who have negotiated with him have noted, Aziz is smooth and suave, but loyal to the core. He always follows instructions.

This "acceptable face" of the Iraqi regime was born in the village of Tell Kaif, near the city of Mosul. After moving the family to Baghdad, his father reportedly worked as a waiter. Aziz went on to study English literature at the Baghdad College of Fine Arts, where he became a militant Ba'thist. In 1968 he found himself on the wrong side of a factional struggle within the party. Thanks to Saddam, then the number-two man in the regime, he was rescued and soon made editor of the official newspaper, *Al-Thawra*. By 1973, he was information minister and had control over all media. In 1983, his role as chief apologist for the regime was confirmed and he became the foreign minister. Like other Christians in the regime, Aziz played his role in a very low-key manner.

He and I exchanged cordial banalities briefly, then he retired to lunch with his officers.

To pass the time I decided I might as well be a tourist, too, and go sightseeing. I loved Washington. It had a European style and pace, and it seemed so quiet after the roar of New York. Compared with the crowding skyscrapers, the low, gracious architecture was a welcome relief. So this was what they called the Capital of the Free World. Maybe it wasn't, but in the sunshine it felt like it.

First I wanted to go to the Aerospace Museum to see at last the real evidence of the American space program. I had imagined what it was like from the stamps I'd collected in my boyhood: Mercury, Apollo, John Glenn, the Eagle — all magical names to me. I learned about Sputnik and the Soviet cosmonauts, too; we were supposed to admire them more. To me they were all wonderful creatures of fantasy. And at the museum, they seemed even more fantastic. To actually stand there beside Glenn's capsule, to see the tiny space from which he watched our planet, to wander through the replica of the space lab . . . I was in heaven.

I was brought down to earth when I went to the Vietnam War Memorial. Sorrow seemed to surround it like a cloud. Before I even got out of the car, I was almost engulfed in pain. The closer I came to the people touching the stone, feeling the names carved into it, pressing their lips to it as though somehow the dead would feel the love, the more pain I felt. I thought about how we had been taught that the Americans were invaders who deserved everything they got, how the Vietcong were freedom fighters who felled a giant. All I felt now was a deep sorrow for all the misery and loss.

Maybe the Americans had been wrong. Maybe all war was wrong. But at least the Americans cared about their losses. My own people had lost almost a million fathers and sons in the stupid war with Iran, and yet they were not allowed even to post the traditional mark of mourning and the name of the deceased on their doors except very briefly. Our government forbade it to keep from making obvious the full extent of the losses; every door in Baghdad would have been a reproach for Saddam's war. The Americans, by contrast, had lost only about 60,000 men, and every single one was openly mourned at this very public, and yet somehow very private, memorial.

Perhaps this was the most fundamental difference between the two cultures. It wasn't that "life is cheap" in the Mideast, as so many westerners like to say; life is not cheap to my mama, or Bibi, or my friends. Life is dear; sons and daughters are dear. But we are trapped in a vicious circle of patriarchal regimes that kill to survive. Death is their currency, their lifeblood. Sentiment and mourning are repressed in a vice of grief and terror. Iraqi male children are taught that credo. I was soon to learn just how easy it was to teach, using fear as the ultimate weapon.

Late that afternoon our convoy of black limousines rolled through the sunny streets of the American capital again, back to Andrews Air Force Base. Once again we passed though a special gate in the chain-link fence directly onto the tarmac beside the plane. No American authority ever checked us, our papers, our bags, or the boxes originally loaded on board in New York. We could have been carrying anything from plastic explosives to dead bodies.

At first I sat up front with the delegates again, but I soon grew bored and wandered into the back section, where Aziz's body-guard sat. His name was Karim, but he liked to be called Hakim, because that means "wise guy" while Karim means "generous." He was something of a buffoon, a bit full of himself, but a decent-enough fellow. He had once applied to enter the Mukhabarat, a career particularly coveted by the lower and uned-ucated classes, for the Mukhabarat was the best way up the social ladder. All that was needed was total loyalty and adherence to dogma. But Karim had been rejected. He wasn't from the *right* lower class. His family and tribal connections weren't considered as desirable as the Tikritis who, as Saddam's blood brothers, now thoroughly dominated the scene.

Karim was a talker. He chatted about the conferences and summits, and was especially fond of talking about girls — like most Iraqi men — and sightseeing. He wasn't interested in geopolitics. It seemed that part of his job was to round up girls to take to Aziz's farm just outside Baghdad where, from time to time, there were parties. He was utterly, devotedly, loyal to Tariq Aziz and the regime. I joined Karim and we talked for a while of innocuous things. Then I noticed a lone figure by the rear window.

"He's the man from the Jihaz al-Khas," Karim whispered.

He didn't need to say any more. The Jihaz was a powerful entity that handled all military procurement. Its men traveled on the diplomatic flights but were never put on the official list of delegate-passengers handed to the host country. As far as the official records were concerned, this man did not exist. He'd been able to come into the United States, do his business and leave with complete impunity. I wondered if the American authorities knew. Did they turn a blind eye? Did they keep him under surveillance? Or were they simply unaware?

I was idly pondering such things when we began our descent into Baghdad. As I walked along the ramp from the plane into the terminal, I felt as though I was entering prison, on a long sentence.

The senior official from the Makteb al-Khas, the private office of the foreign ministry, met me. He was pleasant, and even ordered us some Cokes while we waited for our baggage, but to me he seemed like a jailer. Waiters in black suits brought us the Cokes with elaborate and incongruous formality, but as far as I was concerned, they were just prison guards.

After I was dropped off at home I fell wearily into bed, too tired and depressed to talk even to Bibi, who was full of questions about my return. This is my new life, I thought. Inside the circle. Trapped inside the circle.

From the moment I'd been ordered back to Baghdad, I'd known my future was bleak, yet somehow I had pushed thoughts of it all aside and actually enjoyed my day in Washington. Rationalization and denial had been my tools. But here in Baghdad those tools were useless. My fears began to return.

No one came for me the first few days. I wandered the streets, had coffee in the cafés, looked disinterestedly in stores which, despite the war, had the usual array of goods. The main shortages were in basic foodstuffs like flour and sugar, and oil, of all things.

In the streets, shopkeepers were engaged in loud conversation with friends who dropped in at their tiny stores, crowded with everything from Kurdish textiles to American toothpaste. Some men lounged on the curbsides under the overhanging roofs, and the distinctive aroma of oriental spices drifted into the air from nearby restaurants. Police and security agents were on every corner. Like most cities, Baghdad teemed with life, but unlike other cities, Paris, for instance, there was no anarchic spontaneity. Spontaneity had zero chance of survival here. Even in the souk, the ancient covered market with its labyrinth of winding lanes and rickety stalls, where one could easily imagine intrigue, the police and Mukhabarat had succeeded in banishing all mystery.

There was instead a sense of furtiveness and treachery. Baghdad had changed since my childhood, or perhaps it was just that I was old enough now to recognize what I saw. And what I saw and felt was the law of the jungle. In this regime, no one trusted anyone because no one was trustworthy. Trust had been replaced by fear. Everyone informed on everyone else, because if you didn't, someone would inform that you had not informed. Whatever the infraction, real or imagined, whoever committed it, friend or foe, it was reported. Children were taught to turn in their parents for the slightest criticism of the government. Brothers killed brothers for the smallest disobedience to the superior powers, just for the sake of a higher rank. This system meant that people abused small powers to gain greater ones. Traffic cops extorted money from motorists. The black market flourished. The treachery was most evident in the lower classes, from whose ranks Saddam preferred to recruit his intimates, but in the upper classes, too, the insidious cancer spread. I was living proof of that.

As each day passed and still no one came to fetch me, I grew jumpy. One day I just took a taxi to the Mukhabarat headquarters and at the gate told the guard I wanted to see someone named Radhi. I thought I'd best go at least as high as the Gorilla. I must have been the only civilian ever to try to get into the dreaded place. The guard was still arguing with me when Khaled, the blond, showed up.

"Hi," he said. "When did you get back?"

Apparently they had not informed him of my abrupt departure from the United States — or so he told me. He came to see me regularly for a few days, asking more questions. He asked about everything except the fiasco with the British police over the Visa card. I never knew why he didn't ask about that.

One morning he took me to Baghdad University to register. As we walked across the campus past the modern buildings with their labs and libraries and lecture halls, I could feel everyone staring at me. I wondered if it was my flashy clothes, my hair or my companion from the Mukhabarat. People always had a sixth sense about Mukhabarat men.

Khaled advised me to wear a plain shirt and gray trousers like the other boys if I wanted to be inconspicuous. As it turned out, there was nothing at Baghdad University similar to the courses in electrical engineering I had been taking in Manchester, so another presidential order was issued to enroll me at the University of Technology. This may sound rather grand, but in Iraq a presidential order has to be obtained for almost everything. If you want permission to carry a portable cassette deck, for instance, you need a presidential order. This mountain of paperwork actually comes from the Presidential Office, and everything is signed by its overseer, Ahmed Hussein. So off I went to the University of Technology.

There, too, I was greeted with silent stares. Then I realized what they all found so fascinating and repellent; I was somehow different. It may have been my mannerisms or even my slight stutter. In Iraq being different meant I must be a homosexual. It was just one more feature of the social landscape here that made me shudder. I was accustomed to western attitudes on this sort of thing. The West was a more or less tolerant mosaic of just about every human type; even a ring in a male ear did not necessarily make him gay. Here, the slightest deviation was suspected, judged and condemned in one glance.

I had difficulty with the deputy of the dean, who took an instant dislike to me and tried to create obstacles to my admission. Under instructions from the Mukhabarat, the deputy was quickly waved aside by the dean. It was my first small taste of the world that security agents lived in, a world where the rules did not apply, where all doors could be greased. No, not simply greased, but ordered opened. I was not sure I liked it.

But in another area I had some satisfaction. The girls loved me. While the male students still eyed me suspiciously, the girls found I was easy to talk to. "You're not primitive like our own fellows," they said. Their "own fellows" could only relate to women as bed meat — which for the most part they could not eat. Conversely the girls seemed to think I was an embodiment of the western male. I was more open, offering genuine conversation and friendship. True, there is more male-female friendship in the West, but I could not convince them that there were "primitives" in all societies.

There were a lot of girls for me to be friends with at the University of Technology. Perhaps the only accomplishment of Saddam's Ba'th Party was opening the doors of education and the professions to women. Saddam had achieved this by holding a gun to the head of virtually every male in Iraq, a country in which the age-old repression of women was the bedrock of religion, society and politics. It would be hard to find a male of the species more chauvinist than the Arab.

In reality the change in the status of Iraqi women was only on the surface. Saddam might have dragged the laws into the twentieth century, but he could not change minds that stayed in the Middle Ages. The war with Iran made the problem even worse. With so many fathers and brothers killed in the war, many of the girls were now free of the traditional unquestioning obedience to their male keepers. Many went wild. It was like going from a nunnery to a bordello overnight. No one was really ready either to accept change or cope with it, least of all the girls. They found that social scandal could still destroy their lives, and that other male relatives, taking on the roles left vacant by fathers or brothers, could be brutal in their condemnation of and punishment for such "crimes." Many girls were killed by family members for ruining the family honor.

Like so many vicious patriarchal cultures, Iraq despised its girl children. Once a couple had three or four sons, they often stopped conceiving for fear their luck wouldn't hold and they would yet be saddled with a shameful girl. But contraception was illegal, because Saddam wanted everybody to be busy making as many little Ba'thist babies as possible. Once again, the black market was the only recourse for amenities like condoms.

Despite all the reforms, little had really changed for women in Saddam's Iraq, because the men had remained the same. But at least females had emerged from the worst of the traditional purdah, and so it was that I found love in an engineering class.

One day I walked into class and saw her. She was the prettiest girl there. Beautiful, actually, with thick dark wavy hair and wide sensitive eyes. She smiled readily, but quietly, as though to herself. And she was, I soon learned, a Christian. I had grown to prefer Christians, as they were more like westerners. Her name was Ban. She seemed quiet and shy, and at first I hesitated to approach her. After years of chasing girls this was a novel experience for me. One day as we were leaving the class, I summoned my courage and managed to move up beside her. "What do you think of the course so far?" I asked. Not a brilliant opening, but it worked.

"It's very interesting," she said. "I like the professor."

She walked on, head bent over her books. I caught up. Now that I had begun the chase, I wasn't going to give up. Usually I didn't have to do much chasing. Still, I sensed this girl was not going to be a pushover. Her seeming lack of interest made her more attractive and aroused my hunting instincts.

"So what made you want to be an engineer?" I asked. "It's still pretty unusual, even here in the new Iraq."

She looked up at me and said evenly, "The same reasons as you, I expect. I want a good job that's a real challenge."

This girl was a real challenge. The old approach would not do. I backed off, and said I didn't mean to bother her.

"That's all right," she said. "I didn't mean to be rude."

"Maybe we could talk a bit better over lunch?" I ventured. For the first time in my career as a ladies' man, I was nervous.

"I can't today."

My heart fell. A refusal. "Tomorrow?"

She hesitated, looking me in the eye. "All right. See you tomorrow."

I was happy out of all proportion to a mere lunch date. But I didn't realize at that moment what was happening to me. At first we saw each other rarely, and always with a group of friends. And slowly I began to wonder if it was possible that I was falling in love. For so long, that kind of love had simply not been a part of my life. I just assumed that I was incapable of it. And now this one gentle girl was changing all that.

We soon knew just about everybody in the university, which had a total of about eighty students. I was actually beginning to enjoy myself. Then I was reminded that in my life now, nothing would be as it seemed.

* * *

It was late at night and the house was still. The ring of the telephone, as harsh as a dentist's drill, jerked me awake.

"I'm a friend of yours," said an unfamiliar voice. "I want to see you."

Terror and panic arose in me. Oh, God, could it be the Mossad? I had simply walked out on them without a word of explanation. I'd vanished because once I knew my own people were on to the connection, the best thing I could do was avoid contact, for my sake and theirs. But the Mossad wouldn't necessarily see it that way. The Mossad was not a sentimental organization.

I hedged. "I'm not sure. Give me your number and I'll call back."

A westerner would immediately and automatically have said, "Who is this?" Not an Iraqi. Certainly not this Iraqi. One simply did not ask such a direct question. If you did you would only get a question in reply. I saved a step by asking him an indirect question, his phone number.

"No. You name a time and place we can meet."

I was afraid to respond and afraid not to.

"Saturday at six. In front of the Mustanseria University," I finally replied. Today was Thursday, the beginning of the Muslim weekend. Friday was the sabbath. So I could at least delay until Saturday.

"I'll be in a blue Toyota, license 155302," he informed me. Then he hung up.

I was terrified. What if it was a setup? What if it was a test by the Mukhabarat to see if I would meet someone from the Mossad?

11

THE WORLD OF THE MUKHABARAT

THE SABBATH WAS QUIET. IT gave me time to think, to collect myself. The more I thought about the strange phone call, the more likely it seemed that this was a setup. First, the approach was just not the Mossad style. It was too raw. They would not make a rendezvous in an open space in broad daylight, with me specifying time and place. The man who had phoned had a northern Iraqi accent. This would be rare in foreign agents, but common in our own service.

No, it had to be a trap.

I called the Mukhabarat and said I wanted to talk to Radhi.

They hung up.

I dialed back, and before they could hang up again, I blurted out, "It's about spying and it's urgent. Something strange has happened." Soon Khaled came on the line. I said I had to see him.

When Khaled picked me up he did not appear to be his usual confident Aryan self. He was nervous and grew more so as I told him my story. "Go to the appointment," he ordered. "We will be in the vicinity."

On Saturday at six sharp the blue Toyota drew up to where I stood in front of the university. License 155302. I still remember that license plate. Under pressure I retain everything. When I'm relaxed I can scarcely remember what day it is.

I also vividly remember the man inside the car: a big man, extraordinarily handsome, with piercing black eyes, the kind one cannot look at directly for very long. As I got into the car, those eyes burned into me. I watched his hands as he handled the car, guiding it through the traffic. He had huge hands, with long strong fingers.

"My name is Abu Firas," he said. "I am with the Special Department. Are you with the Mukhabarat?"

"No, where did you get that idea? I don't know any Mukhabarat."

"Well, some of my friends want to see you."

"Why me?" I asked plaintively. I hoped he did not see through me. "I'm just an ordinary guy."

"Don't worry. We're here for your own good. We're friends of your father."

That was possibly the least-reassuring thing he could have said. My father's words suddenly thundered into my thoughts: "I'll destroy you before you destroy me!"

We drove aimlessly for about fifteen minutes. It didn't seem to matter anymore if Khaled and his people were on our tail or not. I no longer had any idea which tiger was behind which door. The man who called himself Abu Firas talked about computers and technology, Fortran, Pascal. He was clearly a computer buff, if not a professional. Fortunately a nod or two from me seemed adequate response.

He left me back at the university, telling me someone else would pick me up there the next day at six o'clock.

Khaled told me they had no idea who the mysterious Abu Firas was. "We're checking him out. And the car, too," he said gravely. "You go to the next meeting as arranged, and we'll be ready."

It sounded as though they were setting an ambush for this Abu Firas. I hardly noticed the man who picked me up the next day — and drove me straight into the Mukhabarat headquarters. What was going on? Just who was being ambushed by whom here? We drove right up to the first building where I had been questioned. This time I was taken into the large conference room on the right.

Abu Firas came in. "You passed the exam," he said, fixing me with those brilliant eyes. Then his grim expression turned to a smile. "And you called the Mukhabarat to pick me up!" He laughed. It must have been one of their favorite jokes.

"Now someone important wants to see you," he said.

Probably the Terminator, I thought wearily, tired of this up-and-down, cat-and-mouse, now-we-like-you-now-we're-going-to-kill-you game. I was tired of mysterious phone calls and setups. Once again we got into the white Cutlass to drive to the other side of the compound, and once again the cry of "Hussein Ali!" opened the gate.

Back in the same room as before, another man awaited us. He had sharp eyes and a thin face, crowned by a bald dome with a few strands of hair brushed over it. He looked like a hungry old eagle. He was the only one in military uniform. He was Fadhil Selfige al-Azzawi, the Mukhabarat second-in-command. It was said that at home he kept king cobras as pets, souvenirs of his days as ambassador to India.

Abu Firas saluted him. I later learned that Abu Firas was a full colonel, the son of a Bedouin sheikh, and his real name was Farid Shaharabeli. He was head of field operations. To me he remained Abu Firas.

Abu Firas drew out a file from his case and spread out some of the papers before me. "Your case has been settled," he announced.

I looked and saw a document signed by Saddam Hussein himself. "The matter," it read, "is to be left to his father."

There was also a letter in my father's handwriting. Two lines only. It read, "Traitors should always get what they deserve, according to the rules, without regard to family ties."

A death sentence. I *was* going to die. My father's decree did not surprise me. In fact, he must have been almost exultant when he wrote it. Still, death . . . I shivered and felt more alone than I ever had. Perhaps if I'd been older I could have faced it. I was barely twenty.

Everything I had done I had done out of revulsion for Saddam Hussein and the Ba'th Party and everything they represented on earth. But most of all I had done it out of hatred for my father, who represented all of that and worse. For my father and his kind, power was a god named Saddam and Israel was the devil incarnate. Nothing displaced those two icons in his soul. Not friend or family, and above all not his son. Like Abraham he had offered up the life of his Isaac to his god. He had literally signed my death warrant.

Islam teaches the story of Abraham and Isaac, just as the Jewish and Christian faiths do. The sacred stone in the Kaaba in Mecca, to which all Muslims bow when they pray, is said to have been raised there by Abraham and Isaac. Not far away, Mina is said to be the place where Abraham offered his son in sacrifice. Every year pilgrims go there and throw stones at it to chase away the devil. In the Islamic story, it is the devil, not God, who demands the terrible sacrifice. It is God who stops him.

My father, it seemed, had forgotten that this was the devil's work, and he did it for his god, Saddam.

Another letter was produced. "Whose handwriting is this?" I asked shakily.

"His Excellency Saddam Hussein, may his life be preserved by God," was the reply.

I read the words on Saddam's letter. They were incredible. "He is pardoned. But on the conditions of the Mukhabarat."

I could hardly believe it. Saddam Hussein pardoned no one. He even killed his closest allies if there was the slightest indication they might one day surpass him. And now in a supreme irony he had spared my life in return for my father's loyalty. He had stayed Abraham's hand just as he was about to plunge the knife into Isaac's heart. But this Abraham — my own father — would rather, I knew, the deed had been carried out.

"We follow instructions," said Fadhil Selfige portentously.

"We don't ask why. Your case is special. You should thank His Excellency for giving you a chance to live . . ."

He went on and on in this vein and I ceased to listen. He was interrupted by the eight-o'clock news on the television, which as always featured a long speech by His Excellency. It was listened to reverently by all present. Except me. Mercifully on this night the speech was over in a brief ten minutes.

The Eagle called in a servant to bring soft drinks, then turned to me once again. "You are with us now. Abu Firas will take control of you, direct you, show you true life."

I was unsure what this meant.

"Is there anything you would like to ask for?" he said.

"I'm still having problems with that deputy at the university, the one who doesn't like me. He keeps harassing me, lowering my grades, and — "

"See to it!" he ordered Abu Firas.

Suddenly it seemed that they were doing my bidding, rather than the other way around. I was astounded.

The deputy must have been astounded as well; he was taken to the Mukhabarat compound for three days and, upon his return, treated me with deference. I found the knowledge that I could cause someone this kind of trouble vaguely disquieting. It was as if my mind had not caught up to events. I still failed to realize fully that I was now part of the fearful machine. In fact I was beginning to feel as though I had escaped unscathed. I lived like any other young student, enjoying nights out with my friends and with Ban. The only ripple on the seemingly normal surface of my life was Abu Firas, who came almost daily to the house — to indoctrinate me in the ways of the Mukhabarat.

There was one lesson to be learned above all: the Mukhabarat existed to preserve the life and power of Saddam. The Mossad existed to protect Israel, MI5 and MI6 to protect England, and the CIA made the whole world its business. But the Mukhabarat was there for one reason: Saddam Hussein.

"Forget your past," Abu Firas instructed me. "It is over. This is your new life, like a new country. Your promotion to our ranks is unique, especially in a war situation, where we face other enemies, as well: the communists, the Da'wah. They're all trying to destroy Saddam. Saddam is Iraq, and they are trying to destroy Iraq, understand?"

I understood. Most Iraqis understood. There were rows of graves that offered a silent testimony to their understanding.

Abu Firas told me that first they were going to use my talent for getting to know people. "You will report on them. You are one of us now, and you must feel that completely. You are often undisciplined, and we will correct that. So forgive us if we are critical, but it is for your own good. You must report any time you leave Baghdad. You can call me any time you need advice, or help. I am your brother now. If you like we can get some girls and go out. I'm married, but that doesn't matter . . ."

The sudden friendship, the insistence that I now belonged, was mind-boggling. I began to ask myself, is this the dread Mukhabarat?

But soon I realized that Abu Firas hated my guts, hated me for having been an agent of the archenemy, Israel, and he hated what he was doing. But he had to follow orders. The orders had come from Saddam. I was to be enlisted into the service and shown every respect. More than any act of brutality could have done, his enforced kindness made me realize the full power of the word of Saddam. It was more powerful than the word of God.

Abu Firas was afraid of Saddam. So afraid that he could not say, even in private, what his real feelings about me were. I might have informed on him.

It was beautiful. Perfectly symmetrical. The system worked.

I later learned that Saddam had given my father a prize piece of land in reward for his loyalty. It became clear that, to protect my father from the scandal, only the very top few officers I dealt with knew about my crime, my involvement with the Mossad. That was when I realized the full extent of my father's power.

* * *

I was first given a basic introduction to Mukhabarat techniques in the field. Abu Firas and I would sit in the formal living room, which must have been the only room in the world furnished with a combination of Louis XVI chaises, Chinese carpets, Austrian crystal chandeliers and a giant oriental screen of black wood inlaid with shells. The screen divided the living room from the next room. We would drink hot thick Turkish coffee as we worked, interrupted from time to time by Abu Firas's pager. It rang whenever someone at the office needed his advice. The atmosphere was just as if I was his client and he was an ordinary businessman.

On one occasion he brought some maps with him, which he spread out on the coffee table. They were mainly of European cities. "Now then," he said, smoothing out the first one, "a bit about working on unfamiliar turf." It was a map of the city of

Zurich. He then outlined a brief course on what to do when arriving in a foreign city, how to study the map in advance and note all the routes to and from the target address, the surroundings, the possible hiding places. It turned out that all this was academic, because the agent never did any of this groundwork himself. That was not how the Mukhabarat worked.

In the Iraqi service, a team of officers did all the reconnoitering beforehand, set up all the necessary logistics and the cover. The agent was handed an ID kit, complete with passport, credit cards (American Express was the preferred Mukhabarat plastic money), real money ($100 American bills tossed about like small change) and other papers. Usually they would all be genuine, either stolen or those of a corpse, preferably with the citizenship of the country in question.

A car was provided if needed, complete with changeable license plates. The route and timing was worked out. All the agent had to do was follow instructions and carry out the actual shooting, bombing or robbery. There was no actual elite team of saboteurs or assassins; an agent was picked specially, from the general pool of officers and agents, for each individual operation.

Abu Firas explained a horrible phantom organization called the Kisim Alightialat — the assassination department. It had no fixed staff, no real offices, no senior supervisor. What it had was an open unlimited bank account. When an operation was initiated, it was financed through this account, by whomever is ordered to carry out the operation. The choice of the assassin depended on the nature of the victim and the method to be used. The chosen man was given a bit of special training in explosives, or whatever was required, and sent on his way. There was only one basic requirement: blind loyalty. In some way, the agent must have proven to the satisfaction of the authorities that if necessary he would kill his whole family on command and never blink an eye. It seems there are a frightening number of people who, given enough money, are prepared to do such deeds.

With a shock, I realized that eventually, if not immediately, I was to be one of the chosen. For what? I looked at the map of Zurich he was spreading out and felt sick inside.

"You've already proven, of course, that you qualify for this type of work," Abu Firas said in a suddenly cold voice as he continued to study the map.

"What do you mean? I haven't killed anyone."

"Haven't you? The PLO man in Brussels was hit by your old acquaintances. Remember?"

I felt a chill. My "old acquaintances," of course, were the Mossad. People like Abu Firas would go to any lengths not to say the name Mossad.

I thought about Firas's information. So, the Mossad had assassinated al-Arabeh, the Palestinian representative in Brussels whom I had reconnoitered for Daniel.

"You did a terrible thing," Abu Firas said. He was aiming to play on my guilty conscience. But I didn't really have one. I'd been just a small part of what had happened; I hadn't been the one to pull the trigger. I'm not defending what I did, but even now it just didn't seem that significant in the overall Mossad operation.

"But that's over," said Abu Firas. "There is nothing to be done about it. It is closed."

Later I could find no official PLO or media reports of such a killing. Perhaps al-Arabe wasn't official PLO. Perhaps Abu Firas was only playing more games with me.

Then he went on to tell me stories about agents who failed or defected. About the officer who was sent to Kuwait to supervise the sabotage of a refinery there. It was to be carried out by an Iraqi-Kuwaiti agent from Basra, who was to smuggle the explosives across the border near Basra. Somehow the mission failed, and the Basra agent was executed. The officer managed to escape to Sweden, only to be killed two years later by a Mukhabarat assassin, an Iraqi meat butcher selected for the task.

"This is what happens to traitors," said Abu Firas. It was the closest he ever came to expressing his real feelings about me. The Mukhabarat, it seemed, never tortured its victims. It either killed them or kept them. Torture was handled by the Amn, the secret police. If the fastidious Mukhabarat wanted someone tortured they sent him to the Amn for the dirty work. Most of the lower orders of the Amn were drawn from the ranks of ex-convicts, rapists and the like. The officers of most of the Mukhabarat departments, however, came from the elite National Security College.

Apart from my case, Abu Firas was a man happy in his work. In addition to casework, he taught the recruits at the National Security College. I later took to calling it the Goon School. Since they apparently considered that I'd already had enough experience and training, I was not sent to the college. All I ever saw of it were the antennae that rise above the walled compound near Saddam's bunker under the lake.

Every year several thousand apply to the college, and only seventy-six are accepted. The Mukhabarat needs to replenish its ranks every year with about a hundred men, which is the number it loses on operations, mainly inside Syria and Lebanon. It draws its elite from the top five graduates of the police academy and the top five from the Military Intelligence School. Some are brought from other places, too — specialists in linguistics, for instance, especially Hebrew.

The Mukhabarat gets a large number of recruits from the Goon School. Many of the students are from Tikrit, Saddam's hometown, as they are the most likely to be loyal. The criterion is always loyalty, not ability. To get into the school some of the Shi'a even turn in their own family members, saying they are Da'wah.

Many of the others are from the northwest, from the Bedouin there. So that their sons can go to Saddam's school, these traditional tribesmen offer them for military service. The Bedouin are fierce and loyal and unbelievably backward. Desert nomads, they live in the old manner, in tents, and who go barefoot in the sands, with camels as their means of transportation. They live this way by choice, not out of poverty. Many are, in fact, extremely wealthy and also drive Mercedes Benzes. At mealtime, they sit around a roasted sheep on the floor. They feed with their fingers, reaching out to rip off the flesh or scraping out the brains, which are considered a delicacy.

All of this is, ironically, quite civilized compared with what they become at the college. Their traditional manner of living at least has the dignity of ritual. But the college takes this crude oil, so to speak, and processes it, changing the physical properties while the chemical makeup remains almost the same. Exactly as in a refinery.

Recruits are painstakingly taught from the feet up. They must first learn how to wear shoes, how to use a knife and fork, how to speak, how to use a wristwatch, how to put on a tie, how to match a shirt with it — every last detail to make them ready for western society, or for escorting westerners around Iraq, especially journalists. That means learning all about whiskey-and-sodas, rum-and-Cokes and gin tonics. Given the proclivity the press has for reporting from the firm base of a bar stool, this is quite necessary training.

As a diversion I used to like imagining the classrooms. In my mind's eye I saw everyone sitting uncomfortably in chairs, feet pinched and squirming, fists clutching knives and forks and stabbing at rubber-chicken dinners; trying to learn whether one should order the white wine or the red.

Some recruits are also brought from the Fine Arts College, where they have displayed special talent in painting or acting. Such skills can be extremely useful to the agent in the field. Quite often, the Mukhabarat will send one of its "artists" along with a trade delegation, when it wants an inside look at a facility not easily penetrated with cameras. For instance, if the Mukhabarat wants to check out a Japanese petrochemical plant, they will manufacture a trade delegation. The artist goes along and later sketches what he has seen in great detail. If he needs another look the Mukhabarat will wangle a second and even a third visit.

Agents are usually used when dealing with mechanical technology. Electronics are smuggled. On the surface these agents are urbane, well-dressed men of the world. But though the surface has been changed, their minds and souls remain the same: they are fierce sons of the desert, whose obedience to their sheikh, Saddam, is absolute. They do not have, nor would they even understand, the concept of changing sides. They obey blindly.

I had disdained their crude ways of dealing with me at first, but day by day I came to understand that this core of elite officers and their ranks of robots made a formidable and competent organization. They knew exactly what they were doing and how to do it. Sometimes with great subtlety, as with the artist-spies, sometimes with sheer brutality. It worked. It was deadly efficient. My disdain was gradually replaced by the fear and caution I had originally felt.

I was brought up short one evening when Ban and I and some friends were enjoying a fine meal at the Crystal restaurant on Abu Newas Street, on the banks of the Tigris. It was, after the big hotels, one of the best places to eat in Baghdad, with white linen tablecloths and prices to match. Suddenly there was a great flurry of activity, and a parade of black limousines drew up outside. A big black man emerged, one of Saddam's personal bodyguards. He was followed into the restaurant by a gaggle of very garish hookers and a small orchestra. The whole lot of them swept up the stairs to a private room.

The next day I mentioned the incident to Abu Firas, not in a report but out of curiosity. I wanted to know whether this was the normal behavior of the guardians of the revolution. That bodyguard was never seen again. Not by anybody.

Bodyguards were supposed to be virtually untouchable, invulnerable. It was then that I realized with a shock what just a few words from me could do. For the first time I felt the power of being Mukhabarat, and I was afraid.

Finally I cracked under the stress. I was jumpy, unable to eat properly, unable to sleep peacefully and unable to handle my studies. Abu Firas recognized the beginnings of a complete breakdown and ordered me to rest at home. It was odd, being cared for by the Mukhabarat. I stayed home for five months with Ban as my only visitor. During that time, I turned twenty-one. It was the worst birthday of my life. Without Ban I think I might have slit my wrists.

More and more, Ban was becoming the light in the darkness for me. She, though, was unaware of my situation, of my association with the Mukhabarat and the Mossad and the world of spies and assassins. She was from a Christian family, and in Iraq Christians tend to be very quiet, unassuming people who stay out of politics altogether. It was one of the reasons I liked them. So I was not ready to shatter Ban's peace of mind with any revelations about my nefarious activities or the reality of my entrapment.

When she visited me at the house during the day, she would come in the front entrance and have a little chat with Bibi and sometimes help with the cooking before we settled in the salon to talk or watch television. If someone had recently arrived from the States or Europe we might have the treat of a new movie on the video machine, such as *Raiders of the Lost Ark*. If she visited in the evening she would come to a side entrance and avoid explanations to Bibi, who was very old-world in her ways. Then we would usually curl up on the sofa in the drawing room where I met with Abu Firas, surrounded by all those valuables from Louis XVI and Hong Kong.

One night when Ban came over, she looked troubled. "What's wrong with you?" she asked. "Sometimes you seem so nervous and, I don't know, just worried about something."

"It's nothing. Just overwork. Too much studying, maybe."

"Are you sure? It's nothing I've said or done, is it? I mean . . ."

It's funny how women are always quick to assume that a problem with a man is their fault. I guess men have trained them well over the centuries. But that was the last thing I wanted her to think.

"No, no, no. You're the best thing in my life! Don't worry. All I need is some rest and your company."

So she moved closer to me on the couch and leaned against me, and I began to discover that the woman I'd thought shy and withdrawn was very warm and quite daring.

* * *

In the fall I was ready to go back to university — and once again ran into problems with the administration. They used the pretext of my failure to appear at a lecture to finally expel me completely. But I was no ordinary student. Another wave of the Mukhabarat wand, and I was in again. If necessary, my bosses were prepared to fix my grades, as well. Miraculously, I passed the term exams without their help.

What it all meant, I reflected, was that the whole foundation of society was undermined by corruption. Partisans of the regime got ahead without any real merit. A degree was meaningless, because one could not know who'd earned one and who'd extorted one. This rot had spread to almost every facet of life. An example was the airport the Yugoslavs built.

It was a military facility, the Al Baghdadi Military Air Base, near Hadithah, northwest of Baghdad. The Yugoslavs had been given the contract to build it, in partnership with Iraqi military. As in so many of the communist countries, the Yugoslav company was operated by the Yugoslav intelligence service, since most of its work was of a military nature. Given the way the system worked, it was a gold mine for all the officers involved.

The Iraqi inspectors discovered that they had a profitable racket going: our people would order and pay for high-grade materials, the Yugoslavs would supply cheaper stuff, and each side would pocket a share of the difference. Everybody was happy except the inspectors. If they exposed the scam they would be up against powerful military and Mukhabarat officers who could eliminate them in one stroke. If they didn't and signed an okay on the construction, someone else might reveal the truth and they would be in even hotter water. For example, pipes to carry acid wastes were made of easily corroded material; electricity lines were of the lowest quality; fewer electrical outlets were installed than were officially paid for; even the airstrip itself was shaved by a foot on each side for the entire length of the runways. Considering the size of the project, it was worth a fortune to everybody involved. In the end, the Yugoslavs delivered something that looked very much like an air base, but beneath the surface it was a piece of junk. Just like the whole society.

When I told Abu Firas about the kickbacks he ordered me to find a way to penetrate the network. The Yugoslavs had a Palestinian interpreter, who by virtue of his job had to know absolutely everything about the operation. Luckily for me, he was an acquaintance of friends of mine, so arranging a meeting was a fairly simple matter. My superior officers always seemed to know enough to assign me to tasks some parts of which were already in my bailiwick.

One rainy day, I brought the Palestinian to a coffee shop about fifty yards from the Mukhabarat headquarters and introduced him to Abu Firas. After a brief conversation over coffee about innocuous subjects like the weather, Abu Firas took the Palestinian into the compound and presumably instructed him on his new role as stool pigeon. Or perhaps the man was ordered to remain silent, if Abu Firas was on the take, too; after what I eventually knew of the Mukhabarat and its operations, this was a distinct possibility.

In Saddam's Iraq, everyone who could be was on the take. That's how the system worked. It wasn't a system really; it was an *anti*-system.

Take my own case. My official pay was 30 dinars a month, about $100 U.S. at the official rate, $10 U.S. on the black market (the real value). My real pay was in the form of "permissions." Since virtually everything is forbidden in Iraq, one needs a special permit to do just about anything. I had been bringing computer disks back into the country to sell in my own little black market every time I traveled abroad. A box of floppies that would sell for $8 or $9 in the West, I could easily sell for $45 or $50. Especially the 3.5-inch format. Now Abu Firas arranged for me to have a license to do this on a grand scale.

He also set me up in the spare auto-parts business. The Mukhabarat wanted to keep one dealer under surveillance to see whom he was supplying. They suspected that he had partners in the army who gave him army supplies, which he then sold on the public market at high prices. Then he and his partners all split the difference.

He was a young fellow, about my age, so it was easy for me to start up a conversation with him. After the usual talk about girls and movies, I broached the subject of our doing a bit of business together. We soon shook hands on a deal.

The Mukhabarat issued an order paper authorizing the government-supplies people to give me some of their stock. I drove to the huge government warehouses in the Jurf-Al-Nadaf, a government-controlled market just outside Baghdad. There were long rows of huge sheds full of spare parts for Toyotas, Volkswagens and electrical appliances. It was a bonanza. I would load the stuff into a pickup truck loaned for the purpose, then sell it at my own price to the dealer and pocket the difference while my colleagues followed the trail of goods.

The young dealer disappeared for two months, then reappeared, reopened his shop and carried on.

All this is possible only if commodities are scarce in the first place and if the market is tightly controlled by the security service. That's why I call it an anti-system. And in a horrible way, it works. It's a system of terrible beauty. It means that everyone is to some degree beholden to the Mukhabarat that terrorizes them. Even beggars are employees of the Mukhabarat. Everybody is plotting with everybody else, nobody knows who anybody really is, and everybody is kept busy running around in circles inside the circles. No one has time or room left to mount any kind of opposition. You are running around and everybody is running around you. Saddam is at the center, the still point of the turning wheel.

12

SINKING INTO THE MIRE

In the autumn of 1986, my superiors sent me off for Mukhabarat-style military training. The training was held at a base near Taji, northwest of Baghdad. A spartan place, it had rows of undistinguished brick barracks. The large mess hall featured wooden tables and huge windows.

The most intriguing aspect of Taji, however, were the rows of fake wooden barracks. These empty shells were like sets on a Hollywood back lot. They looked real, but they were decoys, built to deceive enemy bombers. A bit farther out on the grounds, I could see equally phony mockups of SAM-6 missile launchers, all set up, ready and loaded with their three "missiles" aimed at the skies.

In 1991, when American planes filled the skies, these primitive-looking stage sets would foil many a "smart" bomb. This sort of mock military base was used by the Allies during World War II when an entire cardboard invasion force was assembled in England to fool the Germans and hide the fact that the real invasion force was assembling elsewhere for a surprise landing on the continent.

My training began in a classroom, though I was the only student and was privately tutored by a young officer. It amused me that he ignored the intimacy of our situation and acted as if he was before a large class, managing to look and sound as if he had given this same lecture every day for a hundred years. He showed me how to strip and clean an AK-47, and then we moved on to a Browning pistol. This part of my training was easy. Then came target practice, shooting at a stationary target on a firing range. I did very well at that; maybe they wondered if the Mossad had taught me, but in fact they had not. I simply had a very useful natural ability.

The rest of my training consisted mainly of being shot at. They would make me stand on the range, holding a waist-high wooden dummy. Then a big Peugeot would come roaring around one of the buildings, its shrieking tires kicking up the dirt as it careered toward me, its occupants firing at the dummy.

At first I wondered just who was the dummy here. I certainly felt like one, standing there in the heat, covered with the dirt flung up by the car. Initially I thought my superiors were dummies, calling this inane routine training. After a while, I reconsidered. Perhaps they had found that in the field our boys were the shootees more often than the shooters. I realized that the idea was to steel the nerves of the trainee to just about anything. Many agents are great shots but go to pieces the first time they are shot at. The Mukhabarat, once again, was not as unsophisticated as it first appeared. Spying, I was learning, was usually boring and routine, relieved, as the saying goes, only by moments of sheer terror.

One of my assignments was to get to know a man named Assad. He was a Syrian student the Mukhabarat was planning to send back to Syria to act as an agent and perform routine missions to penetrate Syrian intelligence. In Iraq the Syrians were hated only slightly less than the Israelis in those days. Saddam had had a personal falling-out with Syria's president, Hafiz al-Assad, the only other Ba'thist leader to head an Arab country. The Ba'thist fraternity had not survived the bitter feud between Saddam and Assad, whose fight was over nothing less than who was going to dominate the Arab world.

Iraqi intelligence had been so successful in penetrating the Syrians that whenever Damascus sent agents to perform sabotage operations in Iraq, the Mukhabarat had their photographs before they even left Syria. They never got farther than just over the border.

I gave a neutral report on my Syrian student. The last thing I wanted was to get innocent people in trouble with the Mukhabarat. I walked a very thin line trying to please my masters and keep my own humanity.

There were no reports in our newspapers or on television of our Arab-versus-Arab activities in other Arab countries. On the surface, we were supposed to maintain the ridiculous myth of Arab brotherhood, even though everybody knew that we were all mortal enemies. Iraq and Syria hated each other, and both despised the Egyptians for betraying the Palestinian cause by signing the Camp David accord. Each Arab nation backed different warring Arabs in Lebanon, and they all envied and hated the wealthy Saudis, whom they considered ill-mannered snobs. The oil-rich Kuwaitis were despised as lazy fat cats. Nobody ever knew what the unpredictable Qaddafi of Libya would do, and so alliances with him were always tempered by fear.

The poor Palestinians were just a political football, and were kicked around, not least of all by the PLO. Sometimes it seems that the PLO wants to keep its people in violent exile, afraid of losing its power if territorial claims are somehow settled, and peace and stability break out. The Palestinian question, as it is called, was similarly useful to all the other Arab leaders. It has been either a rallying cry or a red herring, whichever is needed to distract people from reality. Saddam gave a perfect example of this when he needed an issue to distract people from his crimes in Kuwait and focus them on the perfidious Americans.

One thing and one thing only unites the Arab nations: a pathological hatred of Israel. Even war against the Arabs' other traditional enemy, the Persians, wasn't enough to make them bury their differences. The Saudi and Kuwaiti rulers were terrified that the Islamic revolution might spread across their borders to their own poorer people especially. In response, they reluctantly sided with the equally dangerous Saddam. The Syrians were deeply involved with one of the factions in Iran — the most powerful as it turned out: the mullahs led by Hashemi Rafsanjani. Qaddafi was tied in with another mullah faction. The PLO changes sides according to which Arab leader is backing them at any given moment. A lot of factional wars were played out by these powers in Lebanon where they used their local allies and militia to turn the country into a tribal-political killing ground.

In this atmosphere of factionalism it was easy for spies and agents to cause no end of mischief and mayhem. A favorite locale for operations was the annual *hajj*, or pilgrimage, to Mecca. It was the Saudis' worst headache. They are the guardians of the Holy of Holies, and any trouble reflected badly on them. This factionalism came in handy for Saddam when the tide in the war with Iran turned dramatically against him.

In February 1986 the Iranians had stunned the world in general, and Baghdad in particular, when they captured Fao. A strategic oil-storage facility in the south, Fao was right next to the besieged town of Basra. It was a slaughter. Fifty-eight thousand Iraqi soldiers fell. They had fought fiercely but were overwhelmed by waves of Khomeini's teenage suicidal martyrs.

The Iraqi commanders called a strategic retreat to regroup and were summarily executed by Saddam. Poor bastards. The Iranian maniacs in front of them and Saddam's guns up their backsides.

Later, in 1991, they would have a very different choice: the armed might of the United States and an international alliance in the Saudi desert facing them, and Saddam's ever present knife at their backs.

Saddam had formed special squads from the Republican Guards, his personal elite force, to keep an eye on the officers sent to the front. Since he had decimated the ranks of real military career officers, Saddam now had on his hands a bunch of pampered sycophants. He knew they would run for their lives at the front the moment the enemy attacked. As a result, he needed a backup force to round up the deserters and send them back — or execute them. This worked so well that the new squads were sent to cover the rear of the entire army, to snare any deserters or cowards. They were called the Execution Battalions. The families of those executed by these squads received the body of their loved one in a bag and were denied any military pension.

On the one side, many of the officers faced capture by the Iranians, who would literally tear them limb from limb; on the other, they faced death at the hands of the execution squads. Given the choice, some shot themselves, knowing that at least their families might have some meager financial compensation.

One of the better army commanders tried a desperate tactic against the Iranians. He sent a suicide squad behind Iranian lines. When the squad tried to penetrate the Iranian line by going around Kuwait's Bubiyan Island, at the head of the Persian Gulf, all its members were massacred. The mission was an utter catastrophe and nothing was gained. Predictably Saddam had the commander executed.

Saddam needed help desperately now. Big help. So in order to galvanize more Arab brothers against the Iranians, he launched an operation aimed at the *hajj*.

Two agents, disguised as shepherds, were sent to Mecca. They were to set off "terrorist" explosions at strategic points, carefully orchestrating events to lay the blame on Iranian terrorists. The idea was to promote strong anti-Iranian emotions throughout the Arab world so that other Arab nations would join the war. As the war was against the hated Persians, they could always call it a *jihad*, that now shopworn phrase used to cover every political goal imaginable. The trick was to make sure Iraq would never be connected with the attacks at the *hajj*; Iraq was taking great pains to avoid any taint of terrorism. The great terrorist himself, Saddam, wanted a public image as clean as the desert sand. In the end, the operation was aborted because the Iranians themselves obligingly started mass riots at the *hajj*, resulting in a stampede that killed many hapless pilgrims. The riots, however, weren't enough to drag more Arab nations into the struggle against the ayatollahs. The deadly war was to continue for a long time yet.

Through my work with the Mukhabarat I learned more information about Saddam's arsenal and his strategies than was healthy for any Iraqi to know. I discovered that if you want to know something you should ask a secretary, a driver, a translator or someone like Nasar.

Poor Nasar was an old school friend of mine. His Uncle Amir was a high-ranking officer responsible for the department handling all arms modifications. Nasar was his "special escort," that is, his bodyguard. Nasar knew a lot.

Nasar and I looked enough alike to be twins, and we soon became buddies, as the Americans say. We liked to go and spend a day at Habanniya, the French-built luxury resort on a lake ninety kilometers west of Baghdad. The resort was just past the huge air base that was home to all Saddam's MiG-25s.

Habanniya was a place for tourists, but because of the war there was a singular absence of tourists. As a result, in 1986 it was used mainly by the Iraqi upper classes. There was also a heavily guarded section of the resort restricted to party members. One of Saddam's palaces was on the other side of the lake, protected by everything from anti-aircraft guns to foot soldiers. But I always thought of it as being shielded by some kind of evil blessing.

At Habanniya, there was horseback riding, golf, swimming, water skiing and even carnival rides for kids. In the hotel there's fine dining and disco dancing. I liked to go horseback riding, such as it was, slowly plodding around a small enclosure.

Nasar liked to sit at the patio bar and drink and talk about girls, then drink some more and chase the girls, whom he dropped as soon as he caught them. I joined him in the drinking, but I was wary of the little pills he took to get a buzz. Abu Firas had been clear on that: no drugs. So I declined the pills.

Over the weeks, Nasar kept me up on the latest in weapons improvements, confident that the weapons meant an eventual victory in the war with Iran. It was strange how that war went on and on and yet didn't seem to affect our lives in Baghdad at all. The only exception was during the war of the cities, when Tehran and Baghdad exchanged bombs and rockets; even then, the damage was limited to the area hit. Everyone in the vicinity would rush out to the aid of the unlucky ones.

It was a grotesque war, an obscene war, in which millions of citizens played out the vicious feud between two implacable tyrants, Khomeini and Saddam. Each man was expert at orchestrating the emotions of his public, teaching them to hate the other. It was easy to teach hatred in our countries. There was no free exchange of information, and no one left alive to argue against what we were told. Lately the Iranians had been doing so well it was getting easier every day to hate them.

Nasar assured me that Iraq had been working overtime to gain the tactical and technological edge.

French radar systems were modified to capture a larger field.

The range was almost doubled, from eighteen kilometers to thirty-four kilometers. This made it a bit less accurate and more easily jammed, but to the Iraqi army, range was everything. The Soviet Mi-24 Hind gunships were modified to carry air-to-air missiles, two at a time. They used the Soviet missiles we called "Atul." At first they fitted only five and found the same old problem: the accuracy had been diminished by the modifications.

There was yet another improvement that the American forces seemed unaware of at the beginning of hostilities with Iraq in January 1991: the heavily armored Soviet T-72 tanks were given new computer software programs and night-vision equipment. The Americans seemed to be counting on having the sole advantage of night vision. But the T-72s would be ready for them. The big Soviet tanks were dubbed the "Lions of Babylon." The Soviet shells were also replaced by new ones that had greater range and, alas, less accuracy on the move. Both Iraq and Iran tended to use tanks as cannon, dug in and defended, rather than as assault weapons, so accuracy mattered less than it might to those using a more conventional strategy. The weapons were there to do the job. But the men weren't, as it turned out.

Soviet MiG-23s were equipped with new suspension points to allow them to carry French-made "Magic" missiles, instead of the Soviet ones. The French product was much "smarter" and had nearly 100 percent accuracy. The MiGs were also given new French and German communications systems that improved contact with ground control. The small components were copied and produced at a plant in Eskanderia.

French and German technology was used to enhance Brazilian-made weapons systems. As usual, the equipment was taken apart and copied. It was used mainly in armed personnel carriers and other armored vehicles.

If England was a playground for Iraqi agents and terrorists, then

France was a supermarket for our armed forces. Anything could be had there, from the famous Exocets to Christian Dior fashions for officers' wives and daughters.

Soviet Ilyushin cargo planes were converted into midair refueling craft. Later, toward the end of the war with Iran, Ilyushins were also fitted with the special saucerlike attachment that gave the AWAC (Advance Warning Air Command) its singular profile. These converted Ilyushins were designed and built at Saddam Airport. The first test of one of these lumbering contraptions was a disaster: the behemoth crashed to the ground shortly after liftoff.

As happened so often in modification projects, the Iraqis looked only at the advantages of the improvements, not at the disadvantages. While they might have increased the range of a gun, they might have decreased its accuracy. In the case of the AWAC/Ilyushin, there was a problem with the tail fin that had not been taken into account.

Later I would learn more about the plants in which the ballistic missiles themselves were modified and completed. In a few years the modified SS1 would be a household word around the world: Scud. Meanwhile, I learned that a great many of the engineers in these plants worked under extreme duress. Many were forced into such work against their will. So deep was the distrust and hatred of intellectuals by the party goons that the engineers were routinely beaten by overseers, punished severely for being even fifteen minutes late. A sick child at home, a motor accident or a death in the family — no excuse was acceptable. These were grown men, skilled professionals, being treated like insubordinate privates in the army. Dignity and self-respect were, in effect, forbidden.

As I pondered everything Nasar had told me about these things, I began to worry. Was he, too, a plant? Was the Mukhabarat checking on whether I would report to them? The more I thought about it, the more likely it seemed. Otherwise why would he tell me all these military secrets?

I decided to express my concern to Abu Firas. I expected a knowing look and a casual dismissal of the matter.

Abu Firas hit the roof.

"I don't think he means anything by it," I said, trying to downplay the whole thing. "He's usually a bit high on drugs, you know."

Abu Firas grew apoplectic.

Poor Nasar was immediately transferred to the war front. He was fortunate to have Uncle Amir to intervene for him, and he was brought back from that inferno and put into a safe junior position.

I finally realized that poor Nasar had been talking to me because he thought that, since my father was important, I must be, too, and it would be quite safe to talk to me about anything at all. He got caught between the circles. When he returned, he never called on me again. I could hardly blame him.

It was soon after this that the world learned that Colonel Oliver North and many other misguided fools in the basement of the White House had been selling arms to Iran in hopes of having American hostages held in Lebanon released. It transpired that this activity was directed by President Ronald Reagan himself, even though he couldn't seem to "remember" anything about it. North and his partners claimed they had been dealing with "moderates" in Tehran — moderates like Rafsanjani. Of course Rafsanjani is about as moderate as Heinrich Himmler, Hitler's Gestapo chief. Few who know the Middle East were very surprised at this further evidence of American naiveté and ignorance in dealing with the region. They were learning, but not fast enough.

Everyone knew that the Americans had been playing a not-so-subtle game in the war all along. They gave limited support to Iraq, but did little to stop illicit arms shipments to Iran. The hope was that the two nations would pulverize each other. The Americans weren't the only ones to play this game. France, the USSR, China and Israel itself were having an arms bazaar bonanza.

But Iraq had always been led to believe that Washington tilted toward Baghdad as the lesser of two evils. Oliver North's Iran scam made Saddam livid. As a partial appeasement, Washington reflagged Kuwaiti oil tankers, which carried most of Iraq's oil, to put them under American protection from threatened Iranian attack. Both sides had taken the war into the shipping lanes of the Persian Gulf. It was slowly throttling both nations, who depended on oil exports from the gulf terminals for their financial lives. Saddam was only slightly placated by the American move.

Saddam had been trying to get Iran to agree to a negotiated ceasefire for almost six years of the seven years of combat, ever since it had become clear that the war could not be won. But Iran's mullahs seemed to love the bloodbath.

Saddam came up with a novel Mideastern tactic. The Revolutionary Command Council was accustomed to being called for special sessions during the war, but this meeting promised to be more momentous than any of the others. The members assembled in the central conference room in the Karradat Mariam, the fortified presidential compound on the west bank of the Tigris. The General Command of the Armed Forces was there, too. When Saddam arrived, it seemed that he was, if humanly possible, grimmer than usual. (The avuncular, smiling facade he presents to the television cameras is strictly public relations. Offstage, Saddam is cold and forbidding. Unlike my father, he has control of his passions, and that makes him far more dangerous.)

In his customary precise manner, Saddam set forth the current situation to the council — those who had survived his numerous purges and now served as his intimates. They all nodded as he incisively made point after point: the Iranians' infinite supply of martyrs, their intractability, the option of further bombing of Tehran, the uselessness of that option, the possibility of massive attacks on Iranian ships in the gulf, the dangers then to Kuwaiti shipping, the American policy, apparent for all to see, of sitting on a fence . . . What was needed was to blast America off that fence.

"You are ordered to destroy an American warship in the gulf," he said, turning to his air-force commander, General Hamid Shaaban. "Use the Exocets."

Only in the Middle East would an attack on an American ship be considered a good way to end a war.

I learned all this from my old acquaintance from the *Qadissiya* flight, Karim, who, as the bodyguard of one of the men present, was actually in the room. As I said, when you want to know something, ask the guards and the secretaries. Karim no doubt thought that, in telling me, he was safely praising the ingenuity of his master's master. Karim is now serving fifteen years in prison for similar mistakes, all no doubt made in good faith. But such motivations are not taken into account in Saddam's Iraq.

The attack on an American warship was a perfect example of Saddam's cunning and his unpredictable and extravagant ways. Moreover, there was perfect logic beneath the seeming insanity. America was sitting on the fence because it could afford to. Kuwait and Iran and Iraq were sustaining all the real losses, while America and France and the Soviets and every other nation on earth, it seemed, were supplying arms to both sides. It was just one big weapons-testing ground.

Only pressure from America and the Soviets could possibly end the war now. Real pressure. Pressure that would cut the arms arteries of Iran. Bit by bit, Iraq was already being curtailed by the Soviets.

The Americans would move to end the war only if she herself began to sustain unacceptable losses. Like a naval vessel. And above all, the sailors on board. Saddam believed the Vietnam experience had left Americans deeply concerned about casualties. In his view, they could not bear to have their sons brought home in body bags, and certainly not for the sake of the ruler of Baghdad. Why they were so sentimental puzzled Saddam. But he was convinced they were.

On May 17, 1987, one of Saddam's French-built Mirage fighters streaked out of the blue sky over the gulf waters, headed for the USS *Stark*. The Mirage pilots were the elite, the best trained with the best equipment. For that reason they were also the most intensely screened for loyalty to Saddam. He wanted no Mirage defections. The French fighter jets had been enhanced, so that they could carry not just one, but two, of the deadly accurate Exocet missiles that had proven so devastating to the British navy in its battle with the Argentinians over the Falklands.

On board the *Stark*, radar operators saw the Mirage, but the commander realized too late that it was homing in with deadly intent. The USS *Stark* was hit broadside by two Exocets, and after they exploded the incident exploded into headlines around the world. The *Stark* was able to limp to safe port, but thirty-seven of its men were sent home for burial in flag-draped coffins. Saddam made elaborate apologies, saying it had all been a terrible accident. Exactly how a Mirage could accidentally fire two Exocets at point-blank range by accident was never made clear. The Americans and international agencies were refused permission to interview the pilot. Not aware of the enhancement to the Mirage, western analysts thought two Mirages must have attacked. But both parties let the matter drop after Saddam paid the families of the victims a total of $27 million in compensation.

For Saddam it was cheap at twice the price. America's fence-sitting days were over. Washington began to work in earnest for a ceasefire, bringing massive pressure to bear in all quarters. The war, which would have cost Saddam billions more had it continued, was almost over. The pilot who caused this "accident" was promoted and given charge of the air-force college.

* * *

Throughout the war I was spared military duty because I was Mukhabarat. My life went on uneventfully. I continued to be a student at the University of Technology, went out with friends in the evenings and spent more and more time with Ban.

We both loved to walk in al-Jadriya, the park by the Tigris. We'd just talk, and enjoy some peace and each other's company. I still said nothing to her about the darker side of my life, not wanting to distress her. It would be pointless. She was in no danger from her association with me as long as I was obedient to Abu Firas. I was as obedient as a Boy Scout.

I thought, too, that Ban would simply be bewildered if I tried to explain my activities. Even though she lived in Saddam's Iraq, her background had not prepared her for the nefarious world of spies and assassins. As I've said, Iraqi Christians, with rare exception, minded their own business and kept their peace. Later I realized that I had underestimated Ban, and that beneath her gentle ways was a resilience and strength far greater than mine.

I should have had an inkling of that strength because of the way she handled the difficulties of getting together with me. She had to invent any number of excuses at home, for her parents would have been as happy about her seeing a Muslim as mine would have been about my seeing a Christian. We were an Iraqi Romeo and Juliet, and true to the classic, it was Juliet who was the stronger. But we were happy, and I grew happier as I discovered that my ability to love had not died as a result of my father's persistent cruelty.

This happiness was marred slightly by the presence of Hatem, another student and lieutenant in the Amn, who regarded my turf as his turf. He was tall and clean-shaven, with an arrogant air of superiority. One day he simply walked up to me, flashed his Amn ID and said some of his people wanted to talk to me. He drove me across the city to the Amn headquarters, which was just west of the Mukhabarat headquarters, in the same quarter of the city, Sahat al-Andalus. I could not tell the Amn that I was Mukhabarat. So they took me into the Amn compound, which like the Mukhabarat compound consisted of whole city blocks simply taken over wholesale. The houses were all Amn offices and covered an area even larger than the Mukhabarat compound, like a city within a city.

I was left cooling my heels in a waiting room in one of these houses. Finally someone came out and told me there had been a mistake. I could go.

I was angry, and went over to the Mukhabarat offices and told Abu Firas so. He said to ignore it.

Then Hatem pulled the same stunt again. After I left the Amn that time, I stormed over to our offices once more and told Abu Firas I was fed up with this Amn game.

A week later, Hatem, the Amn lieutenant, was gone. No doubt remained in my mind about who ruled the security-service roost.

I don't know when it was that I realized I both loved and hated being the property of the Mukhabarat. I hated informing, and went out of my way to avoid groups or conversations where sensitive subjects might come up. That meant just about any conversation, since everything in this paranoid regime involved national security. But finally I had to admit to myself that I loved the special powers. If someone was making life a little inconvenient for me, such as the deputy or Hatem, then abracadabra! They were gone. I was now thinking of the Mukhabarat as *us*, their headquarters as *our* offices.

At the same time, I began to see how easy it was for Saddam to create his goon squads. I hated the man, and yet look how his ways had seduced me! It was a depressing insight into human nature, and I began to think for the first time of getting out. I was barely in, not even used yet on any major assignments, and already I was beginning to hate myself. I knew what I was becoming bit by bit. I even started cheating on Ban. I met another girl at the university, whose come-hither smile was too much to resist. But I didn't really try to resist. I was just going along with whatever came my way. It was a kind of sickness of the soul, a deep malaise.

When someone is sinking into the mire as I was, even the finer emotions sink with him. On top of everything else, I had hurt Ban. I was part of the anti-system. I was becoming a goon.

Until now I had just accepted it as my fate. But looking at Ban's loving face one evening, I suddenly realized what was happening to me. And I decided then and there to find a way out for us both. I began to watch for an avenue of escape, waiting for a chance. I knew I must not make a mistake, not even a small mistake. I would have to play their game better than they could. If I did not, they would eat me alive.

Just in time I returned to myself and to Ban. I returned before I destroyed everything worthwhile in my life.

13

"MY LIFE IS WITH YOU"

NEW YEAR'S DAY 1987 I WAS invited to a birthday party for one of the Mukhabarat men. The party was to be held in a special neighborhood on Umm al-Khanazir, an island in the Tigris, located where the river bends at the southern edge of Baghdad. On the surface it looks like any well-to-do neighborhood: large homes with tended gardens, guarded by armed sentries.

The whole island is owned by the Ba'thist Party, and the houses are used for the entertainment of its elite. I learned that to have a party in Umm al-Khanazir one needed special permission from the office of the Ba'thist Party headquarters, Internal Affairs — a horribly apt title, as it turned out.

Inside, each house is comfortable, but in order to leave room for dancing, the L-shaped salons are sparsely furnished. Our birthday party was an ordinary-enough affair, with twenty or so agents and as many girls. I played deejay while everyone ate, drank and danced to western pop music.

That night, I learned more about this neighborhood and what went on behind its closed doors. The person who told me was an officer in one of the Amn security departments. After a few drinks, he entertained the group — "sickened" might be more accurate — with stories about other parties that went on in these houses, affairs attended by party higher-ups. Like everything else in this Iraqi-Arabian nightmare, sex is deformed, perverted and full of terror. The story I heard was not a tale filled with romantic clichés about dark-eyed desert sheikhs and pampered harem beauties who drift about in gauzy silk, eating figs until summoned to the royal cushions. Many of Saddam's men have quite different tastes.

A party bigwig reserves the houses, has the furniture moved out of the salon leaving only the cushions. When the host arrives, he brings with him his own privately sponsored musical group. The party bigwigs all have groups who cater to their individual taste in entertainment. There is usually a singer, backed up by a small band, who has a repertoire of old Bedouin and modern Iraqi numbers. Such musical groups are bought and paid for, and preferably, its members are all blind.

The Ba'th has been a bonanza for blind musicians. They're preferred because the feature attraction at these soirées is erotic dancing by young Egyptian boys. They bend and writhe, stripping off scanty costumes down to their smooth young skin. As the nude dancing boys excite them, the men begin to beat the boys with special batons and whips brought for the occasion. Most of the boys are male prostitutes of sixteen or seventeen. Some never grow older.

The climax of the evening is the rape of the boys by these Iraqi rulers who profess such an abhorrence of homosexuals. Grunting and yelling obscenities, they brutalize their "lovers," competing to see who can make his victim scream the loudest in agony. Many of the boys end up in hospital, presumably to be mended for further use. Others, it is said, die of their injuries.

I know that prisoners in Iraqi jails are often subjected to the same sadism, a hideous form of hypocrisy and cruelty that says more about these men than any other single fact. Worse, there is nothing new about this intimate horror. It's not unique to Iraq or to the Ba'th Party. Others have written of the same tortures in Iranian, Turkish and Greek prisons. Sexual sadism seems to be a common denominator of male tyrants. I won't even pretend to understand what it means, but it's dark and evil.

Iraqi sadists prefer to act out their perversions on Egyptians because they can never be sure if an Iraqi victim might turn out to be an agent for one of the other security branches, or might have powerful family relatives. Moreover, Iraqis are renowned for pride and arrogance. It is said we love to lord it over those considered inferior. The Egyptians are considered inferior, and they are submissive and available in large numbers. Iraqis like to say the Egyptians are easy to jump over, like a low wall.

Egyptians have always been present in Iraq, where they are employed in menial jobs that Iraqis refused to do. Many more Egyptians arrived after the war with Iran began to deplete the work force. They soon filled the posts left vacant by the military draft. After a few years of the conflict, it was hard to find an Iraqi in any of the businesses along Rashid Street. Egyptians literally became the lifeblood of the economy. Those who weren't drug addicts were forced to donate blood to the military medical banks. The medics even relieved them of their kidneys and other parts for transplants. The Egyptians became warehouses for human spare parts.

Many Egyptians brought drugs and pimps with them, and so were hated for being a corruptive element. In 1985 Saddam set up the mysterious Egyptian Department of the Mukhabarat. Five Egyptians were assigned to head this operation. Incredibly they were immediately given the rank of major. No one knew why they were chosen, or who they really were. They were appointed by Saddam's personal decree. Their job was to act as a strike force within the Egyptian community and go after every undesirable element, every potential threat. These five, it was said, never slept.

When the war ended and the soldiers came back to find that their jobs were filled by these foreigners, open war was declared on them. Egyptians were simply gunned down in the streets.

* * *

I was learning that, human nature being what it is, sex of one kind or another plays a large role in espionage, politics and just about everything else. Shortly after I learned about the homosexual affairs of state behind the closed doors of Umm al-Khanazir, one of Abu Firas's men assigned me to gather information about a woman named Abir Abdal Rahman. She was what westerners call a knockout. Stunningly beautiful, she looked like those exotic creatures in the paintings of the harems of ancient Iraq's legendary ruler Harun al-Rashid. When my preliminary inquiries revealed that she was the girlfriend of Saddam's son, Oday, I was ordered to stop my snooping. Such was my vital contribution to national security.

This incident once again reminded me that feelings toward women in Iraq are little better than Iraqi attitudes toward their Egyptian "guest workers." The emancipation of women is strictly on the surface. The longer I stayed in Iraq, the clearer this became. Beneath the surface, the old attitudes live on. Women are playthings and domestic servants.

Officially there is no prostitution in Iraq. In its place there is a platoon of girls, mostly in their teens, run by the Mukhabarat. The girls are not "agents" but are at the disposal of the Mukhabarat for the entertainment of important foreigners, from politicians to businessmen. Most westerners have tended to avoid this obvious trap, but others from Tokyo to Islamabad were well looked after. If young boys were preferred, they were supplied, too. The

Mukhabarat officers themselves were usually careful not to avail themselves of this convenient service, as they knew that no one could be trusted, no one was safe. Even a lowly hooker could be their undoing. So to speak.

* * *

As I found myself mired deeper and deeper in this squalid world, Ban became my lifeline. I knew that with her I had a chance of becoming a decent human being again, if I ever had been. She constantly pulled me back to my better self. At first I needed her, and then I loved her.

One night when we were together in my room I confessed my feelings. "I can't survive without genuine emotion — without love." She said nothing, but her eyes told me she understood.

"I didn't mean to hurt you when I went out with that other girl. She meant nothing."

Quietly, almost in a whisper, she breathed, "I forgive you."

I held her close and our kisses grew more urgent. As I stroked her hair and nuzzled her neck, I could feel her passion match my own. She pulled me down on the bed and we made love like two ravenous lions.

With most Iraqi men, that would have been the end of the love story. According to the old hypocritical code, you never marry a woman you seduce. The woman you marry is a virgin. You hope. Deceiving and seducing virgins is a national sport among the male population. The younger the girl, the better. Men give promises of gifts, love, honor and marriage. When the girl gives in to a man's sexual desires, the fun is over and the man dumps her. Often the girl is left pregnant. I know this kind of Don Juanism exists worldwide, but in Iraq it is still in its most virulent form.

I could never understand this ancient double standard. It

seemed to me that both men and women lose something as a result of this attitude. For me, when Ban and I became lovers, that sealed our bond. We belonged to each other. Given our new intimacy, I decided it was only right that she know at last just with whom she was involved. Over dinner one evening at our favorite haunt, the Crystal restaurant, by the Tigris, I decided the time was right.

I told her about the Mossad and my "escape" into the arms of the Mukhabarat. At first she was utterly nonplussed.

"You mean, you're an intelligence agent?" she asked unbelievingly.

"I'm afraid so. A halfhearted one, though. I try not to get anybody in trouble, but it's almost impossible. And the worst of it is, it's getting to me. I mean the special privileges and the power. Ban, I have to get out of this."

"You mean you're a spy?"

"Yes. I'm a spy. And I hate it."

"You mean the Israelis are after you?"

"Not that I know of. They've tried to contact me, but they must know by now I haven't done anything to damage them."

In 1985, after my five days in Baghdad, there had been a strange phone call for me at my father's house in New York. I believe it could only have come from the Mossad. My father answered the phone and a stranger asked for me, saying he was a friend of mine. When my father demanded to know who he was, the caller hung up. My father was angry and disturbed, because his phone number was supposed to be unobtainable.

"No," I assured Ban, "the problem for me is our own Iraqi agents."

"Then what can you do? Can you resign? Will they let you out?"

I realized she hadn't grasped yet what I meant by "out of this."

"No, my love," I said as gently as I could. "They don't let anyone resign. I don't know how yet, but I have to get out of the country. Permanently. And then I'll need you more than ever . . ."

Her face fell. The full import of what I was saying was beginning to dawn on her. She began drawing on the place mat, putting dots on the *i*'s, filling in the holes. I did the same, as we both tried to think of what to say or do next. After a time, she spoke.

"I don't understand about the Mukhabarat and how it works. But I know you, and I know you share my feelings about life. That's enough for me. My life is with you. Wherever it is."

For the first time in months, I felt that I might have a future.

* * *

After my confession to Ban, I went on as usual. I was buying time and waiting for an opportunity.

As far as my dubious career was concerned, I began to relax a little, once again lulled into a false sense of security. I began to believe that I had got off easily. I felt destined to continue being a student and a junior agent for trivial affairs. Then the Palestinian phoned.

"I have a letter for you from your father," the unfamiliar voice informed me.

A letter? From my father? He might as well have said he had a pouch of diamonds for me from the Queen of England. That would have been more likely.

"Can you meet me at the Meridian Hotel?" he asked politely.

Was it the Mossad? I sat on the edge of my bed and tried to make sense of what I knew. First, my caller's accent was Palestinian; that could mean he was Mossad. Second, my father never writes; the Mossad knows this, so maybe the call was a signal from them. But, third, the technique was not Mossad. It was too direct, too raw.

So, out of three factors, two fit the Mossad. The third did not. I decided it had to be a plant, perhaps by the Mukhabarat.

I called Abu Firas. When his office staffer said he was out, I left an urgent message for him to call me. I gave my code name, Ahmed. Leaving that name always felt a bit ridiculous; in English it was the equivalent of being code-named "John."

When I met with Abu Firas later, he warned me to be extremely careful. "There's something wrong with this guy," he said. Then he handed me a flat, thin rectangular metal case, about the size of my hand, marked "Made in Switzerland." It was a tape recorder. Concealed in my jacket, it was wired to a microphone attached inside my collar.

"Why not a cordless mike?" I asked.

"We don't trust them. Leave the machine on the whole time," he instructed. Off I went to the Meridian to meet the mysterious Palestinian.

The lobby was busy, mainly with journalists there to cover the latest in the eternal war with Iran. On the house phone I called the room number I'd been given. The Palestinian told me I'd know him by his white hair. Within minutes he appeared. An older man whose white hair was curly, he looked like any businessman, dressed as he was in a beige jacket and brown trousers. But I still had no way of knowing if he was a Mossad agent brazenly setting up a meeting, or a Mukhabarat agent pretending to be a Mossad agent to find out if I would still play ball with the Israelis. Or he might have been as advertised — a Palestinian.

He greeted me warmly, then steered me out through the garden to a secluded table in the breakfast café. He was just beginning to explain his business to me when I saw Abu Firas come in and head our way. Frightened of a trap, I began to stammer.

Abu Firas came right up to the table and looked at me. "Hi, Hussein. How are ya?"

The Palestinian laughed and said to me, "Did you call him here to catch me? What did you think I was? A spy?" He laughed some more.

Very funny, I thought. As it turned out, the Palestinian was genuine. He was in Baghdad as a delegate to a PLO-Iraqi government conference. The Mukhabarat had set me up — probably, I thought bitterly, with my father's help. He would have been part of the conference arrangements at the United Nations end. Another test. I was fed up with being tested. My nerves were twisted into knots all the time.

Still, I was rewarded, in a way, for having passed all my tests so well. They let me go to New York for a holiday, accompanied by my father — and my shadows. Even if I had attempted to defect at this point, I was almost certain to be caught. But I could not run for it just yet. In the first place, there was Ban; I had to get her out of the country. And I wanted to finish my degree and get my diploma, or I would have to start all over again in the West. Given Iraq's very well-known success in the engineering field, particularly weapons enhancement, an Iraqi degree was not without value. So I decided to bide my time.

In New York, I hadn't much choice. If I tried to go out of the house in Westchester, someone tailed me. So I stayed indoors, watching movies on HBO. My father and I barely exchanged three words. I realized he and my mother were at odds, for he was constantly angry and cruel with her. I decided to talk to her.

"He blames me for everything," she said, crying. "I don't even know what it is he's blaming me for."

So I told her that, like many young people, I had got myself mixed up in a bit of trouble, but it was going to be okay. Then I told her that my father, however, had ordered in effect that I should be executed for what I'd done.

When she heard that, she became furious and hysterical at the same time. She was beside herself with the knowledge that her husband would order the death of her son. The rest she didn't really understand. But she understood he had ordered my death. It was the last straw.

After a monumental fight with my father, she began to pack with the intention of leaving him forever. Soon after I left New York — after spending any time with my father, it was almost a relief to return to Baghdad and the Mukhabarat — she, too, moved back to Baghdad.

By now I was in my third year of university, and in spite of everything my grades were acceptable. Abu Firas and his men kept me busy watching this student and that professor, and I almost always found there was little or nothing to report. Iraqis were already held in such a vicelike grip.

The rest of my time was spent managing my various financial scams on the anti-system market, with my computer disks — a fresh load from my vacation — and my auto parts. I had come a long way from the days of selling girlie magazines to my high school class.

I had passed my tests so well that at the end of 1987 the Mukhabarat assigned me to do a security check on a man being considered for employment in a missile factory.

Northwest of Baghdad, near Taji, was a large industrial facility called the Munsha'at Nasar, the Victory Factory. The final welding and assembly on most of the large ballistic missiles was done here. The man I was to check out was Ahmed Hassan. In the course of that effort, I learned a great deal about this assembly line of death. In this case, my informant must be protected.

The Nasar plant was enormous. It had been producing missiles twenty-four hours a day since 1988. Two of its main products were the Al Hussein and the Al Abbas missiles, hybrids made from the design of the Russian SS1 — the Scud. Iraqi scientists and engineers dismantled then studied the SS1s in order to reproduce the parts, to which they added their own improvements. All the work in the Nasar factory was directed by a German scientist who ruled there like a god. No one knew his name, except those in the very highest echelons.

Deep inside the factory was a protected core called the Al-Mauka'Al Sirri — the Secret Position. I was never certain, but perhaps it had to do with the adaptation of unconventional warheads.

The Al Hussein was a qualified success: though it could achieve a range of 600 kilometers, the designers forgot to make the appropriate changes to strengthen the fixed launching pads, and as a result only six missiles could be fired at a time.

The Al Abbas was a dream machine. Its range was up to 800 kilometers, and the fixed pads could accommodate thirty at a time, each one capable of delivering a 250-kilogram payload.

The drawback of both missiles was the lack of a guidance system that could accurately aim them. But that was a minor matter to our leaders, who simply shot and prayed, and cared little about precision. For them, it was quantity that mattered. Something was bound to hit something important. As always, the target in mind was tiny Israel.

Since the beginning of 1988 the Nasar had been producing about two missiles a day, seven days a week. Taking into account those used against Iran until the ceasefire in August of that year, it meant that by the time the gulf crisis erupted, Saddam would have at least 1,400 of the things. And the Americans would be frantic to hit the mobile launchers; they estimated thirty or so. The Mossad calculated there were closer to 150 mobile launchers.

Originally the Nasar plant manufactured containers for everything from household fuel to oil storage tanks. Whenever American or other suppliers of alloys wanted to inspect the Nasar to make sure their vital materials and technology were in fact being used for peaceful purposes, the stagehands would go into action. The missile-factory set would be struck, and the machines and other paraphernalia from a genuine container factory nearby would be hauled over as replacements. A half-finished container from the original plant was kept on hand for these presentations. It lent an air of authenticity.

The American inspectors, sometimes from a company, sometimes from government, would then be courteously shown through every inch of the "factory"; they would look closely at it all and nod wisely, sign the required forms and leave. Their backs would hardly be turned before the stagehands reappeared to change the scenery back to Act I, the Victory Factory.

Abu Firas and my other colleagues loved this and laughed at how completely they had duped the Americans. I was never sure if the Americans needed duping. Money talks, and business is business, especially in the arms business.

Perhaps the playacting kept everybody happy. The Germans, the Swedes and the Swiss were openly helping Saddam build bunkers and underground hangars for his air force. All of this construction was designed to withstand any attack, including nuclear. One had to assume they knew who the potential enemy was supposed to be.

Once again I had been assigned to check out someone with whom it was easy to strike up an acquaintance. Ahmed Hassan lived in our neighborhood and that gave me the pretext. It is the custom for neighbors to gather together when someone in the neighborhood dies. And thanks to the war, there was always a house in mourning nearby.

I simply went to Hassan's, knocked on the door and asked him to come with me, because I did not want to go alone to the mourning service. In the Mideast, this kind of thing is quite natural and easy between relative strangers.

So we set off together for the big tent pitched in the middle of the street for the purpose. It was an army-type khaki-colored tent, and it might as well have been left there permanently, because the supply of dead never stopped. All over the city, streets were closed to accommodate the tents for the three-day mourning period called the *fat'ha*. After a while, the traffic became so bottled up the government restricted the number of tents. At the same time, they forbade posting the victim's name on front doors, as is the custom. But even without the posting of names everybody knew that we were paying a terrible price for Saddam's rash invasion of Iran.

It was cold that day, a bitter day in December, when we entered the tent and muttered the *fat'ha* verses as we paid our respects to the corpse.

Besme Allah, Rahman al-Rahim . . .

Al hamdou l'illa rab al alemin al Rahman al Rahim . . .

There was always something hypnotic about the rolling sounds of the benediction and prayer, even though for me they were hollow sounds. Ahmed and I joined the line of mourners to offer consolation and help to the relatives, who were overwhelmed by grief but stoically stood to receive commiserations. Then we sat in a couple of the chairs placed around the walls of the tent in a circle. We shivered with the other men as we listened to the long plaintive chants from the Koran intoned by the mullah hired for the service. Less well-to-do people had the option of using a taped mullah on a loudspeaker system.

Piercing the male chanting in the tent were the heartbreaking sounds of weeping and wailing from the women, segregated from us inside the house. The poor women, who had spent long loving hours day and night nursing and nurturing their children, only to

have them die so young and so uselessly. On these days they wore
the long black *ab'a* veils that used to be so rare in modern Baghdad.

As we listened to the old mullah droning the *suras*, I was
reminded of the fate of my cousin. He had been whisked away
seven years before for "questioning" by the Amn. Sometime later
two agents came to the door and informed my uncle his son had
drowned accidentally. They handed him papers to sign to receive
the body. He protested and began to ask questions, but they thrust
the papers at him, then dumped a coffin on the doorstep, ordering
him to take it straightaway for burial and not to open it. My uncle,
a very religious man, could not bury a body without performing
the ritual cleansing. So with help from friends he took the coffin
inside and opened it.

My cousin had had dark hair. The body of this man, covered
with bruises and burns, had white hair and did not resemble him
at all. He was shorter, too. My uncle washed the body anyway and
saw that it was given a proper burial. He believed that since he
had done this, other strangers would do the same for his own son.
We all went to the Shi'a cemetery to bury this unknown man. My
father was not in the country, which made it easier. He would have
disapproved, and my mother never told him. Seven years later my
uncle died, and we returned to the same family plot to bury him
beside the stranger who was supposed to be his son.

I had never minded the Sunni cemetery, with its wreaths and
its earthly grief, but the Shi'a cemetery is on another plane.
Outside of town in the hot dry sands of the wadi, where once a
wide river ran, it is near the Shi'a shrine of Al Najaf, the tomb of
Ali, son-in-law of the Prophet Muhammad. All the Shi'a of Iraq
are buried there, as well as some from afar who have requested
burial near the holy shrine. When I was there to bury my uncle,
my second visit, I was deeply affected. As far as the eye could see
was endless desert. A feeling of utter hopelessness rose up from

the graves and enveloped me. It was a place of utter desolation. According to the Koran, the wicked are punished after death by eternal torment in hell, where they find no peace, no drink but boiling water, no food but thorny herbage that leaves them famished. They pray for release but release will not come. And the worst punishment is that Allah will not speak to them.

The righteous are promised a reward of eternal bliss in the Gardens of Eternity, with rivers of water, milk, wine and honey where they live forever in communion with Allah.

To me, the Shi'a burial ground whispered only of death, final and absolute. Here I could only feel defeat and annihilation.

I was brought back to the present abruptly when the mullah in the tent stopped chanting. This ritual would continue for the first two days, then on the third the family was expected to supply a feast for everyone. The feast would include a whole sheep stuffed with spiced rice. Coffee and cigarettes were also given out, not just to the mourners, but to passersby. Nothing but the best would do. It all cost a small fortune for the bereaved family. But then, it is not so different really in the West.

The main difference at this ritual was the presence of Mukhabarat agents, who blended into the crowd of friends, relatives, neighbors and strangers, listening keenly for any complaint about the war, for even small utterings that indicated rebelliousness. I was glad to be spared that kind of spying, even though for me this was still a working funeral.

After the funeral, Ahmed Hassan and I discovered we had a mutual interest in chess. We began getting together for matches, sometimes at his house, sometimes at mine. Ahmed, it turned out, was a brilliant engineer and other than that a very ordinary guy, not interested in politics, drinking, girls or other dangerous distractions. Though I tried halfheartedly to get him to talk about politics or the war, he was only interested in chess and money. He knew how the engineers were treated in these factories by the overseers, but he knew also that the engineers were well paid and often given land and a car. He needed the money. So I gave him a neutral report, and I suppose he continued working in the Victory Factory.

* * *

The Nasar wasn't the only facility that produced items whose designs were stolen from cannibalized technology. Iraq also had a thriving computer business going, based on the best of IBM and Apple. I learned a lot about this sort of thing from other Mukhabarat officers and agents I dealt with, as well as from some of the people I cultivated for them.

There was an enterprising fellow from Basra who had a computer business in southern Iraq near the Kuwaiti border. Since he mainly supplied the military with their weapons-enhancement designing, he had a great business going. His only problem was that, since he supplied the military, Apple wouldn't supply him. To solve the problem, he simply acquired the components in Kuwait and the United Arab Emirates, where Apple did a lot of business. Then he shipped the components to phony companies. False end-user certificates — the end user is simply the person, company or country for whom the shipment is ultimately destined — were made out to get around laws that barred export to Iraq and other bellicose countries. Then the parts were put all together in his plant, and presto, Iraqintosh Apples.

The main assembly plant is in Baghdad, near Fourteenth Ramadan Street. I was told the computer factory operates sixteen hours a day, two full shifts. These computers have helped in programs such as the improvement of the heat-seeking SAM-6 missile. When the Americans developed the phantom "heat balloons" to fool the missile and draw it away from an aircraft, our researchers went to work and designed special censors to equip the SAMs to distinguish between the balloons and the jets.

When government importers ran into problems in negotiations with IBM for the XT model computer, other ingenious Iraqis dismantled the ones they had, copied the parts and went into business. If they needed actual components, those, too, could be had in Kuwait.

This was Kuwait's main function as far as Baghdad was concerned. It was all pretty much business as usual, in the Mideast tradition. No one thought in their wildest nightmares that Saddam would turn those missiles and guns on Kuwait. Except when we lost a football game to them. Then the fans would start to grumble that Kuwait used to be a part of Iraq, so we should take it back.

14

OUR MODERN-DAY
NEBUCHADNEZZAR

Just before the new year marking the beginning of 1988, my sister and I were invited to visit friends of hers in Kirkuk. Their father worked in the giant oil refinery there. I went to Abu Firas for permission to travel outside Baghdad.

"No problem," he said, "and while you're there, get me a full report on the place, the refinery, the defense system. I want to know what someone could find out just from looking around."

"You mean, if a spy or someone would be able just to get in somehow?"

"More or less. Learn everything you can."

I knew the Mukhabarat had detailed reports already — in fact, they probably received daily reports from informers inside the refinery. So, I thought resignedly, I was either being tested again or I was testing the other agent's reports. Circles within circles, eyes upon eyes.

We left early in the morning in the freezing cold. There were two routes to Kirkuk, in the northeast corner of the country. The new highway, which conveniently goes through Saddam's home-town, Tikrit, was easiest because of the new paving. The old way was shorter, but was closed after 6 p.m. because of the risk of raids, robbery and rape by the marauding Peshmarga — the Kurdish militants. Still, we took the old route because it was more scenic.

We picked our way through the streets of Baghdad, then up through the poorest areas of the city in the north end. When we reached open land on the outskirts, I floored the accelerator on my Volkswagen Passat (which I'd bought with my special earnings). We rolled north through the countryside, which changed from desert to rocky scrub, then to green open spaces as the lowland began to rise toward the mountains. I loved the mountains, the way they soared serenely into the sky like freedom, their peaks white with snow.

As we climbed into the higher ground, rain began to fall. Light at first, it turned to driving sleet, and we slowed. Along the way, we glimpsed the wire enclosures marked with signs to keep out the curious: Archaeological Site. No Trespassing. There were dozens of these sites, some two thousand years old, still buried, waiting for the scientists' shovels and brushes.

By the time we reached Kirkuk, well ahead of the 6 p.m. deadline, the sun was out again, shining on the puddles in the muddy streets of this old town. It was like a trip into the more recent past, for there were relics of the first days of the revolution everywhere: signs that advertised the Victory of the People, of Ba'thist Brotherhood, all the promises of a new life. Such signs were now long gone in the rest of the country, where posters like the ones in Kirkuk had been replaced by giant images of Saddam in military dress, Saddam in Arab robes wearing a burnoose, Saddam surrounded by small children, Saddam in a business suit talking to other men in business suits.

Kirkuk was a unique place. Within the town there was an entire separate compound for the refinery workers and officers and their families. Within that, the refinery itself. We passed the inevitable military base, then, near the town's police station, turned into the main gate of the refinery "city." Ten or so guards stood at the gate, the only entrance through the chain-link fence and the trenches around the perimeter. As guests of my sister's friend who worked there, we were taken inside for a tour, first of the refinery city, then of the refinery itself.

The refinery city was literally a city within a city, with its own houses, restaurants, discos and private clubs, though some of it had been damaged by Iranian artillery and rockets. There were three lines of anti-aircraft defenses around it, and a special brigade of infantry to guard it. The Kirkuk refinery is the largest in Iraq, though smaller than the Iranian installations at Abadan, which our artillery had been pounding night and day for years now. It was like a mythical battle of giants.

All around us, the ground was lit by small eerie fires, the result of gas seeping from the deposits in the ground. The refinery itself loomed across an open space that separated it from the oil city. It looked like something out of *Star Wars*, a huge fretwork of pipes, catwalks and girders, with fire and smoke belching from its chimneys. Overhead, the sky had a perpetual reddish glow.

Parts of the complex had been totally destroyed by the Iranian barrages, but since the refinery was compartmentalized, those sections were shut down while the rest kept right on producing. In order to baffle the enemy — it's more vulnerable when in operation — the refinery was operated on a random schedule, sometimes from 1 to 3 p.m., sometimes from 6 to 9 a.m. But inside, I found it was a sitting duck for a suicide strike, and the Iranians were, we knew by now, given to suicide missions. The guards had grown careless, and the main emplacements of the Russian-made Doushka anti-aircraft guns were on open hilltops around the plant with no real protection. The infantry was no-where in sight. The most vulnerable part of the refinery was where the oil was separated into different streams according to density. This area and the two-dimensional and three-dimensional radar equipment was unfortified.

Some Iranian commandos had once got through as far as the houses in the oil city, but they had been caught and immediately killed. With a bit more determination and a firm sight on martyrdom, though, they could inflict mortal wounds with as little as a shoulder-held RPG-7. I said as much in my report to Abu Firas.

In truth, my report to Abu Firas was secondary. I was more interested in having a good time and in visiting this famous town. The houses were old, but had been renovated with all the modern conveniences. Soon we were settled comfortably with our friends. Most of the engineers at Kirkuk seemed to have been married to British or Irish women. This was a legacy, I suppose, of the days of British control here. Our hostess was British, and so the house was full of Christmas trappings. There was a big decorated tree and a genuine feeling of Christmas as we exchanged gifts and feasted on roast beef and apple pie.

In the evening we all went to the Club, one of the perks for senior staff, for dining and dancing. At first, everyone wanted western pop music, but as they got drunker, they wanted the old eastern sounds played on the new electronic keyboards. These were strong driving rhythms in a minor key, twanging faster and faster. The pulse of life in a minor key — that is still in our blood, no matter how westernized our outward appearance.

We partied there until three in the morning. The next day we all trooped off to the old bazaar with its stalls offering baskets of spices, mounds of bright dyes, fruits and vegetables, all the rich smells of the East.

A Baghdad native was as obvious here as an American businessman or a Russian adviser. To blend in with the mix of Turkoman, Kurd and Arab who live in Kirkuk, I wore Kurdish dress, with the traditional baggy pants. I also bought a magnificent peacock feather for Ban. For a time, I had almost managed to forget about Abu Firas and the circles.

When we returned to Baghdad I was again, to my surprise, sent to the United States on "vacation." As usual, it was a desultory, hostile time with my father, and I was not unhappy when he came to me one day and said abruptly, "You leave in one week. Abu Firas says hello. Someone will join you on the plane out of Amsterdam. You are to be his friend, understand?"

I understood. Someone else for me to vet.

I slept as much as I could on the transatlantic flight, so when an Irish doctor took the seat next to me on our Jordanian Airways flight to Baghdad, I was awake enough to engage him in conversation. His name was John Donohue, a kidney specialist going to Iraq for ten days. He'd been invited there by the Al Betar Hospital as a guest and consultant. When the plane landed in Jordan on a stopover, I picked up some computer disks for my customers and together we boarded for the final leg of the flight. Our seating had been arranged by the Mukhabarat, which has always had a close working relationship with the Jordanians. In any event, Jordan had to do pretty much as Iraq dictated, as it was totally dependent on Iraqi oil. So the Jordanian airline was as much a creature of the Iraqi service as our own airline.

It was clear to me that Donohue was exactly what he was supposed to be: a doctor, offering medical help, and I told Abu Firas so. Having got along so well on the flight, Donohue and I arranged to have dinner at the Al Rashid a few days later. We met first for drinks in the Shaharazad bar.

All the night spots I mention were named as much for Saddam and his grandiose ideas of Iraqi history as for western visitors who cherished myths of Arabian romance. During the war these places were wasted on journalists, arms dealers and spies, whose idea of romance was a junket to the front lines with their courteous "guides" from the Ministry of Information.

Dr. Donohue and I left the bar and arrived at one of the Rashid's restaurants only to find everyone leaving it in careful haste. It seemed that inside at one of the tables sat none other than Barazan Ibrahim al-Tikriti, Saddam's brother. He was renowned as a bloodthirsty monster. It takes great application to achieve this much notoriety for brutality in Iraq, but Barazan had managed it in his term as head of the Mukhabarat. His bloodthirstiness was too much even for Saddam's idea of public relations, and he was replaced by Fadhil al-Barak, who didn't last long either. He had been replaced by Fadhil Selfige al-Azzawi, the Eagle. Even now people were afraid to be in the same room with Barazan.

But I was Mukhabarat, part of the circle, so we brushed past the fleeing diners and settled ourselves comfortably to eat with this former Butcher of Baghdad. His table, across the room from ours, was on the upper level. He and another man were dining with two expensive-looking women and relishing the endless parade of *mazza*, small portions of every Arab dish under the sun, from kebabs to humous, brought by the groveling waiters. They behaved like any wealthy, well-brought-up patrons.

We had a perfect chateaubriand. And once again I realized I had to get out of this vicious circle that was growing so materially comfortable.

* * *

The war with Iran was still being fought by an exhausted, and now resentful, army. It was the spring of 1988. If the war had ever been justified, it wasn't now. The soldiers knew they were dying in a lost cause.

One of the heroes of the war so far was General Abdul Maher

Rashid, commander of the Third Army Corps. When the Iranians pushed into the area of southern swamps near Basra, known as the Majnoon, Rashid was brought up from the Seventh Army in the southernmost sector near Fao, to save the situation. He did, stopping the Iranians just in time to save Basra. Rashid was a flamboyant, swashbuckling type with natural military skill. He even had the self-confidence — and permission — to talk to the foreign press.

These talents would have made him an invaluable asset in any western army. In Iraq, it meant he was doomed simply because he might one day be a rival to Saddam. Rashid must have known this when he and his brother, a tank-corps commander, began to plot a coup. They had the admiration and respect of their men, and if they could get rid of Saddam, the men would follow.

They never came close to success. Saddam had ears in their operation, and the tank corps was seized on its way to Baghdad by Saddam's elite Republican Guards. Rashid's brother was killed with great style: Saddam replaced his helicopter pilot with one of his own men and ordered Rashid's brother flown to Baghdad. The new pilot waited until the commander was approaching the helicopter, then turned on the blades, cutting his head off.

General Rashid himself would have suffered a similar fate, but his daughter was married to Saddam's son, Kusai. Saddam balked at condemning him to death. Rashid was placed under house arrest.

Sadly, for Iraq, for the gulf region and for the world, Saddam has done such a thorough job of eliminating his opposition that there is scarcely an organization or a leader left who could assume power and run the country properly even if the opportunity presented itself.

Saddam deported, tortured and killed opposition among the Shi'a. The gassing of the Kurds, another group who might have risen against him, is also well-known. The actions of the Mukhabarat against the Kurds is less well-known. The Mukhabarat used to send a female agent to sell a popular home-made yogurt to the Kurds. The yogurt, contaminated with cyanide or rat poison, would kill everyone who ate it. This was also done in Europe, to kill those judged to be a threat to Saddam. It was an alternative to the infamous "diplomatic box."

Members of the Da'wah, Kurds, rebellious party members, and military officers who offered competition to Saddam, all had been eliminated. They were delivered in boxes to their front doors after being gassed, shot, bombed or beheaded by a helicopter blade.

Even Saddam's closest colleagues were not safe. Naim Haddad, a Shi'ite in the Revolutionary Command Council itself, made the mistake of suggesting that Saddam announce he was "stepping aside" to facilitate an end to the war with Khomeini while in reality remaining in power from the wings. Haddad was planning with forty officers to overthrow Saddam. The officers were executed and Haddad vanished.

In Haddad's hometown of Nasseria, south of Baghdad, his followers attacked a police station and burned cars. The whole area was placed under siege, and Saddam ordered Haddad's release. He was kept under house arrest in Nasseria. Later he was executed.

In 1989 Saddam killed Sabah Murzah, his own bodyguard of twenty years. It was discovered that Murzah was using his considerable power and influence to help his friends in the army attain the ranks and postings they wanted. It wasn't Murzah's influence peddling that caused his downfall, for all manner of favoritism is permitted to certain people in the regime. What is not permitted, however, is personal popularity in the armed forces. Murzah had used favoritism to become popular with some of the officers and soldiers. He became dangerous. He had to be killed.

In this atmosphere, it is hardly surprising that there is virtually no significant democratic opposition group. There is a collection known as the Liberal Democratic Front, based mainly in England. They have been creatures of the British government since the fall of the Iraqi monarchy. Their leader is the son of Salih Jabur, who was the prime minister under King Faisal.

The Liberal Democratic Front busies itself in London with newsletters, pamphlets and meetings, but for the Iraqi people living under Saddam's boot, they are distant, irrelevant and seen as pampered in their London homes.

Perhaps the most telling thing I can say about them, and Saddam, is that the Mukhabarat wasn't even interested in killing them.

We all began to wonder if there was going to be anybody left alive to run either the army or the country after Saddam. Ironically, Saddam would turn to Rashid after the humiliating defeat by the Americans in 1991, to help him try to salvage the ruins. Rashid, still popular with the rank and file, and with whatever capable officers were left, would bear watching.

At the beginning of the war with Iran, the only organization in the country that was not hopelessly corrupt was the army. But the battle with the Ayatollah changed that. Soon all the officers were in business for themselves. I am not referring to the petty thievery of military supplies and abuse of privilege that can attend just about anybody's war. Our Ba'thist commanders went into racketeering and nest-feathering on a grand scale. In fact, they didn't just feather their nests, they got the whole birdcage.

It was done like this: General X, head of Armored Division Y, is given a prime piece of land by his grateful commander-in-chief, Saddam. The land was given for winning, or just surviving, a land battle. General X wants to enhance the property with a magnificent home for himself and his family. The general then orders his subaltern to put together a list of the soldiers under his command who suit his needs: bricklayers, painters, electricians, carpenters, designers and those who own or have contacts in cement companies or who are involved in glass manufacture. These soldiers are then rounded up and set to work on the general's new house. Soldier-craftsmen make him exquisite handmade furniture. Modern appliances appear, though no one else could have them.

In return, the soldiers are all given a year's leave of absence from the war. The men work free and supply thousands of dollars worth of labor and materials in order to escape the carnage at the front. The general receives a free home from which he can continue to conduct the war, sitting comfortably in his handmade armchair.

I know personally of a few who did this and learned that it was a common practice. Officers from heads of brigades to heads of entire army corps were routinely given these pieces of land. Naturally the practice left a lot of holes in the army forces, but in a million-man army, nobody seems to miss ten thousand men, off building houses. It was one of the reasons they needed a million men in the first place.

For the officers, everything from sewing needles to cars was free. Eventually they virtually controlled the car market. The government imported all cars and then controlled their distribution, as part of the anti-system. During the war, cars were given out to officers like candy, from Mercedes Benzes to Toyotas. Some got a new vehicle as often as every two months or six months. Some were given none at all. It depended on how the battles went and who you knew at the presidential office. Those who got cars regularly would sell the "old" car to a civilian buyer. A Mercedes could bring 100,000 dinars, about enough for a fine house.

A pilot would receive one of the best cars after every successful mission: a bombing run on Sirri Island or an attack on Tehran itself. If there was a major battle, the price of cars dropped, because there would be so many on the market.

The value depended less on the quality of the car than the availability of parts — also controlled by the anti-system — and, even more, on its color. A high value was given to cars that were the easiest to paint after an accident, so they could be resold. Some paint colors were common; red was as rare as rubies, and equally expensive.

At the beginning of the war with Iran there were about 50,000 private cars in Baghdad. By the end of the war there were 300,000.

Army officers made still more money on everything from power generators to surplus uniforms (the better-quality ones were made in Yugoslavia and Romania). They had access to everything including food and medicine. Such items were "military priority." A whole new black market sprang up, run by the military officers.

It was like living on New York Mafia turf, where one family controls the Bronx, another Brooklyn, another Queens . . . In our case, one officer controlled prostitutes, another cocaine. Large powerful fish ate smaller fish. A new officer war hero would be backed by the Mukhabarat, or the Estikhbarat might kill another officer and take over his turf. In return for their backing, the Mukhabarat and the Estikhbarat would take a financial cut.

The ordinary civilians and foot soldiers paid the price for this new form of corruption.

Customs agents were part of the corruption, too. They would confiscate incoming items on a whim and store them in huge warehouses. Every province and every major town had one or more warehouses where black-market goods were stored. There would be one room full of television sets, one with video machines, one with large appliances, and so on. At any given time, an armed-forces or Mukhabarat officer could come in and say, "I'll take that room. I'll pay you one dinar." The room's goods might be worth 100,000 dinars on the market. Often the officer who took the goods would hold an auction so that more could be obtained from their sale. That was the anti-system.

Then suddenly, after eight years of killing fields, both Iran and Iraq declared victory, signed a ceasefire and the shooting stopped. It was August 8, 1988.

After thousands of tons of mortars, bombs and rockets, after billions of bullets and millions of dead and maimed, Iran had been brought to its knees by economics. The Iranian economy was bankrupt, its society crumbling, as the war in the gulf shipping lanes cut off the country's financial lifeline. Even then, Khomeini refused to cave in. He preferred instead to take his country and every man, woman and child down with him, rather than negotiate with his rival Saddam. But Rafsanjani, the second most powerful man in the revolution, somehow twisted the old man's arm. Furious, spitting out his hatred, Khomeini gave in. "This is worse than poison," he said, signing the decree that stopped the carnage.

In Baghdad, people celebrated by shouting, dancing and shooting guns into the sky. The hospitals had several patients wounded by falling bullets, but hardly anyone cared. That night we went out into the streets of Baghdad to join the throngs throwing buckets of water at each other or tossing baskets of olives in the air. It was a rare time of total, open joy in Saddam's Iraq.

It seemed the right time to ask Ban to marry me. I wasn't much of a prospect. I was an ex-Mossad spy working for the Mukhabarat and trying to run away from both organizations. I did not seem to have a very bright future; in fact, perhaps a short future. Still, we had to believe otherwise, or there would be no point in living.

When I made my proposal we were at a Chinese restaurant drinking hot jasmine tea following a delicious meal. "I know I may bring you only trouble for a while, but one day we'll be free of all this. And I love you. I need you more than life. I know I'm a bit crazy, but I won't be so bad if we can just start a new life. Please be crazy and say you'll marry me."

"Of course I'll marry you," she said simply. "What did you think?"

Overjoyed, I gave her a beautiful diamond ring I had found for her. She was incredibly happy, smiling through tears, looking at the ring and then at me. I could not believe how lucky I was.

* * *

In October Iraq had a festive spectacle in Babylon to celebrate our modern-day Nebuchadnezzar, Saddam. He was like the last Iranian Shah, who also likened himself to the powerful rulers of the ancient Persian Empire, Cyrus, Darius and Xerxes. The Shah had announced this to the world in 1968, when he held a multi-million-dollar extravaganza at Persepolis, the royal city of Darius. I had read about it in my father's censored library, which also had American magazines like *Life*, with its photo stories. Dignitaries from around the world were invited to a display of brightly colored silk tents and magnificent banquets, crowned by a procession of soldiers and cavalry dressed as the warriors of the past, while women dressed in the costumes of the old court. The Shah was trying to remold Iran to revive its pre-Islamic past, before the Muslim conquests. Ayatollah Khomeini put an abrupt halt to that.

Ancient Iraq had two main cultures, one in the north and one in the south. In the north were the people of stone, the Assyrians. They once ruled that plateau with brutal but brilliant efficiency. Though they built their palaces and cities to last, ultimately the Assyrian empire fell to a Chaldean and Medean coalition. The Assyrians left behind only their giant monuments of stone. In a way they achieved a kind of immortality. When you gaze upon the huge figures, it is easy to imagine their Assyrian creators as lords of their universe. Some of the identical figures are twenty feet high, and each depicts the body of a mythological bull with outspread wings and the head of a man-god bearing a tall crown.

Most of the Assyrian remains are near Mosul, northwest of Kirkuk. All Iraqi children are taken there on picnic trips to learn about the ancient times. Except me. Because of my father's position, my mother was in constant fear for my life and was afraid to let me go. I would plead and beg, but the other children went off on the adventure while I stayed home with my bodyguard. Ironically I finally saw these wonders of my country in Paris when I was much older. There I could wander through the Louvre, a place I loved. For me, the museum was a kind of cathedral. I would walk for hours through its halls, through the past, and one day I turned a corner and there were the Winged Bulls of the Assyrians, silent and eternal.

Iraq's second ancient culture, in the south, was that of the Sumerians and Babylonians — the people of the mud. The relics of these desert people did not survive as well as the relics of the Assyrians because they had no stone. Their monuments were of a different nature, and their ingenuity wrought the Seventh Wonder of the Ancient World — the Hanging Gardens of Babylon. Drawings and writings survive to tell us of the magnificence of this palace of flowers in the desert.

But Iraqi minds were filled more with another of Nebuchadnezzar's accomplishments: the defeat and enslavement of the Jews. We not only studied this in school, but we also were reminded of it regularly as adults. Propagandists drew attention to the parallel in modern times, our glorious Saddam facing the Jewish enemy, ready to conquer Israel.

Saddam decided to build a replica of the ancient palace in Babylon. It was a reconstruction that must have caused howls of anguish from archaeologists around the world. Saddam's idea of restoration was simply to build a new palace over the foundations of the old, burying even deeper the streets and walls of the lost city.

Saddam set about re-creating the Hanging Gardens, too. A public contest was held for the best design for the new Gardens and, above all, its irrigation system. To accomplish the final effect he wanted and to irrigate the gardens, Saddam diverted the waters of the Euphrates so that they ran past the doors of the palace he had built on the ruins of the halls of Nebuchadnezzar. It seemed Saddam was a man-god, too.

Nevertheless, like any mortal tyrant, he needed bodyguards. So when he went to Babylon for the great spectacle, I was assigned to go, as well. I was one of many to guard the great ruler. I had missed the picnics to Babylon as a child, so now I was finally rounding out my education — at a fashion show. Yes, the great spectacle was to be a fashion show. This was the doing of Saddam's wife (and first cousin), Sajidah, who otherwise stayed out of the limelight.

It was wiser to stay out of the limelight. Seven months after this spectacle, her own brother, Adnan, learned the hard way what happened to those who tried to take over the stage. He made the mistake of refusing to sign execution orders against his fellow officers, and as a result became enormously popular with the armed forces.

At about the same time, Saddam's older son, Oday, with whom I used to play at the Hunt Club, took up another form of rebellion. He murdered one of the bodyguards who used to supply Saddam, it was said, with women. Rumor had it that he acted with his mother's blessing. In any case, Oday was a rash sort. A family feud developed and Adnan made the further mistake of siding with Oday. Adnan was terminated in one of those helicopter accidents that kept happening to soldiers who crossed Saddam. It was also a public lesson to the family about obedience.

Sajidah confined her activities to harmless pursuits like fashion and had established the House of Fashion to cater to her tastes. Sajidah's designers took apart the Diors and St. Laurents she had sent home from Paris. Like the missiles and tanks, she had them altered and improved to incorporate the Iraqi features she preferred. Since almost every Iraqi Airways flight carried these Paris designs, people called the flights the *Airlift*. Inexplicably her designers were mainly from Thailand and the Philippines.

Now the House of Fashion was going to give a special presentation of ancient Babylonian costume. Saddam himself would preside. It was a warm night with a soft wind whispering across the desert. Ban and I arrived in Babylon and followed the crowds to the brand-new ancient amphitheater, because we Mukhabarat guards were supposed to be part of the public and not evident in our official capacity. We did not have time to see the new palace, and I was vaguely disappointed. But we climbed the stairs to my position near the upper right-hand entrance and took our seats at the back, where I was to be ready to jump up and go into action if necessary. There were guards like me everywhere, the elite being in the circle immediately surrounding Saddam. Before us the tiers of seats curved in a graceful circle, descending to the stage. Saddam, Sajidah and their party sat on a special dais near the curved stage.

On all these public occasions, Saddam was surrounded by three circles of security. The first was made up of heavily armed men handpicked from the Presidential Guards, usually relatives of Saddam. They stayed right by the president's side. This circle was directed by a special branch of the Jihaz al-Amn al-Khas, headed by his cousin and son-in-law Hussein Kamel, who became a general after a mere ten years in the military. These apes would shoot first and ask questions later. They'd shoot many poor unsuspecting people who'd approached Saddam and without thinking reached into their pockets to pull out their letters of supplication for help with this problem or that. The second circle was made up of Mukhabarat officers and agents. The officers were in uniform and armed. The agents, of which I was one, were in plainclothes and unarmed. Our job was to handle the public in Saddam's vicinity. Finally there was an outer third circle drawn from the Amn forces of whatever town or city Saddam was visiting. Since their job was to handle overall security and any emergency evacuation, local people who knew the terrain were preferable. The idea was to have security from several different branches in case one branch proved disloyal. Saddam did not want to suffer the same fate as Anwar Sadat of Egypt, who was assassinated on a reviewing stand by his own soldiers.

The amphitheater was lit by torches, which flickered to the strains of ancient Babylonian music. Then war drums announced the beginning of the show. Mercifully I did not have to watch the parade of ersatz fashions, as I was obliged to keep my back to the stage and keep a watch on the audience. My mind was completely taken up by the task at hand, because the punishment for failing to protect Saddam would be unimaginable. Still, I thought the vigilance wasn't really necessary. The devil himself protects Saddam.

On these occasions, and this night was no exception, Saddam presented himself as a kind of godfather, like Marlon Brando, aloof, disdainful, giving lordly blessings with an slight wave of his hand. He was powerful, and a mere blink of his eyes was enough to command his men to obey orders. But he does not have a real natural charisma. His aura, such as it is, grows out of raw power. Rather than inspire devotion, he instills fear.

Maybe Saddam felt as I did about his wife's pet fashion house, because he left in the middle of the show. I had to go with him, leaving Ban to her own devices.

Along with the army of bodyguards, there was, as always, a photographer with Saddam to capture every moment of his public life. Every day, every hour, every minute, every second. Saddam wanted to be sure that any attempt on his life would be recorded. His intimates said he liked to sit later and watch films of failed assassination attempts. He was to have a new one to watch very soon.

We junior guards were dismissed before I had a chance to follow him to his palace, where he went to commune, I imagine, with Nebuchadnezzar.

15

DELIVERYMAN TO ABU AL-ABBAS

ONE AUTUMN EVENING IN 1988, soon after the spectacle at Babylon, I was visiting the home of one of my computer-disk customers. He was an old acquaintance from school named Ahmed Zaki. I had always envied Ahmed his father. Mr. Zaki was not like any other father I knew, least of all my own. He was warm and friendly and loving with his son. When I visited, we would sometimes play a game called Risk until six in the morning. Then we would arrange for his father to lose, so he would have to fix breakfast. Ahmed Zaki's house wasn't at all like our house. His house was alive.

Mr. Zaki had fought on the side of the PLO in the war in Lebanon in 1975 and 1976. Hundreds of Iraqis like him were part of what they called the Jabhat al-Tahrir al-Arabia, the Arab Liberation Front, a force of volunteer fighters sent by Baghdad to aid the Palestinians. They were trained by the Estikhbarat under Sabir al-Dhoury, who also directed the training of the PLO factions, as well as the Iranian Mudjahedeen, who were staying as guests in Iraq. The Mudjahedeen were one of numerous Iranian groups in exile opposed to Khomeini. This was kept as discreet as possible since Saddam did not want to be viewed by the world as a terrorist leader like Qaddafi. Mr. Zaki's fighting days in Lebanon ended when he was hit by a dumdum bullet, the kind that do the maximum damage by exploding inside you. When he was dragged into the hospital by his wife and friends, the doctors just shook their heads hopelessly. His wife pulled out a hand grenade and informed the doctors that if they didn't operate she would detonate the thing. They operated. Mr. Zaki lived.

Given Mr. Zaki's background, it wasn't a total surprise when one evening as we sat having tea together one of the most famous Palestinian terrorists in the world walked in with several of his cronies. He was tall and a bit fat, with light brown hair, but clean-shaven, unlike Arafat and his other rivals. This was none other than Abu al-Abbas, the mastermind behind the 1985 hijacking of the cruise ship *Achille Lauro*.

Abu al-Abbas wasn't the only radical Palestinian who had been welcomed to Baghdad. Long before Abu Al-Abbas moved into town, Abu Nidal, responsible for the hideous attacks at the airports of Rome and Vienna in 1985, also took up residence in Baghdad after his split with Arafat. Abu Nidal had been sent packing to Damascus when Saddam wanted to be removed from Washington's list of terrorists so that he could receive American aid in 1981. No one was really fooled. The Americans went along with the charade because at that time they were beginning to worry that Iraq might actually lose the war with Iran. There were reports that Abu Nidal moved back to Baghdad later. Saddam's special relationship with these men went back to his violent rupture with Arafat's PLO. In the mid-seventies, Iraq had harbored large numbers of PLO fighters, in sympathy with the persecuted victims of Israeli ambitions. But the PLO had done exactly what it had begun to do in Lebanon: try to form a state within a state. And in both cases, the PLO's hosts began to both resent and fear the militant Palestinians. When Saddam learned that the PLO had actually set up its own prisons, its own criminal-justice system for its people, northwest of Baghdad, he decided that they had completely worn out their welcome. He turned the Mukhabarat loose on them. Those who weren't arrested were deported to Syria, and the Mukhabarat confiscated all the weapons they could find.

An all-out war broke out between the PLO and the Iraqi regime. The Syrians aided and abetted the PLO, allowing fighters based in Syria to stage raids into Iraq. In March 1978 the PLO's Fatah group sabotaged the Iraqi Embassy in Brussels. That July Fatah agents just missed their assassination attempt on Baghdad's ambassador to the United Kingdom. The next month they again missed an attempt on the consul in Pakistan. There were attacks on Iraqi Airways offices, as well as car bombs and letter bombs directed at Iraqi targets from Frankfurt to Athens. The Mukhabarat turned on its killing machines in Europe, hitting PLO men from London to Amsterdam. The shooting stopped only when Saddam and Syria's Hafiz al-Assad worked out a very temporary truce.

Both Abu Nidal and Abu al-Abbas led factions of the Palestinians who had broken with Arafat largely over the PLO's too cozy relationship with Syria and over Arafat's moderation. As a result, they were welcomed by Saddam to Iraq. Abu Nidal, whose organization bears his name, is the most ferocious. Abu al-Abbas heads the PLF, the Palestine Liberation Front.

Like a ball of mercury touched by a finger, the PLF in turn split into other factions. The names are almost indistinguishable. This is all a symptom of an almost pathological disease among our so-called leaders: everybody wants to be king. Instead of hammering out ways to work together and form a consensus, they form groups within groups to try to form a base for gaining control of the whole. There is no real ideological difference. Hence, the welter of absurd names: the Democratic Front for the Liberation of Palestine, the Palestine Liberation Front, the Popular Front for the Liberation of Palestine, the Popular Struggle Front, the Organization of the Armed Arab Struggle. I rest my case.

Abu al-Abbas had been in residence in Baghdad ever since his men hijacked the *Achille Lauro* in 1985. In that attack, Leon Klinghoffer, a crippled Jewish American passenger, was killed. When Abbas and his cohorts were pursued, they were taken in by Saddam. Abu al-Abbas lived in Baghdad like royalty. He had the key to the city. Anything he wanted he could have, from weapons to women.

It's odd that cold-blooded killers like this are often so gentlemanly and pleasant at social occasions. In their own eyes, they are not killers of innocent people. To them, there are no innocent Israelis, or Americans or westerners, and they see civilians as much the enemy as the governments. The fact that they know that most Arabs have nothing to do or say about what their governments do is immaterial. The militants' minds are an absolutely closed system. This was clear even from the demeanor and conversation of the men in Mr. Zaki's large salon that evening.

Abbas and his cronies all made themselves comfortable in the room, drinking tea and talking quietly about the arms trade. They discussed where to get automatic rifles and how many pistols each one had in his private cache. It soon became apparent to me that Mr. Zaki was a major player. He was Abu al-Abbas's number-two man, in charge of field training.

Among Abu al-Abbas's close associates was a tall, fair-skinned man of about my age named Mazin Shibly. I had run into him before, so I knew that his father was one of the top men in the Ba'th Party, just below Michel 'Aflaq himself in prestige. Mazin was a sociable sort — and a trained Mukhabarat agent. Seeing him there at the Zakis', I figured he'd had training with Abu al-Abbas's commandos.

In 1989 Mazin was sent to the United States, ostensibly to

study dentistry. First they changed his diplomatic passport, which he had because of his father's position, to an ordinary civilian one, so that he would not be conspicuous. He started off in Columbia, South Carolina, then transferred to Boston. At all times he had an open-ended account for his expenses, whatever they might be, from the Iraqi Embassy in Washington. Mazin himself told me most of this when we talked about changing money on the black market. I could only assume that he was doing a great deal more than studying dentistry in the United States, but I was never certain. That night, the conversation ultimately turned to weapons.

There were a lot of weapons up for grabs after the war. There were also a lot of people who wanted them. After the war ended, there were many unemployed soldiers about, more than a few of whom turned to crime to support themselves and their families. Others sold their weapons. A whole new market grew. Reports abounded of cars full of men in uniform abducting girls and raping them. If the rapists were caught, they were immediately executed. No trial. In such an atmosphere, many ordinary people wanted guns for self-defense.

In the course of the conversation that same evening at Mr. Zaki's, I piped up and said I knew a fellow who had gone into the arms business. "He brings the stuff in from northern Iraq and sells it to anyone who wants it." Everyone's ears pricked up.

"Is he trustworthy?" asked Abu al-Abbas. A great question coming from him, I thought.

"As far as I know," I muttered, and breathed with relief when he changed the subject.

I should have known better. The next day, Mr. Zaki phoned me. "We want to talk to you about the matter you mentioned last night."

Reluctantly I went over to see him.

"We trust you," he said. "We want to arrange to buy some small stuff from your guy. Can you set it up?"

I began to stammer a response. He interrupted. "Nothing big. Pistols, mainly."

I felt like a fly caught in a cobweb. Every strand was sticky with Mossad, PLO and now radical terrorists. Moreover, the Mukhabarat spider could be anywhere. What was Abu al-Abbas up to? Abbas had trained in Iraq, and Saddam had supplied weapons. Abbas had everything from defensive grenades to Katyusha multirocket launchers. Moreover, Abbas could have any pistols he wanted just by knocking on the door at the presidential palace. Why did he seemingly want to go behind Saddam's back? Why go underground? Were they building a secret stockpile? Maybe they planned to do as the PLO had done in Lebanon and eventually become a state within a state (which turned out to be largely true).

What should I do? Say no? Report to the Mukhabarat? But what if I said no and it turned out the regime was just testing my loyalty to its allies? Or were they all just playing another cat-and-mouse game with me? I decided I had to play it right back.

"Okay," I agreed. "I can put you in touch with him."

"And you can be the deliveryman. It's better that way."

Better for whom, I wondered, and off I went off to the Mukhabarat headquarters to report to Abu Firas. All things considered, my reporting to him wasn't going to get Mr. Zaki in trouble, since Abu al-Abbas was, after all, an honored guest of the state, and Mr. Zaki was just being a good host. Whatever the consequences, it was my decision to report.

Abu Firas was inscrutable. He pondered it all for a few moments, then spoke. "We'll supply the weapons. Leave your contact out of it. I'll send a man with you to help deliver them."

Oh great, I thought. So now I was going to sell guns from the

Mukhabarat to al-Abbas, a terrorist. I was going to con some of the most dangerous con artists around. And who was the Mukhabarat conning? I wasn't sure. For all I knew, they were going to rake in a profit with no one the wiser. Including Saddam. Would anyone like to live that dangerously?

I gave up thinking about it. Trying to sort out the maze would drive me crazy. I reported back to Mr. Zaki that I could supply the weapons, without ammunition, for 30,000 dinars. Abu al-Abbas was quiet and businesslike. "I'll check the shipment myself," he told me.

A few days later, one of Abu Firas's agents rolled up to my house in a pickup truck. Another pickup followed. Both were loaded with heavy crates, like the ones used to pack RPGs. In most countries two trucks arriving in broad daylight at a suburban home and unloading boxes of weapons might cause some comment. Not in Baghdad. People were used to seeing the distinctive crates; everybody knew what kind of cargo they contained and nobody cared anymore. We drove to the Zakis' house. Almost immediately a Range Rover came around the corner and stopped beside us. Abu al-Abbas, wearing a light safari suit, stepped out. Taking one of the crates, we all went inside.

Calmly he levered it open, then took out one pistol, then another, giving them each a cursory appraisal. Then he nodded, picked up a brown leather case at his side and opened it for my inspection.

"Do you want to count it?" he asked casually.

"No, thanks," I said, looking at the bundles of money. "That will be fine, I'm sure."

I went into the kitchen and came out with a black garbage bag. I stuffed the money into it, thanked him and went home, later turning over the money to one of Abu Firas's men. I never saw Abu al-Abbas again, but friends told me nothing at all happened to him after our little deal.

Saddam had clearly come to some kind of terms with these Palestinians and was as involved in world terrorism as Iran or Syria or Libya. He simply handled it more discreetly. It was said that even the most famous terrorist of them all was alive and well and living in Baghdad — Carlos, the Jackal. Other Mukhabarat officers used to whisper about this, but even they were not sure. If Carlos was around, it was a top-priority secret. What we did know was that the Ba'th regime was intimately tied to certain very accomplished terrorist organizations and was sure to use them when and if they deemed it an advantage.

Only a few years later, when the American bombers flew their devastating sorties over their Iraqi targets, I wondered if they fully realized just what they were unleashing below. Every bomb, I believed, would eventually be avenged in cities around the world if Saddam or his shadowy allies sent out the orders.

My life in the Mukhabarat again settled back to normal, so to speak. One day during a routine meeting when we were touching base with each other on what I was up to generally, Abu Firas suddenly acted very friendly. He offered me a way to "invest" the money I had made from my own little business enterprises, a small fortune of 20,000 dinars, which is about $70,000 U.S. at the bank rate, $7,000 at the black-market rate. But given that in Baghdad you could rent the finest mansion for 500 dinars a month, it was a lot of money either way. He told me he knew an ex-spy from Syria, Haithem Bashir, who was now managing the Al Qadisiya Hotel and its nightclub. If I invested money in the hotel — no messy papers to be signed — then Abu Firas would give me a 1,000 dinars a month on my investment.

It sounded fishy enough already, and then he told me never to go to the hotel or to discuss this little matter with anyone. By now I almost automatically reported everything even remotely odd, in case they were testing me — but I always reported to Abu Firas.

If this was a test, it was ingenious. Who would I report to about Abu Firas himself? The Eagle. I went to Fadhil Selfige al-Azzawi himself.

The next day Abu Firas came storming over to my house. "You want to get me killed? You want to destroy me? Why the hell did you tell Azzawi about the investment?"

"You were taking money," I replied. "That's the sort of thing I'm supposed to report, isn't it?"

"You don't understand. It's all just a misunderstanding!" he said, and gave me back my money.

Now I realized that in spite of all my conscious efforts, I was one of them. Deep down, I had known it was not a test. I was a Mukhabarat agent informing on another, an Iraqi informing on another Iraqi. No excuses. No rationalizations. And now I knew they would pull me in further and further, so deep that I would forget all my old values. They would be able to brainwash me completely, simply by keeping me doing what I did every day for them.

I realized that I had to stop thinking about escaping and do something about it, or I was going to self-destruct. If I stayed much longer I would inevitably run afoul of my masters. If I made a serious misstep, my original reprieve would be rescinded, and my father's horrible order carried out.

* * *

The only thing that kept me sane and in control was my beloved Ban. Her love for me, and mine for her, carried me through. I decided on a drastic move again, as drastic as that other fateful move I made in Brussels — the move to confess to the Mukhabarat before they got to me. I decided to escape to Beirut.

The Mukhabarat had a program in which it trained a select few men to go to Beirut to aid the anti-Syrian factions fighting in the never-ending fratricidal war in Lebanon. I would volunteer. And once in Lebanon I would make my break.

There can't be many countries in the world from which Beirut looks like a safe haven. The once beautiful Lebanese capital was by now a twilight zone of destruction. Almost every building still standing looked like Swiss cheese; the rest were rubble. The lunatic militias and warlords kept right on pounding each other with their deadly arsenals. When I decided to leave, I think the Israeli-backed Lebanese Christian killers were fighting the Syrian-backed Lebanese Christian killers, both of whom were still locked in mortal combat with all the Muslim warlords, two of whom were at each other's throats. After a while it didn't really matter. They seemed to know only how to kill, and beneath the stupid rhetoric about religious rights and freedom fighting, in the end all these madmen were about was power. Religion was a tool just like an RPG. Saddam was about to figure that out. He suddenly decided to get religion.

Lebanon had got out of hand when the PLO arrived. In 1970 its members had been forced out of Jordan and into Lebanon by Jordan's King Hussein as a result of what has been called Black September. The PLO in Jordan had begun to form a state within a state that threatened the king's government — action that was becoming a familiar PLO pattern. The Palestinians rapidly set about entrenching themselves in Lebanon, especially in the south. The Shi'a Muslims who were in the south of Lebanon at first welcomed the PLO as fellow sufferers of oppression. Their welcome was short-lived as the Palestinian leaders commandeered houses, patrolled the streets and generally acted like an occupying army. With the Christians already opposed to the Palestinians' armed presence, it took only a small spark to ignite the whole lot of them: an attack by Christians on a busload of Palestinians in

1975. They've been at it ever since, in a mad shifting array of alliances. The Israelis, the Syrians, the Soviets, the Americans, the Iranians, the French and we Iraqis all backed one or the other gang of thugs and kept them armed to the teeth. By 1991 about 150,000 men, women and, as always, children, had perished in this madness. The carnage has lessened somewhat, but every week sees a few casualties.

Nonetheless, this is where I decided to go to begin my escape. Since the war with Iran had ended, Iraqis were allowed once again to travel. This made it possible for Ban to meet me in another country later. So my plan was for her to go on a "vacation" somewhere like Paris, and I would come from Beirut to join her. Then, I thought, we would disappear into the world. Ban was horrified.

"Lebanon!" she wailed. "How can you even think of it? It's crazy!"

"But if I don't take this chance, I might never have another one," I argued. "Abu Firas has it in for me after the hotel money business."

"He won't do anything if you behave for now."

"We don't know that. They've got rid of a lot more important people than me. For a lot less reason."

Ban began to cry. "I can't bear it. Already there's so much against us. Your parents, my parents, this whole horrible secret police, this whole mess of a country, and now you want to go to Beirut!"

"I don't want to go." I tried to soothe her. "But I just don't see a better way. And I won't be in Beirut itself. The operation is based in Junieh."

"Don't go! Lebanon's a shooting gallery. They're all crazy there!"

I held her and stroked her hair. She was right. And so was I. I had to try it.

I wrote a formal memo to the Eagle, Fadhil Selfige al-Azzawi, who was now head of the Mukhabarat. I requested assignment to the Lebanese theater of operations.

In the eighties Saddam had changed his tactics with regard to Lebanon. The Arab Liberation Front volunteers were replaced by the more cold-blooded Mukhabarat. Handpicked agents were trained for the assignment. Basically Lebanon was another battleground in his war for Arab supremacy with Syria's Hafiz al-Assad.

Saddam supported the Christian Militia, known as the Lebanese Forces, because they were Syria's current enemies in Lebanon. Since the assassination of their leader, Bashir Gemayel, the Lebanese Forces had been led by two of the bloodiest warlords in Lebanon, Samir Gea Gea and General Amir Aoun. They hated each other, and soon their relationship deteriorated into a vicious war between the Christian forces. Since Damascus supported Gea Gea, Iraq supported Aoun.

Saddam's loyalty shifted with the prevailing winds, just like every other leader in the Mideast. At that point our war was with Syria and Hafiz al-Assad in Damascus, so we swung all our weight behind his enemies in Lebanon.

Most westerners look on these alliances in total confusion and think they will never understand the Middle East. I can assure them that confusion is the only possible state of mind in this welter of madmen. The situation is absolutely not to be understood.

Iraq sent weapons galore to the Lebanese Forces, American- and Soviet-made rifles, larger guns and ammunition, and Soviet T-54 and T-55 tanks that were now out of service. Some of Iraq's allies grumbled that with friends who send T-54s, you don't need enemies. But the T-54 wasn't that bad; it could still do a lot of damage in a small place like Lebanon. Its guns were bound to hit something.

The arms were shipped by land from depots in Haswa, just

outside Baghdad, and sent to the port of Aqaba in Jordan. From there, they could be sent by boat to Junieh Harbor at the northern edge of Beirut. Some of the cargo was unloaded at sea first and marked for other destinations; some fell into the hands of Syria's local thugs.

Mukhabarat agents on their way to Lebanon took a different route. They flew on Iraqi Airways to Larnaka in Cyprus, then continued by sea to Junieh on the ferry. Since Lebanon had collapsed into anarchy, Cyprus had become the main base for just about every intelligence service in the world that operated in the Mideast. It was like Casablanca during World War II. Somebody should make a movie about it.

The reply to the request I made of the Eagle to join in this fray came back almost immediately in the form of an official approval given by Abu Firas. After the hotel fiasco, he was glad to get rid of me.

The first stage was a trip back to the training camp near Taji for a language class made up entirely of fellow-stutterers. We looked and sounded like a scene from a Woody Allen movie. A whole c-c-c-class of us.

But the strategy behind this comedy was in deadly earnest. Iraqis have a very different way of speaking Arabic from the Lebanese. A totally different slang, too. While the Lebanese speech is soft, ours is harsh and dry, like the difference in sound between a Bostonian and a Virginian. It's impossible to teach the Lebanese form of Arabic in only a month, but the stuttering and stammering that my classmates and I were prone to under pressure would mask any mistakes we might make.

While all this was going on, I was finishing my courses at the university, and it looked as if I was going to manage to earn my degree. The problem now was to take proof of that with me.

Normally an Iraqi graduate is not given any document showing his degree. This policy helps to prevent educated, skilled Iraqis from leaving the country.

I went about getting a Tunisian passport. First, I made sure that we, the Mukhabarat, didn't have an agent or informer inside the Tunisian Embassy. Otherwise, someone would report to my office that I was requesting a Tunisian passport, and the game would be up. A few discreet inquiries among my colleagues revealed that Tunisia was one of the few embassies we hadn't bothered about.

Second, I needed my father's old Tunisian papers, so that I could claim a passport as the son of a native Tunisian. I felt nervous as I went through the things he had left in his office at home, as if he would somehow know from across the ocean what I was doing and would fly here on his bat's wings and catch me. I found what I wanted and tucked the papers into my inside jacket pocket and went to class. In the middle of a lecture I slipped out. No one would follow me once they thought I was safely occupied in classes for the rest of the day. I went directly home, though, just in case. Then I crept out the back door, slipped over the neighbor's fence and from there made my way to the car I had borrowed from a friend and parked around the corner.

The Tunisians at the embassy were polite and cooperative. But it took weeks of waiting while I grew more and more anxious. Finally they issued me the precious document. A passport. I was ready.

Ban was numb with the strain, but she bravely agreed to play her part. I went to the last of my language classes, held by one of the Lebanese sent to get us into shape for Beirut. He was one of the Druze Muslims led by Walid Jumblatt, whose father, Kamal, had been renowned for his savagery. Walid was famous chiefly for his habit of sniffing cocaine and arriving at meetings and press conferences under the influence. The Druze fighter sent to teach us spent most of the time talking about his own exploits. I was impatient to leave, impatient to get out of this hole.

Then unexpectedly they called me back in to see Abu Firas. With great trepidation, I went to headquarters.

"You are being taken off the Lebanon assignment," he said.

I was stunned. "Why?"

"There is too much to do here."

16

THE NUCLEAR GOD

TAMMOUZ/OSIRAK — GOD OF the Dead. Saddam wanted his power. It was as though he wanted to *be* Osirak. And what better way to achieve this than to harness the destructive power of the atom? Saddam had named his nuclear reactor after the god, and was on his way to acquiring the Bomb.

But the Israelis had shattered those dreams, when they bombed the reactor in 1981. Progress on the work of rebuilding was going too slowly to suit Saddam. He had left the reconstruction up to a special scientific department for nuclear power. Now he dissolved that department and put the nuclear program under the direct military control of the Amn al-Khas.

All pretense that Osirak was a peaceful civil project was dropped. And the Mukhabarat was ordered to run thorough checks on everyone to be employed on the project, especially the engineers.

This was my new assignment. The assignment that would keep me in Iraq. "You are to screen one of the senior engineers," Abu

Firas informed me. "And report on even the slightest doubts about him. This is to be a top, top secret project now."

Everyone in the West, in the world, in fact, thought that Osirak had been completely destroyed by that lightning Israeli raid in 1981. But Osirak still lived. I was as stunned by this news as any outsider.

"But all the newspapers, the TV, everyone said that the whole thing had been wiped out."

Abu Firas laughed. "That's the news we put out. Otherwise they might have come back to finish the job. But the core of reactor is still intact. Now instead of them coming back to finish the reactor, we're going to finish them!"

I was appalled. He meant exactly what he said. Saddam had always said that if Israel had so much as a grenade, then we had to have the same grenade, only better. So, since Israel had the bomb, we were going to have it, too. And we would use it first. The Israelis, I knew, understood this perfectly. They knew their enemy and of what that enemy was capable. The western powers still found the idea of a first nuclear strike unthinkable, and they failed to realize that a man like Saddam was quite capable of the unthinkable. If Osirak rose from the dead they were going to realize it very quickly.

The general Iraqi population seems to sit with resignation, waiting for the Armageddon that would follow any nuclear attack on Israel.

I was ordered to get to know an engineer named Muhammad Ali. Because he was in fact a relative of mine, it wasn't that difficult to approach him and encourage a friendship, even though he lived an hour's drive outside Baghdad. Like me, he had studied in England. He'd completed a doctorate in nuclear physics in Newcastle. We had a lot in common and we spent afternoons reminiscing about the good old days in England.

For five or six years he had been head of the furnaces operation at the nuclear plant. After the Israeli raid, he was sent to Germany, France, Japan and Kuwait on shopping trips for the parts and materials necessary for reconstruction. It seemed that the air attack had obliterated all the labs and much of the reactor itself. But as it turned out, the Israelis had used special steel-encased bombs, designed to go off after they had penetrated the structure, rather than on impact. Some of those had not gone off as planned. They were disarmed, dismantled or removed. Work to rebuild was proceeding.

For Muhammad Ali, it was simply a job, and he would do it to the best of his ability. Like so many Iraqis, he had completely lost all moral sense in the twisted ethical world of Saddam Hussein. He simply had no concept of what he was doing. Like the westerners he didn't think the unthinkable: a first strike.

Ali was perfect for Saddam. I gave a neutral report on him saying that he was an engineer, pure and simple, without politics, who would do exactly as he was told.

I handed Abu Firas my report in one of the meeting rooms at Mukhabarat headquarters. "The Israelis will know what we're up to and just come back, won't they?" I said to him.

"It won't be so easy this time. We're ready. Those stupid bastards who were sound asleep on the anti-aircraft and the SAMs have been taken care of. The new guys will be awake, you can count on it."

"Even so, the Israelis won't give up."

Abu Firas looked at me with a satisfied smirk. "It isn't all there anymore. We've got a lot of enriched uranium stored in the underground channels at the Dokan Dam."

I decided to shut up. This was dangerous territory, and I didn't want to know more than was healthy for me. The dam was on the Little Zab River, north of Kirkuk, almost at the Iranian border.

Saddam still intended to be the God of the Dead. There were other nuclear projects at Hammam Ali and Irbil, which were to the west, nearer Mosul. Just to be sure, Saddam was still manufacturing other forms of death: nerve gas, mustard gas, typhoid. And the most deadly germ of them all, anthrax. There were chemical facilities around Baghdad, at Madain, Samarra and Al Qaaim.

Just about everyone in Baghdad knew about a mysterious Canadian scientist who was one of the key men on the chemical-weapons program. They would point out his expensive house, which was near the home of the old Mukhabarat chief Barazan in the Al Jadriya district, on the peninsula that jutted out into the river. He lived there with his family, constantly guarded by security men supplied by the government. The scientist was a friend of that other Canadian who had been so vital to Saddam's war schemes, Gerald Bull.

Bull was still working on the Supergun. But the modified Howitzers were being adapted to carry what we called Binaries. Special chemical warheads, they carried two different chemicals that, when exploded together, reacted with each other to create lethal gases. They were being developed by Bull's Canadian friend. At least that was the commonly held belief inside the Mukhabarat.

The ultimate target was, as usual, Israel.

The chemical projects were field-tested on whole villages of Kurdish men, women and children. The first tests were primitive, but effective. They simply flew over in Soviet Ilyushin transport planes and rolled barrels of the stuff out the side. On impact, chemicals in separate compartments combined to form lethal gases.

By March 16, 1988, the Iraqis had refined the process and tried out chemical bombs on the Kurds. The entire village of Halabja was wiped out in seconds. Other villages nearby were treated to a similar fate from the long-range Howitzers. This mass killing did not come to the world's attention until after the ceasefire between Iran and Iraq in July 1988.

The Kurds were Saddam's whipping boys. He had his military officers use them as practice targets for cluster bombs imported from Chile, then for modified cluster bombs called Siggils, fired by multimissile launchers. The Ababil missile was tried out to see what radius of killing field it would produce. It was a roaring success.

In a more traditional exercise, Saddam had his gunships wipe out thirty-six villages in the Imadya sector in the north, leaving not one survivor. And then special units were sent in to demolish what little was left of the frail little village houses. Eventually they annihilated every village within thirty kilometers of the Iranian and Turkish borders. The war was the excuse for this slaughter. The Kurds were to be wiped out in order to create a no-man's-land along the border. Then, to prevent resettlement, the whole area was mined.

Saddam couldn't get to the Jews. So he contented himself in the meantime with the genocide of the Kurds. The world said virtually nothing. In the summer of 1988, the Kurds were again the guinea pigs for biological weapons. The military scientists tried out their typhoid virus, but for reasons that remain obscure, it was not a success.

Biological warfare plants were built in Al Kut and Suwera, both to the southeast of Baghdad along the Tigris. I was never sure what they were busy cooking up in Al Kut, but at Suwera, I knew, they nurtured typhoid. A friend of mine who worked nearby at the technical college came to visit one day and recounted with glee the latest accident at the Suwera typhoid plant.

"Today they had to run around vaccinating everybody in the area because of some big emergency at the laboratory," he said, laughing. "The police were going crazy trying to find out who had been in the area at the time. It was real chaos!" And he laughed some more. Typical Iraqi.

In Iraq people hardly know the difference between life and death anymore, because whether you are dead or alive, it's all the same. Take the case of an extraordinarily clever man. To some, he appears stupid, because he is so clever what he says goes over their heads. It is the same with laughing and crying. Sometimes if you cry long enough, after a while you go right around the circle and start to laugh. In Iraq, if you are going to die, you just take a shortcut through the circle and start to laugh right away. You don't bother with crying.

I think this kind of psychology is part of the reason westerners so often just don't understand what they are dealing with in the Middle East, even on an individual basis. They are completely bewildered, or even antagonized, by the way we react to many situations. It's because for centuries we have had to hide our feelings, and have been so brutalized that some of our feelings have changed.

In the end it means that sometimes, though we may be feeling the same pain or have the same wish as a westerner, our way of showing it is exactly the opposite. When Saddam used chemical weapons on the Iranians, too, during that grisly war, many ordinary Iraqis used to joke that we had simply used pesticide on insects, and had a good laugh over it.

Whether this reaction is the result of living under Saddam's brutal regime or something bred in the bone, Iraqi moral feelings seem stunted. The fact that this death-in-life has wormed its way into our souls may be worse than all the torture and killings.

* * *

I wanted to live. To be really alive. And to do so I needed two things: freedom and Ban. Again we talked about it one day when we took a little trip to a lake outside Baghdad.

"As soon as I figure out a way, we get out of here," I said to her as we drove along the highway.

"But how?" she replied, always practical. "They'll find us."

"No, I know how to disappear," I assured her. "At least I learned something useful from all this shit."

Ban gave a miserable little sigh and leaned against my shoulder.

"They've given me a ticket to go to Manila to visit my wonderful father. He's the honorable ambassador there now," I told her. My father was carrying on the fine tradition of B'ath diplomacy in the Philippines, which has a significant Muslim population.

"Are you going to go?"

"Not if I can help it. But it's one of those tickets with a string attached. If I don't use my exit visa within sixty days, they take my passport and I can't get out of the country for years. So we're going to have to do something pretty soon."

"Did you tell them we were driving here today? You're supposed to, aren't you?" she asked with mild curiosity. Ban still didn't really understand the world I lived in and how it worked. She was about to learn. As it turned out, her question was prophetic.

As we approached a checkpoint, the guards ordered us to stop. There was no way of knowing who they were, as they wore no identifying uniforms. I thought as we pulled over that they were probably Mukhabarat; not far away a new palace was being built for Saddam. They hauled me out and shook me by the shoulders, then pushed me against the car to be searched.

Poor Ban was terrified. I was pissed off. Abu Firas again. I hadn't told him about our little jaunt. His his long arm was reaching out to remind me just who was boss. They demanded identification papers and after a quick perusal turned even uglier.

"So you two aren't married, eh? Then what are you going to do? Find a private little spot and screw each other?" One of them sneered, with a lecherous look at Ban.

The other searched the car for a gun, anything to incriminate me.

"I'm from the Mukhabarat," I finally told them, "and if you don't let us go now, you'll be in trouble. If you don't believe me, call headquarters."

This made them break into nasty laughter. They held us there for three hours, while other motorists drove through the checkpoint without so much as a glance from our captors. My poor Ban was seeing the beast face-to-face for the first time, and though it was barely showing its teeth, she was frightened out of her wits. It was the unknown that was so scary. Not knowing what they were going to do, but knowing all the possibilities. Finally, they released us.

"You didn't need to do that, especially to her!" I complained to Abu Firas the next day at headquarters. "You know she hasn't a clue about any of this."

"It's your own fault," he replied imperturbably. "Next time obey the rules."

"So they *were* your guys then."

"I have a full report," he said ambiguously. "You just forget it."

If I had ever had any doubts, they were gone now. Ban and I had to get out.

"You are to go to the Philippines," Abu Firas continued. "Then you are to return here to be trained to work with foreigners."

"There's something I want to do first. I want to get married."

Abu Firas looked taken aback. Then pleased. A married man was a man with ties that kept him bound to the regime.

"We need your father's approval first," he said cautiously.

"My father says it's okay with him if it's okay with the Mukhabarat and whoever else it's necessary to get permission from."

In the end, we needed the permission of all three security services, the Mukhabarat, the Amn and the Estikhbarat. They all got to work and did a security check on Ban, looking into her background, snooping around asking questions of the neighbors.

She passed these tests, but then Abu Firas had another one. "She has to convert to Islam," he said.

I was furious. "No way! I am not going to ask her to change everything she was brought up to believe. You can't make a person do that anyway. It never works. I won't ask her to do this."

"We'll see about that," he replied, "but in any case we have to have her parents' approval."

I sighed. Her parents had been opposed from the beginning to their daughter's going out with a Muslim. They were no different from most other people in my country, where everything was done to keep the various religions separate. But though there was a law that prevented Muslim women from marrying Christian men, Muslim men could marry Christian women, if they got all the necessary permits. I went to the offices of the Amn to see the person in charge of these matters.

"It's the rules," he said. "Must have parental consent."

So I went hat in hand to Ban's home to plead with her mother. That is the custom when asking for a girl's hand, because a daughter is the mother's charge. In the end, she relented, because ultimately her daughter's happiness was more important to her than anything else. Since Ban's mother had agreed, her father did as well, as is also the custom. We decided to go ahead with the legal ceremony. We were not actually considered truly married until we'd had both a legal and religious service, after which we could live together. Abu Firas was still insisting on her conversion to Islam, but we could at least have the legal procedure done.

Poor Ban. She'd been raised to look forward to a beautiful wedding in white performed in a church, and instead she had a dismal little ceremony in a courthouse. Our witnesses were an old couple I found in the waiting room. I paid them to serve for us.

It was November 11, 1989. I chose the date on purpose, so that our wedding day was the same as Remembrance Day in the West. That way, it seemed even more concrete, something to hang on to in the trials ahead of us. "I promise you," I told her, "when we're out of this country, we'll get married again — your way. We'll have a Christian service in a Christian church, and lots of flowers and a limousine. The works."

"If we get out," she said softly.

I made my first move just before Christmas. Abu Firas's wife was expecting a baby about then, so I counted on that to keep him preoccupied. On the twenty-fourth, I bought a ticket for Jordan, choosing that country because I didn't need a visa to go there. It was going to be a kind of trial run, to see how I was received at the American Embassy. If they were positive about my case and would give me asylum, then I could return to Iraq and finish making financial arrangements and plans for Ban to follow. Then I would leave forever.

At the enormous steel-and-glass expanse of Saddam Airport, I was tense, constantly looking over my shoulder, expecting the long Mukhaberat arm to reach out again. It didn't. With relief I boarded the plane and settled back in my seat. When we lifted off, I felt as if a weight had been lifted from my shoulders. I was up and away.

When we landed in Amman, I was cautious, but my feeling of

elation still grew. Until I noticed him. He was about fifty and dressed like any businessman. As I walked through the crowds in the terminal toward the currency-exchange booth, he carefully, but very definitely, stuck to me.

"Hello!" he said jovially, as he took his place in the line behind me. "You're an Iraqi brother, aren't you?"

"Yes," I replied, my heart sinking. "How are you?"

"Well, well, well," he continued. "Isn't this great!"

I knew when I was defeated. So I decided to turn their little plan around and stick to him, instead of him sticking to me.

"Say," I suggested, "maybe we could help each other out. I'm here to do some shopping, but I don't know Amman very well, so . . ."

"No problem. I can help."

"And we can share some expenses. Maybe even the hotel."

"Good idea."

And off we went to play cat-and-mouse in Jordan. This kind of casual striking up an acquaintance is very common in the Mideast, so there was nothing unusual on the surface. But we both knew that a game was being played. What was unclear was just who was the cat and who the mouse.

So like Felix and Sylvester, off we went shopping and even took in a movie together, one of those double features they have in Jordan where one movie is in Arabic and the other in English. I don't even remember what they were. I do remember coming back to Baghdad two days later with my heart feeling like lead.

Abu Firas had me up on the carpet immediately.

"Why did you leave without reporting your plans?" he said coldly. It was more effective than any angry shouting would have been.

"I did," I said equally calmly. "I phoned you from the airport and left a message that I was going for a shopping trip."

"Not good enough."

"And besides," I added, "I had to make some trip abroad or my exit visa would have been canceled. And I still haven't gone to the Philippines."

He gave me a long, hard look. "Don't play with fire," he hissed in a low voice, as though this were only between the two of us. "I'm doing this for your own good. You don't report something like leaving the country half an hour before you do it. Understand?"

I understood perfectly. Abu Firas was giving me a very un-friendly warning in a friendly way. My time was running out.

I began to make serious preparations for departure, without knowing yet how I was going to do it. I set about getting a passport and exit visa for Ban. Normally this could take weeks, but with my connections I was able to have the precious documents within twenty-four hours. "As soon as I contact you," I told her, "you will go to London. I'll either send for you or join you as soon as possible." I told her where to stay and again promised it would not be long.

The other major consideration was money. Iraqi dinars were worth even less outside the country than they were on the black market. Zero, in fact. So I set about converting my hundreds of thousands of dinars into tens of thousands of dollars' worth of gold and jewelry: necklaces, diamond rings, emerald and diamond bracelets, pearls, an antique bird pin and gold coins.

Alone in my room at night I packed the gold away in small packages secured with tape to keep them from jingling. Then I packed them all tightly inside a Thomas Cook travel bag. But where on earth could I go? And how? Abu Firas seemed able to know wherever I went.

My misery was complete when my father arrived on one of his trips home to the foreign ministry. Then I realized that my father could help me escape. Of all people, my father was my ticket out — if I could play it just right and maneuver him into position without his knowing it. Ironically he now wanted me to change money for him on the black market. This time, I got him the very best rate, so in a way he owed me a favor.

We met at his suite at the Rashid Hotel, where he stayed now that his separation from my mother was irrevocable. The main salon overlooked the garden by the swimming pool. I came in and handed him the money. He was his usual self, mean and blustery.

"Thanks," he said gruffly as I handed him the money. "You'd better be doing what they damn well tell you the rest of the time," he added.

These references were no longer a mystery to me. While searching for my father's Tunisian papers, I had found some papers that revealed the fact that my father was a senior Mukhabarat officer. It seemed clear that, because Saddam had commuted my death sentence, my father regarded the Mukhabarat as my adopted guardian.

"Yeah, sure." As casually as I could, I said, "But I've been having a few little problems with Abu Firas. Nothing big."

"Like what?" he demanded quickly. I knew he'd bitten.

"Nothing much. A little misunderstanding about money. Some hotel deal they have going. Almost took me for a lot."

"What the hell are you talking about?"

So I told him. And added that, since then, Abu Firas had made a point of harassing me, especially about travel abroad. It worked like a dream.

"Who the hell does he think he is, messing with my family!" he exploded. "I'll show him a thing or two."

It was that old rule. Inside the family, the lord and master can treat his wife and children as brutally as he wants. But if an outsider gives them trouble, beware. Then it's the honor of the master that's at stake. I knew my man.

We met again the next day in his hotel suite.

"So," I said carefully, "have you met Abu Firas? That is to say, Shaharabeli," I added, using his real name. I'd almost forgotten he had a real name.

"No. But it doesn't matter. I don't need to see him." And he went over to the writing desk by the window and picked up an envelope. "This is a letter of introduction to my friend in the embassy in Yemen, asking him to give you any help you need, any money while you're visiting there."

Yemen? I wondered why he wanted me to go to Yemen of all places. Then it dawned on me. It killed two birds with one stone. What he wanted to do was to show Abu Firas he was the more powerful. He could send me anywhere he wanted, without any stupid okay from Firas. Yemen was as good as anywhere else. Anywhere but the Philippines. That was the second bird: he averted an unwanted visit from his despised son.

"Here's some money, too, for the trip," he said, handing me another envelope.

"But what do I tell Abu Firas?" I asked nervously.

"Fuck him. I'll show him his place but good."

That was the last time I ever saw my father.

I was to leave on March 17, after my father had departed again for the Philippines. In order to confuse possible pursuers, I changed my reservation on the ninth, a Friday (and the sabbath), when only the Iraqi Airways offices in the Rashid Hotel were open. I arranged to leave the next day.

Now I set about leaving for good. I gave away virtually everything I owned to a few of my friends. On my second-last night, Ban and I decided to take a suite in the Rashid, not knowing when we might see each other alone again.

"Do you have to go now?" she complained. "You won't be here for my birthday."

"I know," I replied, stroking her hair. "But you have to understand. This is my last chance. And there isn't much time. The Mukhabarat are really jumpy these days. They might do anything."

Poor Ban still did not understand the nature of the system, and she couldn't picture my part in it. But recently they had arrested a British journalist of Iranian origin, Farzad Barzoft. He had been caught trying to get into one of their special factories in disguise, and he was to be tried by a special court. People here and abroad were being told that he was going to be tried, convicted and then thrown out of the country, but I had heard differently. No one got any margin from the Mukhabarat these days.

They executed him. The whole world seemed stunned. I don't know why. It was normal procedure in Iraq.

The Eagle was replaced as head of the Mukhabarat for being lax enough to let Barzoft roam the country. Sabaowi Ibrahim al-Tikriti, Saddam's brother, took over as head of the service.

But my main concern was Abu Firas. I wasn't sure exactly what the rift between him and my father might cause. The best course for me was straight out of the country. To anywhere else.

We were discussing all this when there was a knock at the door. Ban jumped in fright. My own heart skipped a beat or two. But the best thing was to answer it as if I was innocent.

"Hello," said the old man at the door. I recognized him straight away. He was one of the escorts for visiting VIPs, from the Ministry of Foreign Affairs. He was short, with wavy white hair and one eye slightly wider than the other, which made him look lopsided.

"Oh, I'm sorry. Hello, Hussein. What are you doing here?"

"What are you doing here?" I returned.

"I must have the wrong room. Is this, wait a minute, let me see," he said, looking for something in his pockets. "I've made a mistake," he finished, drawing out a piece of notepaper with writing on it. "I'm supposed to go to 616, not 610. Please forgive me."

"No, no, not at all, why don't you come in?" I said. "Have a drink with us."

I had said the magic word. He came in and explained that he was expected by the delegation of the Iraqi embassy from Jordan. The ambassador himself was here.

I was extremely pleased by the coincidence. Here was a perfect way to smuggle my gold out of the country. Acting as though he was a trusted confidant, I told him I was taking some gold out of the country and had a pilot friend in Iraqi Airways who would help me for several hundred dollars. He took the bait immediately.

"You can't trust one of their pilots. I can do it for you for less than that!" he said. And we made arrangements to meet the next day. Ban listened to all of this in resigned bewilderment.

When I asked at the desk, I discovered the ambassador was indeed staying in 610. It was an incredible coincidence and a piece of luck for me.

"At least I won't have to worry about us having something to live on," I told Ban.

She nodded miserably. I pulled her onto my lap, then picked her up and carried her to the bed. Kissing her face and her neck, I told her we wouldn't talk of it anymore. Right now, we had to think only of each other. We were each a refuge for the other. We made love, then slept still in each other's arms, far away from the world.

When it came time for me to leave, she cried, but then made an effort to be brave again. I saw her again only briefly before I left. I went to say good-bye formally at her home. Her mother was there. Ban's father had died at Christmas.

Then I went to my home to do the most difficult thing of all. I told my mother and Bibi I was going away for a long time. They understood they would not see me ever again. They were deter-mined to be brave, not to cry, but the tears welled up in their eyes.

"Don't forget your mother," whispered mama.

"Never, mama," I told her. "How could I?"

And I walked away from my father's house forever.

My new contact picked me up at the gate and drove me to the airport. He carried the bag of gold, as we had arranged, and got us through the first security check. After that, he handed the bag to me. They hadn't stopped me at the first post, so I was home free.

As the aircraft lifted off, I took one last look, I hoped, at the country I loved and hated so much. Then it disappeared beneath the gathering clouds.

17

"I'M WITH THE CIA"

T HIS WAS MY LAST CHANCE. I was a spy who had escaped Iraq, trying to come in from the cold. But I was still in the Middle East, and the Middle East, nearly all of it, was a dangerous place where the long arm of the Mukhabarat could still drag me back to a living hell in Iraq, or to a slow death, punishment for my leaving.

Many of the gulf states were grateful to Saddam for taking on Iran. Ayatollah Khomeini and the other mullahs in Tehran had called for an Islamic revolution in virtually every Arab nation. The Saudis, the Kuwaitis, the Yemenis, all had been shivering in their boots as they watched their volatile populations and worried about Iranian agents. When Saddam launched a war against the mullahs and kept it up for eight years, those states had a lot to be thankful for. The Kuwaitis bankrolled Baghdad for the duration of the war. But nobody sent any troops or weapons. Gratitude has its limits.

Of all the Middle Eastern countries, Yemen was the worst country in the world for a renegade Iraqi in 1990. Saddam Hussein owned Yemen. During the war with Iran he had kept it supplied with oil, and that meant Yemen owed Saddam its life. Almost the entire Yemeni army and air force had been trained by Iraqis.

When Saddam "won" the war with Iran, he became a hero in Yemen, as well as in a number of other countries. As a result Yemen was now virtually a fiefdom of Baghdad, and Iraqis were "kings of the mountain" in San'a, the ancient capital of Yemen. The Iraqi Embassy there was a bit like the American Embassy in El Salvador; it was, in fact, the seat of government.

I knew I had to walk a narrow line in this ancient town. I could use my Iraqi status to open doors, but I would have to keep as low a profile as possible. As I walked the streets of San'a I thought the city must look almost as it had centuries ago when it housed the throne of the Queen of Sheba. The elegant mud-brick homes of the wealthy, some five stories high, are like a collection of fantasy castles, with their intricate tracery and filigreed screens. They rise into the clear cool air of the hills at the foot of the towering mountains of Jabal Nuqum. Inside the city, the streets are narrow alleyways winding between the ancient buildings and the hovels of the poor. Baghdad has the reputation of being the city of the Arabian Nights, but it is San'a that looks like the mythical city of Scheherazade's tales. This notion, however, is soon dispelled by the incongruous crush of modern traffic.

I looked up the hill. The newly built American Embassy stands like a fortress overlooking the ancient city. I'd met with the consul earlier in the week and given her a brief written précis of my situation. For the second time since my arrival I climbed toward the iron gates. I was dismayed to see that, as before, there were hundreds of visa-seeking people lined up: men, women and children. The sight of those veiled women, with only their eyes peering out of slits in their long black robes, made me shudder. I am an Arab, but where I come from, most of the women do not wear these awful robes. Those eyes with no faces touched some deep nerve of fear in me. Nevertheless, I hurried up a path, crossed the budding new garden and headed for the consular building. Everything in this compound was ultramodern. Like American embassies all over the world, thought had been given to emergency evacuation. The new garden was flat enough and large enough to land a fleet of helicopters.

The receptionist, a local Yemeni, tried to give me a hard time. "Do you have an appointment card?" He looked at me with narrowed eyes through the bulletproof glass that separated us.

"No, but I was told to come back today — at this time." I tried not to sound impatient.

"I'm not supposed to let in anyone who doesn't have an appointment card." His lips were pressed together and this time he didn't even look up.

"You'll get in trouble. I do have an appointment."

Again he ran his finger down a list he had in front of him. "Do you have any identification?"

"Look . . ." I was getting angry. He suddenly turned around. A short man of about thirty with thick glasses had come out of an inner office and now stood behind the receptionist. The man came around out of the cage and held out his hand warmly. "Hi," he drawled in a southern accent. "I'm Steve. I'm with the CIA."

Nothing is ever as we expect. Here he was, a representative of the Central Intelligence Agency, introducing himself like those waiters in American restaurant chains — "Hi, I'm Steve. I'm going to be your waiter tonight." I half expected this Steve to add, "I'm going to be your agent today." He was just an ordinary guy who looked like a schoolteacher.

The illusion of being in a restaurant continued as Steve ushered me into a small room furnished with a round table, comfortably padded chairs and a bar along the wall. The table had a lace cloth and was set for diners. There were no windows. There was, however a small round bugging device on the ceiling, obvious to anyone who knew what to look for.

It was March, the month in which Ramadan fell that year. Ramadan is the Islamic period of special religious observance.

During the month of Ramadan it is the custom to fast from sunrise to sunset. Steve asked politely if I was fasting.

Not me, I replied. He ordered us soft drinks and food, and while he asked general questions about my personal background, another man appeared with a meal. It was cooked in the Mideastern style. The atmosphere, the meal, everything, seemed so normal, genteel even, considering the subjects we were about to discuss.

I *had* to make this escape good because there was no turning back. I wanted asylum in the United States. I had brought out enough gold to bankroll a new life and was willing to give the Americans whatever information I could. Whatever they asked for. Steve did not have the précis I'd given to the consul earlier, but he had notes.

"Ah!" Steve said, pouncing on my passport. "You have two visas here! One for the Philippines and one for Thailand. Going to pick up drugs for delivery?" he demanded, pleased with his deduction.

I sat there dumbfounded at this ludicrous question. Then the phone beside Steve rang. He picked up the receiver, listened, then hung up and turned to me. For a second he glanced at his notes. Then he looked up. "How did you come to work for the Mossad?" he asked.

Apparently whoever was on the other end of the phone was listening to our conversation and, equally apparently, knew the ropes better than poor Steve.

I told Steve — and our invisible listener — about Mossad operations I had been on in England, about the Syrian informer who worked in the nuclear project in Damascus. I told him how Iraqi agents come and go from the United States and European countries with complete impunity. I revealed how the Iraqi regime kidnaps its opponents in the capitals of the world and ships them home in the so-called diplomatic bag.

I told him what I had learned in the Mukhabarat. I talked about the training schools, the assassination operations, the weapons-modification factories and horrors such as the accident at the typhoid-virus plant. I was prepared to tell more: I knew about the American-based ally of Palestinian terrorist Abu al-Abbas and the truth about the missile attack on the USS *Stark*. But I wanted to keep some of these cards in my hand. I hinted at the darkest secret of all: Osirak, the nuclear phoenix ready to rise from the ashes of the Israeli attack. Everyone believed it was destroyed. It was not.

Nine months later the Americans would hit it again for good measure and announce once again that it was dead. But I had reason to doubt even then that Saddam's nuclear ability was completely destroyed. Underwater in the channels of the Dokan Dam was enriched uranium. And if they had disguised the Nasar facility by moving another entire factory, they might have moved a lot of Osirak.

I continued with my revelations. "I can tell you a fair bit about the surveillance of the American Embassy in Baghdad," I offered Steve, aware of his unseen colleague listening in. "Does that interest you, maybe?"

His ears pricked up. "Of course. Fire away."

The American Embassy is a fortified compound that sits right across the street from the Shahin Hotel. "The Shahin is one big ear for the Mukhabarat," I began. "It's equipped to overhear everything that's even whispered in the washrooms of the embassy."

I told him the next item the Iraqis planned was electronic equipment that can "hear" what a teletype machine is printing. This was more difficult than "hearing" a typewriter, where each key has a distinctive "voice."

I talked about the Al Qadisiya, the hotel owned by the Syrian ex-spy where the government insisted foreign visitors go so they could be kept under surveillance. "Delegations from the United

States and from the Soviet Union merit particular attention. The Americans are taken care of by one Mukhabarat department that tries to learn everything it can about their doings," I revealed.

I went on to explain that the Soviets had two levels of Mukhabarat keeping track of them: one to eavesdrop and learn what they were doing; another to stick to them and make sure none of them tried to use Iraq in order to defect from the USSR. This was part of the Soviet-Iraqi pact, agreed to by Saddam even though he did everything to destroy communists at home. Still, Saddam was obliged to turn back anyone trying to escape communism in the Soviet Union. Given the overall picture, I doubt any Soviets would have been mad enough to try to defect to Iraq.

"Mountains of records of meetings and telephone conversations are gathered every day. They're pored over by Mukhabarat staff. Spying is one of the biggest make-work projects in the country; it's a major source of employment. As a result, the intelligence services have exhaustive information on everything that transpires in the country, from private arms deals to food orders for the American Embassy."

I smiled a little. "You see, if there's an unusual amount of fancy food ordered by the American Embassy for an important guest, then the spies set about finding out who's coming to dinner, and for what purpose. They use that advance knowledge to know when to eavesdrop."

"We run a tight ship," Steve protested.

I shook my head. "In addition to the resident informers on staff, there's one junior staffer in Baghdad who makes money on the side by selling American visas. This comes in handy for the Mukhabarat when they choose to send agents using other means than the diplomatic flights."

Steve looked amazed. He shouldn't have been. Interested, yes. Amazed, no. What I was telling him was pretty much business as usual in the Mideast. I couldn't believe that senior American officials didn't realize this. But I intended to offer them whatever I knew.

Still, Steve waffled. "I'm not sure we can do anything to help you — at least not immediately."

I felt empty inside and defeated. Didn't he realize how valuable my information might be? Saddam was starting to make noises of war again. Surely the Americans could see that Saddam had new military designs. Or were the Americans still clinging to the illusion that Saddam was some kind of ally? Would they never learn? There are no such things as allies in the Middle East. There are only shifting sands. And it was only a matter of time before Saddam shifted again. He had a million-man army with nothing to do. No dictator in the world could let that situation go on for long. He would have to find something to keep them busy before they turned their thoughts to the presidential palace, the way armies do when they have time on their hands.

Saddam had already killed some of the commanders who posed the greatest threat to his power. But there were always others. To keep them busy, he might turn his attention to the Kurds again. Or he might turn south to Kuwait. Saddam nursed a long-standing grudge concerning the disposition of Babiyan and Faylakah, the two islands in the gulf held by the Kuwaitis. When the British drew the new borders that carved up the Ottoman Empire after World War I, they literally cut off Iraq from the sea with one stroke of a pen. The war with Iran had reminded Iraq just how dependent it was on its coastal neighbors. Moreover, Kuwait was making noises about wanting Iraq to repay the billions of dollars Kuwait had supplied for the war against Iran. I wasn't the only one who foresaw the gulf crisis. We Iraqis all knew that Saddam had a very short fuse, and it was burning in the direction of Kuwait.

But Steve and his colleagues at the American Embassy in San'a seemed to live in a world in which some acts were unthinkable. I knew there must be Americans in the CIA, the State Department or the military who realized the true nature of the world around them, but how could I reach them to present my case? Sitting in this little room in the embassy with Steve, I felt a million miles from Washington. Steve and his unseen colleague didn't seem to grasp what I was offering them on a silver platter. Intelligence on Iraq was as rare as camels by the Potomac.

I gave Steve all my papers, even my address book with names and phone numbers. "Well," he said, "how do we know you didn't just make this all up, even the phone numbers?"

I stared at him in disbelief. Was that all he had to say?

Was this man an aberration, or was I his first experience with the spy world?

Once again, the phone rang. After nodding several times, Steve corrected his approach. "Well, we'll have to see," he hedged. "We'd like you to go back to Iraq and carry on working there."

I cut him off. "I've had five years of hell there. My last escape attempt failed. This is it. All I want is to start a new life."

"We can't give you a visa, you know —"

"I don't want a visa," I replied, despairing of this obtuseness. "I need asylum!"

"Is there any other country you could go to? I mean, we might be able to help you later . . . These things take time."

Since the doors of the United States were clearly not going to open right away, I decided to try my other alternative. "I could go to Canada," I said. "I know someone there." At least it was North America.

He nodded. "Right now the main thing is to get you out of here. You've probably been seen coming in here. Yemen won't be safe for you. Why don't you just get yourself to Canada and we'll get in touch with you there." He put his hand on my shoulder. "And then we'll see what we can do for you."

He was clearly anxious to get me out of the embassy, looking for Iraqi agents over his shoulder. Or rather over my shoulder.

"Sure," I answered. "We'll see."

What I saw was that although Americans and their government were always talking about helping freedom and democracy and rescuing people from tyranny, it just doesn't work that way. Geopolitics come first. Just the same I gave him a phone number where he might contact me in Canada. And he gave me a code and number to reach him in San'a if necessary.

Going to the Mossad, even if it had been a good idea, was impossible here. There was no Mossad in Yemen.

"Well," said Steve as I prepared to leave, "you're *sure* you won't go back to Iraq and work for us there?"

I could have screamed with frustration. "I can't! Don't you understand? It's all over for me there." I drew my finger across my throat like a knife.

"Hmm. I see," he said, but I knew he didn't. I couldn't understand his cavalier attitude. He should have seen me as a spy's bonanza.

I left the American Embassy knowing Canada was my best bet. Still, I had to get out of Yemen without arousing the suspicion of any Iraqi higher-ups who might be tracking me. As an extra cautionary measure, I went to the Iraqi Embassy, just as my father and his people would expect, and called on his friend, Ambassador Abdul Hussein. The Iraqi Embassy was large, with two buildings inside the walled compound. The checkpoints were manned by armed Iraqi soldiers. Iraq refused to allow local people to work at the embassy in any capacity. The ambassador's office inside was predictably luxurious, with Louis XVI sofas in the outer room and even more ornate antiques in the inner sanctum. His Iraqi secretary was a young woman in western dress. Abdul Hussein himself was a big bald man, his teeth stained green from his habit of chewing *kat*. Since alcohol is prohibited in Yemen, many Iraqis turn to this drug instead. They wad it in their mouths like chewing tobacco. Kat is a plant, like tobacco, and it is one of Yemen's most profitable crops. A hallucinogen like mescaline, it is also a stimulant. As it seems to have the effect of about a hundred cups of coffee, kat has a tendency to make the user nervous and edgy. Abdul Hussein was visibly so. In fact, there were a lot of nervous, edgy Iraqis with bulging cheeks around town.

He greeted me amiably enough, though, and asked if I needed anything. I assured him I didn't and that everything was fine. Then I detected menace beneath his friendly manner.

"You have been called back to Baghdad immediately," he said. He gave no reason, and I needed none. Abu Firas must have been livid.

I hid my fear that I might have been seen going to the American Embassy. I told myself that if I had been, I wouldn't be able to leave this room. I stayed on for a few minutes chatting, then left with the excuse that I had to make arrangements to go to Baghdad.

It was clear they had no idea what to do with me. So I bought myself a ticket to Canada. The German line, Lufthansa, refused to sell me a ticket. Quite properly, they demanded proof of acceptance into the country of destination. At the Yemeni airline counter, however, I just showed my driver's license and said it was my American Green Card, and they happily sold me a ticket to Toronto.

The problem for the Americans was that they only knew how hard things could be, not how easy things are. They didn't know how to think like Arabs. Our logic is not a straight line, but curled and twisting like our script. Our sense of life and death is not theirs: we laugh where an American cries.

I went back to my hotel and packed my bag. I could just make the flight to Frankfurt. I went through the airport procedure almost in a trance, mechanically going through the motions as they inspected my luggage and checked my passport. The crowds and the noise seemed far away. I felt no elation when the plane lifted off, for I was full of foreboding and worry. After the failure of my meetings with the Americans, I wondered, would anyone help me, anywhere?

The huge Frankfurt airport was depressing, and I took the first available flight to Bonn. I wanted to get to the Canadian Embassy there as soon as possible.

It was raining in Bonn. It was always raining in Bonn. I took a taxi to one of the small, cheaper hotels in the old part of town where the streets are closed to traffic. I checked in under a phony name, which I now did automatically. I paid them cash in advance so they would not request my passport to hold overnight as insurance.

My hopes lifted a bit when I entered the Canadian Embassy. It was a plain office building on a small side street not far from the Iraqi Embassy. I filled out the necessary forms, then handed in my visa application with my ID papers to a woman at the counter. As I was explaining to her how desperate I was to go to Canada right away, the consul himself appeared behind the glass. He was an older man with glasses, an old-world gentleman. He came out and ushered me through into his office, explaining that an instant visa was impossible. "You should have your visa in about three weeks," he reassured me. He was so kind I felt like crying.

"Three weeks! But I got my German visa in one hour!"

"That's the Germans. Ours take fourteen working days, you know."

All of a sudden I felt terribly alone. Ban seemed a million miles away. And here I was stuck in Bonn. Well, better Bonn than Baghdad, I said to myself. Shape up. It could be worse.

So I went back to the hotel, retrieved some of the gold jewelry from the pouch and went in search of a buyer. After asking for estimates in a number of stores, I was directed to a small shop run by a Jewish dealer in a third-floor flat. When I showed him one of the items, a hundred-year-old diamond ring, he exclaimed in admiration. I immediately trusted him because he didn't try to pretend it wasn't worth much. He gave me a fair price for several pieces, and so I had some money to live on while I marked time in Bonn.

Nearly three weeks later, I received a Canadian visa, which is really a temporary visitor's permit. At last. I allowed myself to begin to hope again. But not too much. I knew how closely allied Canada and the United States were, and even though Iraq's relations with Kuwait were deteriorating daily, I was afraid they would still be reluctant to offend Saddam's government by accepting the son of one of his diplomatic corps as a political refugee seeking asylum.

* * *

As the plane began its descent into Toronto I could see Lake Ontario and the tall spire of the CN Tower rising out of the huddle of downtown buildings. It was the end of April, and yet the pilot said the temperature was thirty-one degrees Celsius. I thought he must have made a mistake. In my mind Canada was still freezing in April.

It all looked so peaceful below that I felt hopeful. Maybe Ban and I could live here. I decided to get in touch with her and tell her to leave Iraq right away for England. I would send for her as soon as humanly possible.

The officer at the passport control looked at my visa, then sent me on to be checked by an immigration officer. It was a senior officer, a black woman with salt-and-pepper hair and a wary manner. She asked the reason for my visit. I could see she was suspicious.

"I'm just here for a trip. My father is a diplomat. I travel a lot."

"How much money do you have to look after yourself?"

"About $150 in cash. But the Iraqi Embassy will look after me, anything I need," I lied. "I'll register with them here."

Before I made any move at all in this country, I wanted to make contact with the CIA to see if they might handle my case after all. But I could hardly tell her that I was here to see the CIA.

She was dubious, but finally she seemed to believe me. She wrote down the Iraqi Embassy as my address in Canada and let me through.

It was a beautiful spring day, as warm as the pilot had promised, and my hopes rose again. A trusted friend had given me the number of an Iraqi in Toronto who might give me a room to stay in temporarily. When I called, he welcomed me and gave me directions to his place. It was a beginning.

I waited a week for the CIA to call this contact's number, the one I had given to Steve in San'a. Finally I decided to call Steve.

"I'm sorry," said the woman who answered the phone at the American Embassy in Yemen. "He's been transferred." She recognized my voice, though, and passed my call on to Steve's replacement. But he knew nothing of my case and said he couldn't do anything.

Discouraged and feeling abandoned, I went back to my lodging. The next morning, I received a call from an American who called himself Jackson.

"Steve passed your name along to me. How are you doing? Sorry to be so long getting in touch. Listen, I should be in Toronto soon. Can we meet at the consulate on Monday at 9 a.m.?"

For the first time since leaving Baghdad, I knew I was dealing with a pro. There was something about his voice, his manner, even on the phone, that told me this man knew what he was doing. It was as if we spoke the same language.

"Nine Monday will be great."

"Okay. Tell them you're expected in the office of Mr. Bradley. See you then."

The American Consulate in Toronto is an elegant building on University Avenue. The street is wide and sweeps up to the buildings of the provincial legislature. I used an entrance that avoided the usual lineup of people applying for American visas.

A young man of nineteen or so was at the front desk. I told him I had an appointment and he would find my name on his list. He checked, then slid a book across the desk for me to sign. I left blank the space for "business or profession." Without a word to me, he called someone on his telephone, then handed me a blue badge.

An older woman appeared from the elevator, looked at me, then turned to the young man. "He should have a red badge," she said, and replaced my blue one. Then she escorted me to the small elevator, put a key in the controls and we rose to the upper floor.

There, two men were waiting for me in a comfortable-looking office. One was tall, well dressed, about forty-five and wearing a blue badge. This was Jackson. The other was Bradley.

They began to question me about my story, but not at all about the Mossad. I supposed that meant they must have already checked that out. What they wanted were names of Mukhabarat officers in Iraq, information about people in the nuclear facilities and the chemical- and biological-weapons plants.

"Can you go back to Iraq?" Jackson asked.

"No," I replied, "it's out of the question. Besides, I want to end all that and start a new life, a normal one, in the United States. In return I'll tell you everything I can."

"Well, that kind of decision isn't in our hands, but we'll see what we can do," he promised. "Meanwhile, if you want to go to some other country, we'll vouch for you."

I left disappointed. I had thought it would be so simple. I thought they would jump at the chance of learning more about Saddam and the machine they were about to confront in the gulf. I was mystified.

After a week, they called to say they couldn't help me. Now I was not only mystified, I was depressed and angry. I wanted to help and they wouldn't let me. I wanted to be given help and they wouldn't give.

I decided to apply for asylum in Canada. It was my only option now. On May 23, a few days before my visitor's visa expired, I went to an immigration office and filled out the forms, then submitted them along with a letter explaining why I feared for my life if I went back to Iraq.

Three weeks later I received an appointment to discuss my case. The woman who dealt with me was kind and anxious to help. She even called the welfare department to see if I was eligible if need be.

As the son of an Iraqi diplomat, my case was considered delicate. "This is my second high-profile case," the woman said, "so I'd like to keep track of how you're handled. Please stay in touch. Others will take it from here. You'll just have to wait for now. Meanwhile, I'm sorry but we can't allow your wife to join you, not until you have your status here. And you can't hold a job until then, either."

I appreciated her sympathy. But this seemed ridiculous to me. I could draw welfare but I couldn't work. I would never understand these Canadian rules.

I was waiting anxiously for an answer to my request for asylum when Saddam invaded Kuwait. On August 2, Iraqi armor simply rolled into the defenseless little nation and announced that Kuwait was now Province 19 of the Republic of Iraq.

18

LINES IN THE SAND

As I sat in Toronto, the conquering Iraqi army began to pillage Kuwait, raping its women and brutalizing its men. Thousands of foreign workers and tens of thousands of Kuwaitis fled. Among them were Palestinians who had lived there for thirty years, forced from their homes and obliged to flee, leaving behind their life's savings. This did not stop Saddam from later claiming he had done it all for the sake of the Arab cause, especially that of the Palestinians.

Suddenly the White House was calling Saddam an Arab Hitler, who must not be appeased. But as one American journalist put it, Saddam was more of a Frankenstein's monster than a Hitler. Now the media reported how governments and arms dealers from Paris to Tokyo, from Washington to Moscow, from Bonn to Beijing, had had a field day supplying Baghdad, and to a lesser extent Iran, with weapons, technology and advisers. My own assignments had made me aware of it all, from the British flight schools to the Nasar missile factory with its German overlord.

As usual, no one had thought things through to the next act of the drama. Now their horrible creation was in their own backyard. As far as the industrialized countries were concerned, the oil nations of the Middle East *are* their backyards. To lose Kuwait was bad enough. But right next door was Saudi Arabia. To lose Saudi Arabia was unthinkable.

President George Bush drew a line in the sand. He sent ships, troops, tanks, pilots, bombers and missiles to Saudi Arabia and the United Arab Emirates to back up United Nations' demands that Iraq leave Kuwait. If Saddam refused, he faced the awesome arsenal of the United States and Britain, among others.

I knew there would be war. The minute each man stated his ultimatum it was inevitable. Bush *could* not back down. Saddam *would* not back down. An ultimatum handed to a man like Saddam Hussein guaranteed that he would refuse. The fact that Bush put together an unprecedented alliance of nations from Syria to Bangladesh as his partner in this enterprise, and the fact that everything was done in accordance with United Nations Security Council Resolution Number 678 of 1990, didn't really change the central fact: it was Saddam against the Yanks (and to a lesser extent, the Brits). Saddam played a very clever card when he compared his annexation of Kuwait with the Israeli occupation and settlement of the West Bank, then demanded an international peace conference to deal with all the outstanding Middle East issues, especially those of the Palestinians and the occupied territories. He had a point: the West certainly had a double standard on this issue. Why the Americans had never mustered the political will to buck Israel a bit and do something for the displaced Palestinians, I suppose I shall never understand. It was in their own interest to do so, because it would remove the most powerful psychological weapon the hard-line Arabs had: hatred of America as the ally of Israel's expansionist policy. Now Saddam wielded that weapon.

When situations like this develop there is a lot of knowing talk in the West about how we Arabs need to be allowed a way to save face, and then we will back down. This is a quaint notion that assumes we don't have the West's same hardheaded grasp of the facts. The truth is Saddam couldn't give a damn about saving face, or about the Palestinians. What he was doing was playing every card to try to humiliate the Americans, with no intention of ever getting out of Kuwait, even if they did agree to a Mideast peace conference. He would string it out with one new condition after another, keeping the Americans dangling just like the Iranians did with all their phony hostage negotiations.

The wonder was that Palestinians from Jordan and the West Bank suddenly adopted Saddam Hussein as their hero. It was as if they had instant amnesia about how he had treated the PLO and the Palestinians in general over the years — mere pawns on his chessboard. Either that, or they simply did not have the information in the first place. This is one of the curses of the whole region: people act emotionally, without any access to the full facts of any situation or event. There is almost no free press, nothing but polarized propaganda. Until that changes, there can be no solution or end to the vicious circles of killing and revenge.

I would like to have invited all those deluded Palestinians who were now cheering Saddam as the great Arab hero who would lead them out of the wilderness to visit Baghdad for a while so they might sample life under the Ba'th Party, the Mukhabarat, the Amn, the Estikhbarat and all the rest of Saddam's enforcers.

For a while there was hope that the global economic sanctions against Iraq might bring Saddam to his knees, but that hope assumed Saddam cared about his people. The shortages of food and medicine were hurting children the most, and Saddam and his ministers, including my father, the least. In government propaganda much was made of the cruel shortages, but in fact Saddam couldn't have cared less what happened to his enslaved public. The only place sanctions might have had a real effect was on Saddam's military machine, which needs constant spare parts and technological help to keep running. But the open market and black markets seemed able to keep the arsenals well oiled.

The only reason the United Nations could take a stand in the first place was the collapse of the Soviet empire. For the first time since World War II, local power mongers couldn't play off the White House and the Kremlin against one another. The constant threat of a superpower nuclear confrontation if things got too out of hand had kept something like this from blowing up in the Middle East. But that threat had vanished with the Berlin Wall.

The Soviets had been doing everything to try to pull a diplomatic solution out of the hat right up until the last minute. Soviet envoy Yevgeny Primakov, an accomplished Arabist, traveled to Iraq to try to work out a peace plan with Saddam. The Kremlin was still a bit of a wild card. Gorbachev was under political siege after independence movements in the Balkans were crushed by his tanks; reformers and conservatives alike were shouting for his resignation. A change in the Kremlin could change the whole picture again in the gulf. I shudder at the thought of a new political leadership from the old guard in Moscow suddenly backing Saddam or Syria's Assad. It was to be hoped that the men in Moscow had their hands full and their treasury empty and would not be able to indulge in more adventurism.

When Saddam moved into Kuwait, he seemed to have forgotten that Moscow was no longer a factor. He also banked too much on the Vietnam syndrome, believing the Americans would rather sacrifice Kuwait than get bogged down in the desert in another war. Moreover, he didn't take America's desert expertise into account. The Americans have deserts. They train on them, and it is generally acknowledged that they are far better desert fighters than jungle fighters.

Saddam had completely missed the change of personality America had undergone during the Reagan years. America had accepted Vietnam, had cried its tears at the Vietnam Memorial, and now was ready to face the world again. There would be antiwar protests and much anguished debate, but Americans would fight if they thought they had to.

Everybody knew it was all about oil, no matter how often President Bush stressed the oppression of Kuwait and upholding the principles of the United Nations. Even Bush was candid enough once in a while to say it was a matter of America's strategic interests. And it was. If the United States failed to stand by its Arab allies such as Saudi Arabia and Egypt on this one, those Arab leaders could never again be seen to sit at the American table — if they even lived to tell the tale. As it was, they risked the wrath of considerable numbers of their own populations who would resent American interference, let alone American troops. There wasn't much love for the fat cat Kuwaiti regime in the rest of the Arab world, but there was a great deal of fear of Saddam. So if Egypt, Syria, Saudi Arabia and the Emirates had to go to war over Kuwait to take care of Saddam, so be it. If they had to ally themselves with the ally of Israel, so be it. They hoped to heaven that Israel would stay out of it.

The alliance was a delicate balancing act, like that circus family who could form a human pyramid on a bicycle, and then bicycle across a high wire. George Bush was the guy doing the pedaling.

Where on earth the American media had got the notion that George Bush was a wimp, I don't know. As ex-CIA chief he never had that image where I came from. On the contrary, to us he represented the triumph of the militant conservatives in America. And we were about to see what they were made of.

It became popular to label Saddam a "madman." Several commentators in the media tried to warn that this was a simplistic idea. But the notion stuck.

I knew from the inside that Saddam was not a madman in the

normal sense of the word. He was a megalomaniac, yes, but a ruthlessly efficient one. One of the best judges of human nature in his own country, he was capable of extremely shrewd psychological maneuvers against an enemy.

Sitting in Toronto, waiting, I hoped that the Americans really did have the backbone to take him on. Nothing else would rid Iraq of Saddam. Unless the Israelis did it unilaterally.

I certainly understood the protesters when they shouted, "No blood for oil." I couldn't care less about big oil companies, either. It was a mystery to me why the industrialized nations had left themselves dependent on oil located in such an insane part of the world instead of developing other energy bases decades ago. But they hadn't and here they were, hoist with their own petard. It just happened that at this moment in time the oil companies' interests and mine were the same, though for different reasons. We both wanted to stop Saddam.

As for the innocents who would die, where had all the protesters been for the past couple of decades while Iraq agonized under the heel of the Ba'th? While Saddam gassed whole villages in Kurdistan? While the Iran-Iraq war killed and maimed millions? What about the innocents who would continue to die by Saddam's hand? We had already been dying for years. My view was that even if the war was going to be fought for all the wrong reasons, if it wiped Saddam off the map, it would be worth it.

The threat of war should have meant that the CIA would be more interested in me than they had been up till now. In early October, I left a message for Jackson at the consulate. He called the next day to tell me they were going to be able to work something out and he would be in touch in a few weeks.

I was impatient and frustrated. Ban was alone in England, and now because of the war, her bank account had been frozen along with all other Iraqi accounts, big or small, government or personal. I had gone through most of the gold and about all that was left were the pieces of jewelry that I had meant for her. Though I did not want to break any rules in Canada, I took a small job in a corner store to be able to send her money to live on. I was on my way out for a walk a couple of days after my conversation with Jackson when a stranger phoned the house where I was staying.

"Hussein Sumaida?" he said. "I'm a friend of Abu Firas. He told me to tell you to come back to Baghdad right away."

I froze. There was someone here who knew me, who was looking for me. Someone at this end or that had given away the phone number. Without risking further contact with the CIA, I decided to run. To England. My old stomping grounds would be the last place on earth they would expect to find me. I sold more of the jewelry at a small shop and bought myself a ticket at an Air Canada office — to Cairo, via England. That way, anyone checking the airline's computers would assume, I hoped, that I had gone all the way to Egypt to lose myself in the Muslim masses there.

* * *

Bleary-eyed with strain and the sleepless overnight flight across the Atlantic, I landed in the hands of the authorities at Heathrow Airport in the early morning.

There were no polite questions here. England is as different from Canada as it is from Iraq. For all their veneer of politeness, the English have a lot of the ruthlessness of the Mideasterners. When I told the passport control I wanted to apply for political refugee status, the immediate reaction was hostile. With an "Oh, you do, do you?" the officer roughly shoved me in the direction of a nearby doorway. I was pushed into a room about two meters square.

Over the next thirteen hours, four immigration officers grilled me about my story, each for two or three hours at a time. Once again, I started to recount my frankly unbelievable but true story, and I could see their hostility grow. The issue that seemed to make them angriest was how I had worked for the Mossad in England without British intelligence being informed of the Mossad operations. MI5, MI6 and Scotland Yard were all in the dark.

"You're aware, I assume, that the host country is always to be kept informed?" said one officer rhetorically.

The Thatcher government had expelled two Israeli Embassy employees in 1987 when the authorities found out by accident that a Palestinian they'd arrested in Manchester was in fact a Mossad agent. It caused a lot of strain between Israel and Britain. I imagined they didn't want to repeat the fiasco.

They asked dozens of questions about the chemical- and biological-warfare plants. And more about the foreigners that Saddam was now holding as hostages. He had refused to allow many diplomats and foreign workers to leave the country, instead putting them in areas that were strategic military targets to act as human shields. The West was justifiably furious about this. But it had happened long after I'd left Iraq, and I knew nothing that would help on this score.

Finally they seemed finished with me. I had been given no food all day, and I was exhausted.

"Don't move," said my last interrogator as he left. A few minutes later a burly officer came in, hauled me to my feet and led me firmly through the hallway to a doorway leading to the underground garages. A white police van was waiting. Dumping me in the back, the officer then joined the driver up front, and we drove off. When we stopped I discovered we were at some kind of jail. By now it was nighttime again, and I couldn't distinguish exactly where we were in the few seconds it took them to pull me out of the van and hustle me into a dank cell inside. It was a dungeon, a cold, dark basement cell with no windows. The stone walls were chilly and damp. A concrete platform with a thin blue plastic mattress was my bed, and in the dim light thrown by a low-watt bulb, I could see it was filthy.

They brought me some kind of food, but I was too wrung out even to look at it. I crouched on the floor all night, afraid to have anything to do with the diseased-looking bed. Nothing in my upbringing, such as it was, had prepared me for this. I sat there all night, trying not to imagine what would happen if they deported me to Iraq.

In the morning I was brought brackish coffee, and then they loaded me into the van again. I was taken back to the interrogation room at the airport. At least, I reflected, this wasn't like an interrogation at the Amn where those questioned rarely survived, and if they did they suffered from broken minds and bodies. As rough as the British were, they weren't in the same league.

"So, what do you think of our government, sonny?" asked one of the officers.

"I think —"

"We're a bunch of evil imperialists, I suppose," he interrupted, trying to provoke me.

"Please, you don't understand. I'm telling the truth. I want to help your side. If you don't believe me, let me talk to some of your people in intelligence."

"Not bloody likely, sonny. Think we're a lot of fools, do you?"

It went on like that. They were stupid and nasty and hidebound, with preconceived ideas about everything. As far as they were concerned, I was a terrorist and they knew all the answers. I couldn't blame them for looking for terrorists. But this was hardly the way. As if some terrorist would start ranting about the evils of imperialism! A terrorist would probably come in as a computer salesman.

When they left me alone for a time, I could hear a couple of them outside the door laughing. "Here, take a look at this one! Claims he's been hobnobbing with the CIA!"

I felt like beating my fists on the walls. Then the door opened, and Ban rushed in, jumping with joy.

It was like seeing the sunrise. They had called her to come in and had questioned her, too, but apparently with great kindness. She was laughing and crying and hugging me, touching my shoulders to see if I was real. She was like a little child who had found her lost teddy bear. I kissed her and we clung to each other, trying to shut out the world, saying nothing.

Then to our amazement, one of the officers, one of the better ones, came in and informed us that they had decided I could have a hearing in two months. For now, they were giving me a tempo-rary two-month visa. They let us go.

We took a roomy black London cab back to the city. Jubilant, we hugged and kissed and laughed and cried all the way. We checked into the best hotel I knew, the Regency, and reveled in all the luxury of thick carpets and crystal chandeliers and gilt furni-ture. Feeling we had earned it somehow, we booked an outra-geously expensive suite, beautiful rooms that looked like something out of an old Hollywood movie. After a night in a dungeon, I found the contrast dazzling.

I was exhausted and hungry, but Ban wanted to celebrate. So we ordered champagne and shrimp and lobster and all the most delicious and most expensive things on the elaborate room-service menu. By mutual consent, we didn't talk at all about what had happened to me. We concentrated on the food and on each other, happy to be together again at last, alive and well. We made love that night as though we were the first two people on earth to discover the joy of making two people into one.

The next day, after the shock of paying the bill for all that indulgence, we found a more affordable room at a small hotel and started to prowl about London looking at flats. We finally found one we both loved near Hampstead. I had gone to the bank to see the manager and arranged for them to allow us at least enough money to live on week to week, though they would not lift the freeze on the account. We rented the flat and at last felt we could begin to plan our future.

When the authorities called me to come and see them again at the airport, I went right away, thinking they had finally checked out my story and wanted to begin debriefing me to learn what they could about the regime they were on the verge of going to war against.

"We have to send you back to Canada," said the officer when I had drawn up a chair across from his desk.

My heart stopped. I felt as though I were falling, falling from a high cliff. I was speechless.

"We can't take on your case because you already have an immigration case pending in Canada," he said almost apologetically. "It's against the rules. You'll have to go back and continue the process there."

I began to argue, then stopped, realizing it was useless. I felt for some reason they were just afraid to handle a hot potato like me. They must have imagined the field day the media would have if they were discovered harboring a Mukhabarat agent. Their solution: let Canada have him.

But worse was yet to come. They refused to let Ban go with me. I begged and pleaded, but it was no use.

Ban brought my suitcase, and the gold, to the airport. Her eyes were red from crying and she could hardly speak. For the second time in my adult life I, too, began to cry. Everything was out of reach, no matter where I stretched out my hands. Maybe disabled people feel like that, just unable to do anything for themselves. I felt as if I'd lost my limbs.

Ban clung to me and I to her, weeping, then they gently pried us apart. All I could see was Ban's tearful face as they took me away from her, upstairs to the departure lounge and onto the plane. Then the doors closed, the engines started up, and the aircraft rolled out onto the runway and roared into the sky toward Canada.

I arrived in Toronto on October 19, 1990. The Canadian authorities said Ban could not come until my status was resolved. So I began the long process of immigration hearings for political refugees, alone. In addition, I was interviewed at length by agents of CSIS, the Canadian Security and Intelligence Service. I told them of an informer I knew of in the Canadian Embassy in Baghdad. A Christian Syrian girl who routinely gave detailed reports to the Mukhabarat. Establishing such a person was standard procedure for every foreign legation. Finding out diplomatic and political secrets and having a who's who of foreign visitors to the embassy were secondary to their main purpose: learning which Iraqis were approaching the embassy for visas. Forever keeping the noose tight. The controlling agent for the Mukhabarat department that handled Canadian affairs was a captain named Ziad Haddad, I told them.

The CSIS officers seemed interested in that. No doubt they assumed this sort of thing went on under their diplomatic noses and just factored it in. I had a lot more information to give them, but they told me they didn't need it. They were a "defensive" organization, they said, not a foreign intelligence bureau. I was stunned. Canada was going to war against Iraq. The CSIS agents were pleasant enough, but didn't seem able to take advantage of the intelligence coups I was offering them any more than Steve had in Yemen. I was offering candy to babies, and none of them would bite. I grew more and more despondent.

As fall dragged into winter, I waited for the war to start, and pined for Ban.

19

THE BEST REVENGE OF ALL

ON JANUARY 16, 1991, THE WAR began. As American F-15 fighter bombers streaked across Baghdad's night sky, I sat watching those first astounding live television reports and cheering them on. I wanted the bombs to obliterate Saddam's palaces, the typhoid plants, Osirak, the chemical works, the headquarters of the Mukhabarat, the Nasar and all the other arms factories. I wanted all the grotesque creations of the monster destroyed. Most of all, I wanted the bombs to kill him, to do what Iraqis had not been able to do.

I believed the Americans would strike as precisely as they could, but I knew there would be civilian losses. Even so, I believed the total suffering would be less than would be felt if Saddam and his goons continued to rule. Maybe this was easy for me to say, sitting as I was, safely in Toronto. But I knew that even if I was in Baghdad, I would have been cheering the F-15s from my rooftop.

Like so many others, I realized too late what a total catastrophe the bombing in Baghdad, and other badly hit cities and towns, was for civilians. With water mains and electricity grids in ruins, with the cruel and pointless embargoes on food, medicine and other necessities, the suffering was far worse than instant death. I learned in horror of the hunger and privation, then the spread of disease. Worst were the images of the pathetic children shown in television reports. What had they ever done to deserve this? I had been fool enough to think only the Mukhabarat headquarters and like targets would be hit.

With all communications cut off, I had no idea how my mother and the rest of the family were, and I learned that even my father in Manila couldn't get through to Baghdad. There was a rumor he was asking for "early retirement." And someone who had made it out to Austria got word to me that Bibi had died, not in the bombing, but of illness, a while before. If so, maybe Bibi was the lucky one. But I don't know for certain if the report is true.

The realization that I would have cheered the bombers made me see that life had made me savage, too. The savagery is there in all of us. Western analysts learnedly discuss how Saddam was brutalized by his father and stepfather as if such treatment explained away Saddam's own brutality. I can't go along with that alibi. We all react differently to both kindness and cruelty, but after a certain point of awareness — growth — we are all responsible for who and what we are. Whatever I am, I am. I can't entirely blame my father and his ugly soul. Perhaps I would be different if I'd had a normal father. But I made my own choices; so did Saddam.

As the war continued, I felt I was on an emotional roller coaster. I reached the depths of despair when bombs hit a civilian shelter and killed hundreds of women and children. I knew the neighborhood and I was certain this was not a military target. I cursed the intelligence mistake that caused the horror. Then my spirits soared when I heard how many military plants had been hit and how much of Saddam's war machine had been destroyed. Like others, I waited for the ground war.

Bush's great strength proved to be the fact that he gave Saddam no room to maneuver. And the fact that Saddam had no real idea of the capabilities of the military firepower he faced. He only knew

Iran's limited war machine. At the beginning of the war, I pictured Saddam sitting in one of his palaces, or in his shelter beneath the lake, plotting and planning each deliberate move. He would be assessing just how much damage he could afford to absorb when the Americans struck. Winning didn't matter. What mattered was putting on a good show and gaining the hearts and minds of the smoldering Arab world. The Americans couldn't stay there forever. They couldn't put out revolutionary fires in every nation in the Mideast. When Saddam realized the awesome power unleashed against him his shock and fury must have been devastating. He made yet another call for terrorists to carry out strikes against the Americans and their allies.

In far-off Manila, two Iraqis were blown up by their own bomb while on their way to an American "target." I was certain that my father, now Iraq's ambassador to the Philippines, had somehow been involved in this attempted act of terrorism. The Philippines is fertile ground for the men of the Mukhabarat — my father, and others like him. American military bases are there, and much anti-Americanism to be exploited. Moreover, nearly five percent of the population of the Philippines — more than two million — is Muslim, and it is only a short distance to Malaysia, where more than half the population is Muslim. A concentrated effort is being made to convince Asian Muslims that they should rise up and be a part of the *jihad*. There is an equally concentrated effort by the Arab nations of the Gulf Co-operation Council to preempt such a development with lavish promises of financial-aid packages. It is no accident that my father was sent to the Philippines.

When the coalition forces rejected a so-called Soviet-Iraqi peace plan, and George Bush and his allies sent their armies rolling into Kuwait and Iraq in a massive ground offensive, I knew it was a turning point not only in the war but in America's stand in the Middle East. I felt that for the first time, Washington realized what and with whom it was dealing. The people in the White House and the Pentagon seemed to know as well as we Iraqis that the peace plan was a fraud, just another attempt by Saddam to manipulate the West with its own tools. Unlike his predecessor, Bush was not drawn into phony talks and deals, the kind of thing my people have been expert at for centuries. Protesters in all parts of the world sent up an angry howl, attacking Bush as a warmonger. But he dealt with Saddam in the only possible way.

In the end, the ground war lasted only one hundred hours. Then the guns were silent.

If the Iraqi army had stood and fought, it might have lasted a bit longer. I know that if I had been in uniform I would have been the first to run toward the advancing enemy soldiers to greet them as long-awaited saviors. And that is precisely what more than 60,000 Iraqi men did. Starved by their own commanders, forced to stay at the front with a gun at their backs, they fell weeping at the feet of the allies, half of them not wanting to return to Saddam's Iraq.

Some of those who surrendered must have been friends of mine. As I watched the scene on television, I tried to spot those I knew among the POWs. Perhaps other friends and acquaintances had died in the massive bombardment that preceded the ground offensive. I hoped none of them had been among the monsters who raped, tortured and killed Kuwaitis and then tried to flee with stolen loot. The Americans trapped them and then blew them to pieces from the air. The road back to Iraq was a huge graveyard of charred trucks and stolen cars full of silverware and televisions, and huge Soviet T-72 tanks blasted into small bits, and everywhere there were dead bodies, frozen in this final nightmare. Hardened correspondents were dumbstruck by this ghastly tableau of the new military era.

I like to think that even if I had been among the unwilling soldiers, with death raining in my head, I would still have welcomed the assault if killing me would have helped end Saddam's tyranny. Even so, I know if I'd been one of those soldiers I would have been terrified, bitter and angry at having to die because of Saddam. I wonder how many died with a curse on their lips, either for Saddam or for America.

That is the nub of the question. Who has won the hearts and minds of the most people?

The rich gulf states and their inhabitants are jubilant at the victory. They praise America to the skies.

The poorer Jordanians, and the mass of Palestinians who live there and in the occupied territories, are bitterly angry at the United States. Many citizens of the Arab countries that fought with the coalition are also angry and frustrated. Many parents in the Middle East are teaching their children that Saddam is a hero who stood up to the giant invader. The fact that Saddam was safe and sound in his bunker and left ordinary soldiers (mostly conscripts), mothers and children open to the onslaught, won't phase the Mideastern myth makers.

Radio Baghdad continued its lurid vilification of the satanic infidel invader and hailed the lofty and noble courage of the brave Muslim fighters who repelled the forces of evil in the mighty battle for the glory of Allah . . . and declared victory.

This sort of rhetoric, which in translation sounds utterly asinine, is resonant, powerful and, above all, believable in Arabic. There will be many who know better and have heard from returning soldiers or from the BBC World Service that the war was anything but a victory for Iraq. But just as many will believe it *was* a victory, and be inspired by it.

If, following the war, there is a belated effort to finally force Israel to accept some kind of fair deal for the Palestinian people, many will believe that it is due to Saddam's brave stand. They will believe this in spite of the fact that in the Soviet plan Saddam dropped any demand on behalf of the Palestinians. Facts do not matter. Beliefs do. And to be fair, I believe it is doubtful that the Palestinian question would have been put at the top of any agenda if not for the war with Saddam.

Again, Saddam and Syria's Assad will be locked in verbal conflict. Whatever else happens to him, Saddam will claim the Palestinian question is on the table because of him. Assad will claim it is being considered because Syria was part of the coalition.

In spite of all the horror Saddam has wrought on his nation, it is hard for me to picture him departing from his throne. After his military defeat, he lost no time in settling the terms of the ceasefire. This left him free to crush any incipient opposition at home. Saddam hung on to power after causing the deaths of hundreds of thousands of his people in his ludicrous war with Iran. In the gulf war he lost his hideous arsenal of weapons and most of his army. But these losses would not affect his opinion of himself in the least. He would fight like a tyrannosaur to keep his kingdom. At the time of writing this book, I believed he would survive, though I desperately prayed I was wrong.

Perhaps we can hope that the cynical power brokers and arms dealers will rein themselves in and make a genuine effort to prevent the creation of yet another monster. I am encouraged that there is talk of the need to tighten up arms exports and to enforce controls worldwide. But the powers that be must ensure that unconventional avenues of import are tightened, as well. I am thinking of *Al Qadisiya*, Saddam's private plane, used by Tarik Aziz and a few other high functionaries, and how the Iraqi regime has flown agents into the West and flown them out again with everything from weapons to high-tech devices. These devices were usually used to enhance the death machine with no one the wiser about these "diplomatic" flights. And then worst of all, those grim crates with their drugged prisoners. The Europeans are a more world-weary lot, aware that this abuse of international law is commonplace. I think Americans and Canadians may be much more shocked and angry. North Americans, bless them, still have the capacity to be shocked.

At the age of twenty-six, I am jaded enough to believe that the arms merchants and politicians like things the way they are. They build the tyrants, then fuel the wars that have to be fought against them. I will be very surprised if we do not see another war. The New World Order, which George Bush heralds, is a fine and lofty idea, but I am no longer innocent enough to believe it will mean an end to the profits of arms dealers, tyrannies and evil. All we can do is hope that after the rhetoric the reality will be mitigated somewhat. And I am no longer starry-eyed enough to cherish romantic illusions about Eli Cohen and the Israelis. Instead perhaps I have a more realistic appreciation of the spy and his nation. A dirty, dangerous job, necessary for the survival of a country that is sometimes right and sometimes wrong. But I am still a prodigal Iraqi who can admire it when it is right.

And what of Iraq itself? With or without Saddam, what is there to work with?

Western news correspondents and analysts speak of possible replacements for Saddam as though they are desirable alternatives: names like Taha Yassin Ramadhan, Saddoun Hamadi and Hussein Kamel are bandied about. These men are not moderates; they are Saddam's henchmen.

A bit of background on these potential successors might be useful. Taha Yassin Ramadhan, who used to come to our house to dine with my father, is a former army sergeant who suddenly became the number-three man in the country. His job was to

guide the economic development of Iraq. That is, he was comp-
troller of the anti-system.

Saddoun Hamadi, a Shi'ite, rose from nowhere to ministerial
positions including the foreign ministry. Hamadi has been explic-
itly referred to by some Middle Eastern experts on American
television networks as a moderate. This term has long since fled
the language insofar as Iraq's power elite is concerned. Saddoun
Hamadi is a vicious man who simply knows how to survive in
Saddam's circle of fear. He has no popular base and is incapable
of putting things together or taking anything apart. He was
banned by my father from doing any writing concerning politics
in Iraq after he made some public "mistakes" about Ba'th ideology.

Hussein Kamel, Saddam's cousin and son-in-law, is equally
savage. His chief claim to fame is that he is the husband of
Saddam's eldest daughter, an accomplishment that earned him the
rank of army general in a mere nine years. He was made head of
the Jihaz al-Amn al-Khas, head of the Special Branch for Protection of Saddam, private secretary to Saddam, and minister of
Industry and Military Manufacturing. Later, he became the oil
minister, as well. The fact that he never finished high school was
greatly in his favor as far as Saddam was concerned.

Saddam Kamel, his brother, is married to another daughter of
the Great One. He is a failed actor, who has appeared in some
dismal Iraqi television films, and was accordingly made a captain
in the elite first circle that protected Saddam (I was in the second
circle on fashion night in Babylon). Those in the first circle have
extraordinary power, even over full generals in the armed forces.
They can kill a general, no questions asked. The right to kill is
accorded as a special privilege in this hierarchy.

The slippery Tariq Aziz, foreign minister, who acted as
Saddam's deaf and dumb envoy in peace talks before the war, has

also been mentioned. He is educated, but like the others, has no popular following. He is a yes-man who needs a leader to say yes to. And underneath his stylish suits, he's just another ruthless Ba'thist.

There is also Izzat Ibrahim al-Douri, vice president and number-two man in the regime. He started as an ice-seller in the main *souk*, or market, in Baghdad. Al-Douri has always gone to some lengths to keep a certain distance from Saddam and in fact has not been publicly connected to most of the regime's atrocities. He is at once a sheep and an enigma, said to be a devout individual. It is impossible to imagine such a man as any kind of savior. They are all graduates of the political school of thought that teaches rule by fear.

The ascension of any of these men to Saddam's place will mean a coup every two weeks in Iraq. None of them has a constituency, a power base or the ability to lead. They are consummate followers.

Most of the Iraqi officials who surround Saddam have a poor education. Saddam excuses their lack of schooling by saying, "These men are educated through their struggle to reach the power and heart of the masses." This is typical Ba'thist blather.

Another, sometimes mentioned alternative is the Liberal Democratic Front, headquartered in London and now moved to Saudi Arabia. It has even less of a power base. The Iraqi people have suffered too much while the members of the Liberal Democratic Front have played paper politicians in the West. As I said earlier, even the Mukhabarat was not interested in terminating any of them, regarding them as irrelevant. Unlike Saddam and his Tikritis, or the Da'wah and its Shi'a, the LDF has no core. Iraq is probably not ready for this. The structures are not there for such a disparate group. Again, I foresee a wilderness of coups.

The Americans and their allies may very well wish to see the aforementioned group take over, but it would be an almost impossible task. The logistics of such a takeover are daunting. How could they return to Iraq while the police state still functions? How could elections be held in such a rotten system? How could they run a country that is economically bankrupt and morally exhausted? They would find themselves very much in the same position as the National Front of Iran, which was quickly shoved aside by the clergy in the revolution against the Shah.

Another possibility is that Saddam, or his henchmen, will survive in Baghdad, but lose much of the rest of the country. This is a dreadful and most complicated scenario. It *is* possible that the country might endure a civil war (though there will be nothing civil about it) and chaos much as Lebanon has endured for more than fifteen years. Because of its ethnic/religious structure, Iraq could revert to its pre-colonial sections reflecting regional power structures. The British combined the three ethnic/religious divisions to create modern Iraq. Those divisions were Basra, Mosul and Baghdad. Such a scenario could result in the Da'wah's running southern Iraq with the center of its power in Basra and the Shi'a shrine at Najaf. The Kurds would run northern Iraq with their power base in Mosul. In the meantime Saddam and his forces, or Ba'thist survivors, would control central Iraq from Baghdad. The splitting of the country would be a disaster insofar as the balance of power in the Middle East is concerned. Southern Iraq — from Najaf to Basra — would become the ally of a now greatly enhanced Iran. Northern Iraq — Mosul — might lean toward Turkey, while Baghdad, where almost a third of all Iraqis live, would be reduced to utter poverty, denied the country's natural resources.

The Kurds rose up immediately after the war and began a fierce battle with the army for control of the north. The Balkanization of Iraq seemed to have begun. Ironically, this worst-case scenario is a close cousin of what I believe would be the best: a federation of three, or more, such states. The United States of Iraq. It would be unwieldy and fractious, until somehow each learned to live with the other's rights and simply agreed to differ. That, after all, is the core of democracy.

Unfortunately the group that is best positioned to take over Iraq as a whole is the Da'wah. I came to know them in London and found them to be self-righteous zealots who would kill still more Iraqis in the name of Allah and their bitter dogma. The Da'wah did not have much success garnering support under Saddam, partly because he so efficiently eviscerated their organization, and partly because Iraqis were less than enthusiastic about anybody resembling Khomeini, be he Shi'a or Sunni. But after the war, Shi'a rebellion burst out and Saddam's forces fought back savagely in Karbala, Najaf and Basra. It is highly ominous that Ayatollah Khoi, the senior Shi'a cleric, broke a years-long political silence to call for *jihad*. Khoi and Khomeini did not see eye to eye on religious politics, and Khoi kept his people relatively quiet rather than join Khomeini. Khoi's clarion call from Najaf will reverberate. Saddam, who always kept a tight rein on Khoi, kidnapped the ninety-two-year-old cleric from Najaf and showed him on television, "chastened" and taking tea with the genial president. No one was fooled. That outrage, too, will fuel the flames.

But the situation in Iraq is not exactly as in Iran, where the mosques are supreme. Iraq's mosques are thoroughly penetrated by the Mukhabarat. Ironically the strongest base and network for the Da'wah are the Iraqi POWs who returned from Iran in 1988 full of fervor for the Islamic revolution of their captors. I remembered Noman and the Da'wah gang in Manchester, rationalizing Khomeini's barbarities, fired with righteousness. To them, democracy means rights and freedom — for everybody who agrees with them. The Da'wah would turn Iraq into another Cambodia. My poor people.

An important factor will be whether or not Washington makes the mistake of deciding to live with the Da'wah. George Bush appears to have learned at last what Saddam is. He seems to have taken the measure of the Middle Eastern enemy. But it would be too much to hope that American leaders had suddenly, overnight, learned the lessons of all their mistakes in the region. Again I remembered how Noman and other spokesmen for the Da'wah learned to present themselves to the West as harmless democrats. Moreover Washington does not readily admit to its mistakes. The Americans did, after all, back the Khmer Rouge in Cambodia for years after it was apparent who and what they were. I have no illusions about global political morality. I fear the White House will think that they can do business with the Da'wah.

I know the Da'wah will do business with Washington and then turn and calmly shoot the West in the back. They will do this all over the world if possible. The essence of the Islamic fundamentalist movement is not religion, but rather power through hatred. Hatred of the West in general, America in particular and, beyond all else, Israel.

No peace talks, no settlement for the Palestinians, will change this irrational, visceral enmity felt in the Middle East. Terrorist Abu al-Abbas and his cohorts will continue to fan those flames whether backed by Saddam, the Da'wah or another as yet unknown force emerging from the ashes of Iraq.

The military defeat of Iraq has been followed by some optimistic talk of new hopes for comprehensive peace settlements, as American Secretary of State James Baker swung through the region in March of 1991. But I am not so optimistic. I see only new variations on old, old maneuvers. And Israel is still adamant.

Canadian Foreign Minister Joe Clark said after a meeting with his Iranian counterpart that what was needed was for the people of the Middle East to trust each other more. The naiveté of such a remark is staggering. To westerners who can still think this way, I can only say, read my story and weep. Trust? To trust in my world is to sentence oneself to death. Perhaps these things are truly beyond the grasp of the West. If that is so, then perhaps the lesson to be learned from my story, from our history, is that the West would be better advised to find another energy source and go home. In my world there are no winners. Not for long.

There is one other primal element in this mosaic. And it was illustrated graphically by a young Kuwaiti nurse. When the coalition forces arrived in triumph in Kuwait City, they found a people delirious with joy to be delivered from seven months of hell. Somehow the Kuwaitis had managed to make it through, with the help of a small resistance force keeping everyone supplied with food and water. They demonstrated the remarkable human capacity for ingenuity and courage under duress. The Kuwaitis told of ghastly tortures, parents murdered in front of their children, children shot for scrawling slogans against Saddam on fences, people abducted to an Iraqi twilight zone between life and death. The Kuwaiti nurse, her face half-covered by a veil, told proudly how she had done her part by administering lethal injections to a dozen wounded Iraqi soldiers.

The calm, cool way she told of her act should serve as an illustration to westerners. It should reveal just what they are dealing with in my part of the world — a deep capacity for murderous hatred.

It is a pathology of our culture. It is not just people like my unbalanced father, or megalomaniacs like Saddam. It is, I believe, bred in the bone. If fear is the engine of Saddam's society, hate is the fuel, and it is a deeper resource even than our oil.

I said earlier that when we Iraqis decide we love someone, we do so with enormous passion. And the same is true of the negative emotions. You rarely hear us say we dislike someone. More often we hate them. There is a large room for hate in each of us. All a leader has to do is fill it.

I think the cause lies partly in the heritage of our ancient civilization, one that has seen everything from Tamerlane to T. E. Lawrence. We are stuck in the emotional ruts of history and cannot escape. We are like a train on a circular track. I believe these ancient hatreds are almost incomprehensible to North Americans in particular. The United States and Canada are young nations without centuries of historical baggage, though the conquest of the native peoples may return to haunt them. In a way, people in these two western countries have been able to recreate themselves, because they have had to make something out of a whole variety of peoples and cultures that came together in this new world. For me, it is like encountering a new human race. There are problems and passions, and good and evil, but these are not engraved on the souls of North Americans the way my heritage is on mine.

I have said that we Iraqis seem condemned to be like this, to be slaves to these recurring cycles of violence and circles of fear. But I want to believe that we can change this ancient pattern. I want to believe that this war is the beginning of that change.

The rout of Saddam's feared military machine, its exposure as a fraud and a collection of looters, is, I hope, the first crack in the circles of fear. But the Mukhabarat and the rest of the security apparatus is too complex and powerful to simply fall apart. It is not like the Shah of Iran's brutal but incompetent SAVAK, which collapsed when the mullahs gained momentum. Nor is it like Saddam's pathetic "million-man army" largely made up of unwilling conscripts who embraced their conquerors.

If anything, my story should show that Iraq's secret services are formidable and entrenched. They will remain a force to be reckoned with in some form in any future Iraq. Abu Firas, Radhi the Gorilla, the Eagle, Khaled the blond agent — they will not go gently.

Ba'thism will survive for a time in some form or another. It will survive because such a stain does not come out in one wash. It has not been just a political party, but rather a system of mind control. Children who have been taught to inform on their parents will not embrace the principles of democracy overnight.

My country is a total mess. After so many years of functioning under the anti-system, people's minds and characters have been warped and reshaped until their idea of normal is everyone else's idea of dreadful. Simple things like honesty will take a long while to develop. It was easy for me to be an agent for the Mossad and then the Mukhabarat, because living in Iraq, or anywhere in the Arab Mideast, meant learning from the cradle how to dissemble, cheat and cut corners. I learned how to present one face to one man, and another face to the next. In our world it doesn't take a criminal mind to forge passports, work the black market, deal in arms, cheat on exams; it is all just part of the overall character of life in the culture in which I was raised. Indeed, the attitudes I have described are all part of the religious cloak that shape the personality. It is called *taqiya*. Ali himself, son-in-law of the prophet, gave lessons in the art of the strategic lie to protect believers from imminent danger. *Taqiya* has been extended to cover almost any contingency, sacred or profane.

It is almost impossible to build a democracy out of such raw material. But we must begin somewhere. I don't want to believe we are doomed to tread this horrible path forever. I want to believe that if freed of tyrants, freed of terror and given knowledge and opportunity, we can all learn that giving life is better than taking it. I like to think we will learn that what we have in common is stronger than our differences. Religions and political systems need to teach us tolerance rather than how to despise and conquer. I want us to return to what is beautiful in Arab culture — the long-lost enlightenment of Haroun al-Rashid's age — but nurtured in modern democracy. I know it sounds hopelessly utopian. But if we give up striving, we are truly doomed.

For my part, I will try to escape my past, with Ban. We will try to find a new identity, a new country, and we will dedicate ourselves to the most irrational affirmation of life there is: having children. More than anything in the world, I want a baby with Ban. I want to give life, love a child, cherish it and nurture it so that the beauty I know is possible in the human soul can bloom. I want to give my children fun, knowledge and security. I want to do my part to help make a few more decent human beings on this planet. If my part of the world is to have any hope of peace, we must begin at the cradle. My mother tried, but she was outgunned.

Most of all I want to give love. Then, surely, love will be returned. That, above all, is what was missing in my own father and in the ideology he has served. I will never fully understand why. But now at least I see that seeking revenge the way I did only keeps the circles and the wheels turning. It is the final irony that the best revenge I can take on my father will be to love my children.

These are strange thoughts from a man who served the Mossad and the Mukhabarat. But love is the only way I know to come in from this terrible cold.

INDEX

A note on Arabic names: Many Arabic surnames are prefaced with *al-*, meaning *the*. While retaining this prefix at the beginning of the surname, *al-* is ignored during alphabetical sorting. Note also that throughout this index, a subheading reference to Saddam refers to Saddam Hussein, and a reference to H.S. refers to the author, Hussein Sumaida.

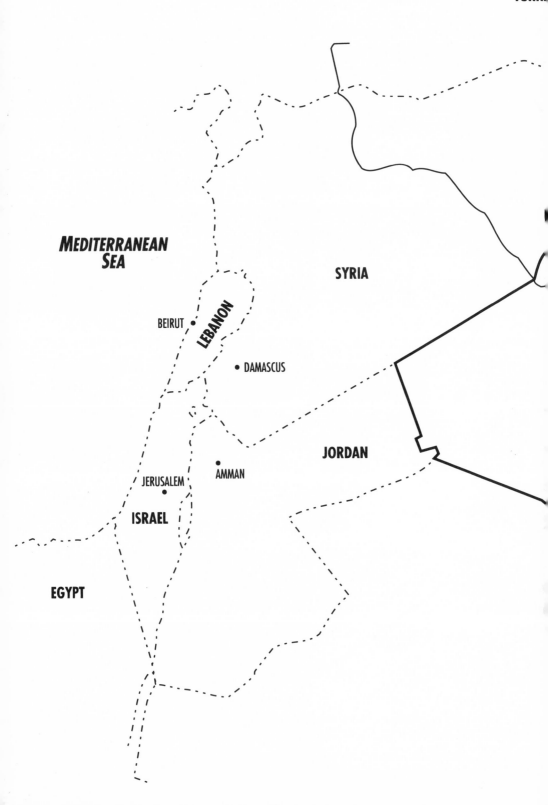